On the Meaning of Human Being

On the Meaning of Human Being

Heidegger and the Bible in Dialogue

Richard Oxenberg

Political Animal Press
Toronto · Chicago

Political Animal Press
www.politicalanimalpress.com
Distributed by the University of Toronto Press

Cataloguing data available from Library and Archives Canada
ISBN 978-1-895131-30-7

Printed and bound in Canada

For Gabriel

Acknowledgments

This work began some number of years ago as my dissertation for the degree of Philosophy at Emory University. It has since gone through many revisions. There are many to thank for supporting me through the process of thinking it through, writing it, and revising it.

First, I would like to thank my dissertation committee members at Emory U., Tom Flynn and Jack Zupko, for their many helpful criticisms and comments. Special thanks are due the Chair of my committee, David Carr, for helping me unravel the complexities of Husserl's and Heidegger's thought, and for his simple willingness to let me be me and write the work I wished to write, despite what seemed to some the unmanageable 'bigness' of my aims. Rudolf Luethe's support and comments were much appreciated as well.

My years teaching in the Core Curriculum at Boston University – in which philosophical, literary, and religious texts were juxtaposed – also helped me see into the meaning of much of what I have tried to present in this work. I would like to especially thank David Eckel for his kindness, wisdom, generosity, and support. My many conversations with David helped sensitize me to the living quality of ancient texts, religious and otherwise.

Beyond this, my work could not have been accomplished without the support and encouragement of family and friends. My parents and siblings have all, in their ways, helped me know something of 'homefulness.' My great friend Vickie Sullivan, who sometimes seemed to believe in me more than I did myself, has been an invaluable support. My wife Pam Greenberg, whose translation of the book of Psalms is an inspiration to all who read it, helped sensitize me to dimensions of Jewish spirituality that I might otherwise have overlooked. And my wonderful philosophical partner and friend Stefan Schindler, with whom I have spent many hours in 'Socratic dialogue,' contributed inestimably to my understanding of matters philosophical and spiritual.

I would also like to mention my friends at New Covenant Community Church of Atlanta, whose dedication to the love preached by Christ is something of a revelation in itself. In particular, Marty Barrett, Jack and Ann Lange, Mort Josephson, Sharon Tan, and Richard Burns, all, in their various ways, helped reveal to me the reality of a life lived in the Spirit. The dedication, love, and wisdom of my good friend and conversation partner, Ann Tempkin, has been a special inspiration.

I am very thankful to Political Animal Press for their efforts in bringing this book to fruition. Lewis Slawsky and Alex Wall of Political Animal both read through my manuscript with great attention and care and made many suggestions that have contributed enormously to the readability and general quality of the work

Last – but certainly not least – I would like to thank my son, Gabriel, to whom the book is dedicated – whose simple presence in the world has accomplished the remarkable feat of making the sun shine more brightly than I had ever known it could.

Contents

Introduction: Religion and *Care*

A few years ago, my wife and I took our son Gabriel to synagogue on the High Holy Days. Gabriel was just turning four at the time and had only been to synagogue a few times before. On this occasion he decided to voice a question that had apparently perplexed him on previous visits as well.

"Dad," he said, just a tad too loudly for comfort, "where's God?"

I was a bit embarrassed, "Quiet, Gabriel, you're in synagogue."

Gabriel, however, was not to be deterred. He had looked carefully around the room and had not seen God anywhere. He now said even louder, "But Dad, I don't *see* God. Everyone is talking to God, but where is he? Is God here?" A few people turned around to look at us.

"Yes, Gabriel, God is here," I whispered quickly, "but you have to be quiet. You're disturbing people."

"But where? Where is he?" Gabriel said, looking around.

"Gabriel, you have to be quiet. People are praying."

"But *where* is God, Dad? I don't see him."

I've thought about this incident many times since. Gabriel's question, of course, is not unique to Gabriel. In many ways, it is a question the entire modern world puts to religion: Where is God? How is it that God is not more manifest? On what grounds can we justify a belief in God given this? These questions haunt religion in the modern age.

Toward the end of the 19th century, the philosopher Friedrich Nietzsche famously declared that "God is dead." By this he meant that the very idea of God is no longer plausible to the modern mind. People still pay lip service to it, they cling to it for comfort and stability, or simply out of habit, but it has lost its potency, its power to provide real direction and meaning for life: "What after all are these churches now," writes Nietzsche, "if they are not the tombs and sepulchers of God?"[1]

More recently, a number of popular critics of religion have suggested that the idea of God is not only false, but pernicious. Religion gives rise to oppressive superstitions and prejudices; it is behind terrorism and ethnic cleansing, sexism, and homophobia. Decency itself demands that we abandon it. Religion – so the title of one recent book tells us – "poisons everything."[2]

And still religion endures. Indeed, in our time the world seems to be dividing into a number of opposing camps with respect to religion: There are those who thoughtfully reject religion – the religious critics mentioned above. There are those who seize hold of their religions with what seems a willful abandonment of thought – the fundamentalists of all stripes, who loudly and contentiously cling to their religious traditions as to a life raft. And there are those who fall somewhere in between; to whom religion presents itself as something of a mystery to be explored and a promise to be pursued – not something to be embraced uncritically or mindlessly, but not to be altogether dismissed either.

This book is written from this third perspective.

This third group can see the dangers and flaws that critics of religion write about, but we see something else as well – what Jesus called "a pearl of great price." We see in religion an endeavor to address and resolve the great dilemmas and fundamental enigmas of human life, in a way that nothing else quite does or can. At the same time, we recognize that religion's truths are not to be found right on the surface. To access this "pearl of great price" will require some deep-sea diving, both into religion and into ourselves.

What I hope to do in this book is make some progress in this "deep-sea diving" – to penetrate into the question Gabriel asked so innocently at synagogue: "Where is God? Why don't we *see* him?" It turns out that this is not a simple question to answer. Whatever God

1 Friedrich Nietzsche, *The Gay Science* (1882, 1887) para. 125; Walter Kaufmann ed. (New York: Vintage, 1974)

2 Christopher Hitchens, *God Is Not Great: How Religion Poisons Everything* (Twelve Books, 2007)

may be – *whether or not* God may be – God is not an empirical thing in the world that we might simply see with our physical eyes. God is "spirit" – whatever this means – and it is only through "spirit" that God may be approached.

I propose to explore these questions through the examination of two interpretations of human existence that coincide with one another but also conflict with one another in significant ways; the one presented by Martin Heidegger in his epochal work *Being and Time*, the other presented in the Hebrew and Christian Bible. The first half of this book presents a reading of Heidegger's *Being and Time* with special emphasis on his treatments of conscience and death. The second half is an interpretive exploration of the Bible's account of human existence, conducted in close association with our reading of Heidegger. I believe that by bringing the two into dialogue we can make progress in approaching the basic questions we wish to address.

But why Heidegger? Heidegger is not generally classed among religious thinkers; in fact, some might even see his work as antithetical to religion. Nevertheless, as some religious thinkers have noted, and as I hope to show, Heidegger's *Being and Time* provides a conceptual framework that allows us to thoughtfully explore religious questions with greater penetration than more traditional, metaphysical approaches. At the same time, stark differences can be found between Heidegger's and the Bible's assessment of human possibility, leading to quite different conclusions as to the way human life may be well lived. As we will discuss, Heidegger's analysis of the human being shows little recognition of the *ethical* dimension of human life; a dimension we find at the very heart of the biblical account. An examination of these differences will help us highlight and explore the issues that we wish to consider.

We will use both Heidegger's phenomenological methodology and his existential analytic of the human being as our interpretive keys for entry into the biblical account, but then contrast what we find there with Heidegger's own assessment of the 'truth' of human Being. Specifically, we will contrast Heidegger's characterization of human existence as essentially bound by finitude (Being-towards-death) with what we take to be the biblical characterization of Man/Woman as essentially, if not always existentially, open to the infinitude of God (Being-towards-*life*).

Although we will be entering into Heidegger's thought in some depth, I have tried to do so in a way that will allow both the Heidegger scholar and those unfamiliar with Heidegger to profit from the book. Key terms and concepts will be clarified as they are introduced throughout.

In this introduction I briefly consider in what way Heidegger's work affords us this new approach to religious ideas, and then provide a brief overview of the work as a whole.

I. The Phenomenological Framework

The new framework we find in Heidegger's work – to give it a name – is that of "phenomenological ontology." By "ontology" is meant the study of Being. "Phenomenology" is a method for achieving knowledge through the careful examination of what appears in direct experience. It will be helpful at the outset to say a bit about how this new framework has emerged and what its relevance may be for the study of religion.

The phenomenological movement in philosophy was begun by the German philosopher Edmund Husserl (1859-1938), whose great insight was to recognize that any investigation of the nature of reality must be grounded in a careful examination of the phenomena that appear to consciousness in direct experience. In the course of his reflections, Husserl came to see that our conscious experience is structured in terms of what he calls "intentionality." By this he meant that all acts, or moments, of consciousness involve a consciousness *of* something that *also* appears in consciousness. Thus, for instance, in the simple conscious act of looking at a desk there is a subject-pole (the *I* who is looking) and an object-pole (the desk I am looking at) and both appear *within* my conscious experience. This is an important point: although I take the object to be other than me the object does not appear *outside* of my consciousness (of course it cannot, for then it would not appear!). Thus, any knowledge we may have of a world *beyond* our own conscious experience must be, somehow, inferred on the basis of that conscious experience. From an Husserlian point of view, the task of phenomenology is to explore conscious experience in order to establish the basis upon which any sound knowledge-claim can be made.

Martin Heidegger, Husserl's most celebrated and controversial student, modifies, extends, and advances Husserl's phenomenological project in three important ways, all of which have great relevance for the study of religion.

First, Heidegger sees that what Husserl calls 'consciousness' cannot be thought of as a mere 'thing' present to us within reality along with other things. Rather, "consciousness" is that through which reality itself – or "Being," to use Heidegger's term – is disclosed. Thus, to state it accurately (as Heidegger sees it), phenomenology isn't an investigation into "consciousness," but into Being; it is an investigation into the self-disclosure of Being. Whereas Husserl sees phenomenology as a method for investigating human cognition, Heidegger sees it as a method for investigating Being itself. Thus, for Heidegger, phenomenology is phenomenological *ontology*, where "ontology" refers to the study of Being.

Heidegger's second and all-important insight is to recognize that what Husserl calls the "intentional structure of consciousness" is permeated through and through with *concern*. We don't just *look* at the desk, we *care* about the desk (that's *why* we look at it), and the desk has meaning for us within the context of our caring about it. Thus, the desk – and more generally, the world – is manifest as something that *matters* to us. Our basic experience of ourselves and the world is continuously infused with concern.

When we couple this insight with Heidegger's recognition that phenomenology explores Being and not simply cognition, we arrive at a conclusion of enormous significance for the study of religion: *Concern is basic to Being itself.*

As we will discuss, this realization is an old one. It is implicit in Plato's understanding of what he calls "the good," as that which ultimately satisfies the soul's fundamental longings. It is taken for granted in most religious thought, where God is said to be the supreme good, and communion with God the supreme satisfaction of the soul's concerns. It has been obscured, however, in modern scientific thought, which deliberately seeks to discount the subjective concerns of the observer in its effort to provide a strictly "objective" account of reality. From the Heideggerian standpoint, this marginalization of subjective concern *distorts* our understanding of Being, for it entails a deliberate neglect of the very concerns that render the world meaningful to us, and that motivate our investigations in the first place.

And this leads to Heidegger's third great insight: Our understanding of the world always involves an *interpretation* through which we apprehend and express the *way* the world matters to us. This need for interpretation arises from the fact that our concerns have a *temporal* structure; that is, they range beyond the present moment of experience, to past and future. Hence our understanding must involve an interpretation of how each moment fits within the broader range of our concerns. Such interpretations provide us with our basic orientation to life.

From this perspective, the religions of the world may be seen as grand-scale interpretations through which we orient ourselves to life as a whole, both as individuals and as societies. That the empirical sciences cannot confirm, or even test, these religious interpretations should not surprise us: God is not an item in the world that can appear to a strictly "objective" observational process. This, of course, is why we cannot simply "see" God in synagogue or elsewhere. God – for those who feel they experience God – is a *concernful* presence, present to us in our concerns and in terms of our concerns. Given this, any attempt to understand religion will require an investigation into the phenomenology of care or concern. This is just what Heidegger provides us in *Being and Time*.

II. THE DIMENSION OF CARE.

At the core of Heidegger's relevance for religious thought, then, is his recognition that Being is primarily manifest in terms of relations of *care* or *concern*. Speaking of *Being and Time* in a later work Heidegger writes: "In the poverty of its first breakthrough, the thinking that tries to advance thought into the truth of Being brings only a small part of that *wholly other dimension* to language"[3] (my emphasis). The 'wholly other dimension' of which Heidegger here speaks is the dimension he dubs 'Care' in *Being and Time*. What Heidegger shows, through his careful phenomenological investigations, confirms the religious contention that relations of care or concern are fundamental to the character of Being itself.

Religion seeks to express the way in which Being 'matters' to us, and takes such 'mattering' to be fundamental to Being itself. When religion says that God is *holy*, for instance, it is not locating God in space and time, but in the dimension of *mattering*. It is saying that God matters supremely. It is, of course, tautologous to say that what matters most about God is just this mattering itself. In other words, what matters about God is not where, when, or how God is, but how God matters. The where, when, and how of God matter only to the extent that they bear upon God's mattering. This may seem obvious when said in this way, but it is often forgotten; as one or another metaphysical assertion about God is given absolute status in the dogmas of religion. This tendency of religion to insist on that which does *not* matter supremely, e.g., God's metaphysical attributes, may itself be recognized as symptomatic of the difficulties of thinking about mattering in general.

To the extent that it is difficult to think about, or speak about, mattering in general, then, it is difficult to think and speak about matters of religion. This, of course, creates a problem for religious discourse. Religion is forced to speak in symbolical, metaphorical terms, i.e., to employ spatio-temporal accounts in suggestive ways so as to give body to that which matters; ever in the hope that the listener will have the 'ears to hear'; i.e., the discernment with which

3 Martin Heidegger, "Letter on Humanism," trans. Frank A. Capuzzi with J. Glenn Gray in *Martin Heidegger: Basic Writings*, ed. David Farrell Krell (San Francisco: HarperCollins Publishers, 1992), 259.

to grasp the meaning behind the outward verbiage. As the twentieth-century theologian Paul Tillich notes, religion is always in danger of elevating that which is of only secondary concern to a position of supremacy and becoming, in its own words, 'idolatrous.' The Bible is a primary example of this. It is, at once, profoundly disclosive of human meanings and perennially subject to absolutistic distortion and abuse. This is why it is ever in need of interpretation; i.e., an account through which its core meaning is brought before us.

It is Heidegger's great insight to see that what biblical hermeneuticists have long recognized to be true about the Bible is more generally true about the world at large. It is not simply the Bible that is in need of, and subject to, interpretation, but Being itself. Indeed, for the religious person, who regards the Bible as revelatory of truth, biblical interpretation is just a special instance of the interpretation of Being. Primarily, then, it is Being that *matters*, and demands interpretation in respect to its mattering: A man and woman sit across a restaurant table from one another. Perhaps they are on a first date. Perhaps they have a sick child. Perhaps they are pondering divorce. What is true about this situation cannot be rendered in strictly spatio-temporal terms. To reduce our cognition of the world to these terms is to exclude from it the very meaning it has to us.

Our world, which presents itself to us sensorily in terms of spatio-temporal relations, is ever in need of interpretation with respect to its mattering. Such interpretation is something we do constantly in the ordinary course of living. To reflect upon these interpretations, to bring them to cognition, to discover the conditions for them, and to evaluate them, is a primary task of philosophy. In this respect, philosophy may be called 'hermeneutical ontology'; it endeavors to understand the meaning(s) of Being. Under the general umbrella of hermeneutical ontology, the specific areas of philosophy – metaphysics, ethics, phenomenology, linguistics, political philosophy, etc. – may each be said to have its place.

Heidegger has criticized the Western theological and metaphysical tradition, dubbing it 'onto-theology,' and meaning by this the reduction of the philosophical and theological enterprise to the investigation of a 'ground' of Being, in the sense of a first cause or condition, naming this ground 'God.' He sees in this an instance of the general Western technological drive to dominate, manipulate, and control Being, rather than live in acceptance and appreciation of it. Our work does not enter into the discussion of onto-theology, except briefly in the last chapter. We take our stance from the conviction that the Bible, read deeply, is not onto-theological in quite the sense Heidegger has in mind. On the other hand, we must acknowledge that the God of the Bible is indeed presented as a 'ground' of sorts, but primarily a ground of *meaning*: God is that through which the meaning of our lives is revealed and fulfilled. To the extent that God is also presented as a causal ground, God's significance as causal ground is just to negate the claim of any *mere* causal ground to supremacy in meaning. To say that *Spirit* created the universe (as opposed to, say, the Big Bang) is to say that relations of meaning, of mattering, are ontologically fundamental. This, it seems to me, is what Heidegger also wishes to say.

On the other hand, the Bible is quite bold in insisting that not all interpretations are of equal merit. Some are better than others, truer than others, more worthy of affirmation and allegiance. Christ's pronouncement 'I am the truth' claims priority for a certain interpretation of Being. To evaluate this claim we must first of all endeavor to understand what it means. This, of course, is a theological task, insofar as theology is interested in exploring the meaning of its central assertions. But it is also a philosophical task, insofar as philosophy is interested in investigating and evaluating ontological truth-claims. In this the two disciplines may be said to overlap.

Our work intends to be a *philosophical* engagement with the Bible. That is, we do not approach the Bible with a commitment to any given religious creed, but merely with the desire to understand its view of human existence, as it may be gleaned from our own interpretive reading of the texts. We make no claim to provide the one 'correct,' best, or authoritative reading of the Bible; nor do we endeavor to ground our reading in any established theological tradition (although it may, of course, show closer affinity to some than to others). We approach the Bible as a book (divinely inspired or not) in which we find a particular existential-ontological hermeneutic, i.e., a particular interpretation of human Being, whose meaning we wish to explore in dialogue with Heidegger. But this is not to say that this philosophical approach should be regarded as without theological or religious significance. On the contrary, among the things I hope to indicate is that the phenomenological approach to religion allows for a new rapprochement between philosophy and religion, one that will allow them to renew a partnership shattered in the modern era by approaches to truth that are incompatible with religious pursuits.

Heidegger's later writings have their own relevance to the questions we will be considering, but for our purposes it will be helpful to restrict our engagement with Heidegger to the Heidegger of *Being and Time*. In that book, Heidegger introduces the term 'Being-towards-death' to refer to the authentic mode of human existence. In Heidegger's later work this term largely drops out. Nevertheless, we find in Heidegger's concept of Being-towards-death an interpretation of human existence highly relevant to the biblical portrayal of human beings.

As subject to death, indeed as *repelled* by death, human beings find themselves in some conflict with the basic contours of their own Being. As Heidegger presents it, this leads us to flee ourselves into a life of inauthenticity. As the Bible presents it, our subjection to 'death' is both a product of, and a condition for, human alienation from God; it is something we must overcome through the life of faith and love.[4] In its treatment of Being-towards-death, then, *Being and Time* presents, with great penetration, one of the basic existential dilemmas that religion seeks to address. Restricting ourselves to *Being and Time* will allow us to bring this out more sharply and with less complication than if we tried to range over Heidegger's entire corpus. To the extent that this may seem an unfair reduction of Heidegger's overall philosophy, I can only plead that my aim is not to provide a treatment or assessment of Heidegger's work *as such*, but rather to employ elements of Heidegger's thought as an opening into the biblical view of human Being. Our focus on *Being and Time* will help us to do so.

A word should be said about the relation of this work to other attempts to employ Heidegger's early thought as an entrée into religious hermeneutic. The two names that spring immediately to mind in this

4 "We know that we have passed out of death into life," writes John in his first epistle, "because we love our brothers. He who does not love abides in death" (1Jn. 3:14).

regard are Rudolf Bultmann and Karl Rahner.[5] Both have found in Heidegger's 'non-objectifying' language a medium for rearticulating the Christian message as they understand it. From one perspective, this work may be viewed as another attempt to do the same. On the other hand, our work differs from theirs in two significant ways. First, as already said, it is intended as a work in philosophy, not theological dogmatics. We do not begin with the assumptions of faith, nor with commitment to a particular confessional tradition, but with 'the question of Being' and proceed from there. Hopefully, this will permit us a fresh look at some traditional material. Second, our aim is not simply to *apply* Heidegger's new conceptuality to theological concepts, but to *contrast* Heidegger's existential ontology with that found in the Bible. Whereas the biblical account affirms many of Heidegger's phenomenological insights, it then places these in a broader context that changes their meaning dramatically. One of our principle goals is to explore these differences. Thus we will be using Heidegger's work to help us more fully understand the Bible's interpretation of human existence, but then we will be using this biblical interpretation itself to help us resolve questions that emerge from Heidegger's work.

Throughout this work I use the hyphenated phrase 'Judeo-Christian' to name the religious point of view developed in this book. Sometimes I will speak of 'the Jewish view' or 'the Christian view' when referring to matters very closely identified with one religion as opposed to the other. In all of these cases, however, I am always referring to *my* understanding of these views, which I recognize may (and at times doubtlessly will) differ from the views of some devoted Jews and Christians. Since it is awkward to continuously write 'In *my*

---

5 For a general overview of Bultmann's theology, endorsed in the preface by Bultmann himself, see André Malet, *The Thought of Rudolf Bultmann*, trans. Richard Strachen (Garden City, NY: Doubleday, 1971). Heidegger's translator, John Macquarrie, provides a comparison of Bultmann's and Heidegger's thought in his: *An Existentialist Theology: A Comparison of Heidegger and Bultmann* (London: SCM Press, 1955). A general review of Karl Rahner's theological thought can be found in his *Foundations of Christian Faith: An Introduction to the Idea of Christianity*, trans. by William V. Dych (New York: Crossroads, 1990). Another theologian often associated with Heidegger is Paul Tillich, who was at the University of Marburg in the early 1920's with both Bultmann and Heidegger. Let me take this opportunity to acknowledge the debt that my own theological orientation, as expressed in the second part of this work, owes to Tillich. Although the interpretations are mine, the general influence of Tillich on my own thinking has been profound. Students of Tillich, I'm sure, will recognize this throughout. Tillich's overall theological statement can be found in his three volume *Systematic Theology* (Chicago: University of Chicago Press, 1951, 1957, 1963).

interpretation of the Judeo-Christian view of human existence . . . etc.' I will, for the most part, simply write, 'From a Judeo-Christian point of view . . ..' This is just for the sake of convenience and not intended as a general claim about Jewish and/or Christian belief. The aim of this work is not to make claims about established religious belief systems, but to explore the meaning of two contrasting views of human Being, one which I read in Heidegger's *Being and Time*, and one which I glean from Jewish and Christian sources. I realize that there are many differing opinions as to what the 'Jewish' and/or 'Christian' view of human existence is or should be, and not all will agree with my own interpretations. Indeed, it is one of the goals of this work to employ Heidegger's phenomenology to penetrate into Jewish and Christian notions in *new* ways, so it may be expected that we will at times diverge from some traditional views.

In this context, let me anticipate a possible objection to my frequent use of the term 'Judeo-Christian.' Some may feel that this term conflates two religious traditions, the Jewish and the Christian, that ought rightly to be kept distinct. My own view is that these two traditions are best seen as complementary.[6] I do not argue for this explicitly here, although the biblical interpretations I offer suggest it. I believe that the phenomenological approach to religious interpretation in general, as explored and presented in this work, will frequently allow us to see commonality where before we had seen only discord and division. This may be a bit jarring for some who are accustomed to drawing sharp divisions between the religions, but I believe it is one of the great merits of the approach we are taking. Still, I recognize that this may not sit well with everyone, and so, again, I emphasize that the interpretations I offer are *mine*. I make no claim to infallibility. I invite the reader – indeed I encourage the reader – to accept my interpretations, criticize them, and/or reject them as he or she sees fit. My hope is that, if nothing else, they will provide some substantial food for thought.

I have adopted the convention of capitalizing *Being* when it would correspond to Heidegger's use of *Sein*, and using the lowercase *being* when it would correspond to *Seiendes*. The distinction between

6 For a discussion of this, see my essay "On the Complementarity of Judaism and Christianity" in *Interreligious Insight*, vol. 15, no. 2, (London: World Council of Faiths, 2017).

these two is important in Heidegger's philosophy. Expressed briefly, 'being' (*Seiendes*) refers to discrete entities, and Being (*Sein*) refers to the ontological 'way' of those entities; i.e., the way they *comport* themselves in their own self-relation and/or in relation to others. If we speak of a human *being*, then, we are referring to a discrete entity, if we speak of human *Being*, however, we are speaking of the specific human *way* of Being. When the word *Being* is used by itself, without qualification, it refers to the general 'space' (or milieu) 'in which' or 'through which' beings have their concernful relation.

III. OVERVIEW OF THE BOOK

Philosophy, says Heidegger, asks after the 'meaning of Being.' The Bible may be said to present us with an *interpretation* of the meaning of Being. But in order to get clear on what this itself means we must first of all examine the meaning of *meaning* itself. Such is especially important in considering religion, because, as we will discuss, the truth-claims of religion primarily pertain to questions of meaning rather than questions of bare factuality. Clarifying the relationship of meaning to fact, then, is of some significance to our work. Our first two chapters are devoted to this task.

In the first chapter we examine the way in which the philosophy of Descartes has helped to condition the displacement, in modern thought, of questions of meaning by questions of causality; a displacement challenged implicitly by the existentialist movement in philosophy and explicitly by Heidegger in *Being and Time*. We discuss the bearing this has had on our understanding of the subject-object relation, and consider the significance of Heidegger's notion of 'Being-in-the-world' in respect to this.

In the second chapter we explore the relationship between the idea of *meaning* and the idea of *value*. Heidegger shies away from any overt development of an ontology of value, a stance that may have some strategic utility in countering the Western tendency to hypostasize value, but one that is, I argue, ultimately inadequate. Value language, although it may need to be modified to express relationality as opposed to substantiality, cannot simply be dispensed with, for it addresses a dimension of Being that cannot be adequately considered without it. This dimension of Being, the *axiological* dimension, is critical to an understanding of meaning in general, and of religious meaning in particular. Chapter two ends with a discussion of the Heideggerian concept of truth as 'unconcealment.' I argue that there is an unacknowledged value claim implicit in Heidegger's distinction between truth and untruth, and suggest that Heidegger's understanding of truth bears strong analogy to that found in religion.

Meaning, we maintain (with Heidegger), has its immediate basis (for us) in the *concerns* of human existence. In order to understand the meaning of Being, then, it is necessary to explore the nature of human concernfulness. This Heidegger sets out to do through his analytic of human existence in *Being and Time*. Chapters three through five of our study are devoted to a reading of *Being and Time*. Chapter three gives a general treatment of *Being and Time* up to Heidegger's introduction of the question of death. Chapter four is a detailed consideration of Heidegger's treatment of Being-towards-death. Chapter five considers Heidegger's phenomenology of conscience, through which, according to Heidegger, the human being's character as Being-towards-death is 'attested to.'

For human beings to live authentically, says Heidegger, we must acknowledge ourselves as "Being-towards-death," i.e., as subject to death. There are questions that arise from this view, however. Being-towards-death, Heidegger tells us, is accompanied by feelings of anxiety and a sense of 'not-at-homeness' (*Unheimlichkeit*). In response, we seek to hide ourselves from ourselves and each other in order to shield ourselves from these repellent feelings. But why, we ask, should human beings feel 'not-at-home' in their very Being? Must we simply accept this as a phenomenological given, or is there a discoverable reason for it? Though Heidegger's *Being and Time* never addresses this question we find a response to it in the biblical interpretation of human existence: Human beings experience themselves as 'toward death' because they are severed from their relationship with the font of *life*: God. God is that through which human beings can find their true "home." Part two of our work, then, is an exploration of this interpretation in relation to Heidegger's.

Chapter six again considers the question of meaning, now with an eye toward an explication of the biblical message. It argues that

Heidegger's hermeneutical-phenomenology provides us with more adequate conceptual tools for understanding the biblical message than does traditional metaphysics. We consider the issues involved in applying Heidegger's methodology to biblical interpretation. This, then, prepares us for our interpretation of the biblical message in relation to Heidegger's work. Chapters seven through nine explore the religious understanding of human Being as Being-towards-*life* through an interpretation of the biblical narrative. Chapter seven considers the meaning of Creation and Fall, chapter eight the meaning of divine Law, chapter nine the meaning of Christ.

Finally, chapter ten presents a summary and reflection on all that has preceded it. We consider the significance of the religious challenge to Heidegger's interpretation of human existence. We conclude with some discussion of the relationship between the philosophical and religious pursuit of truth in this light.

Part One

I

The Question of Meaning

I. Facts and Meanings

What is the *meaning* of my life?

This is a question that almost everyone confronts at some point or other over the course of a lifetime. The religions of the world seek to answer this question, and in the second half of our work we will spend some time considering the biblical response. But in order to think clearly about that response, we must first make some headway in understanding just what we mean by "meaning." This is the goal of this chapter.

It is only relatively recently that philosophers have come to see that an important distinction must be made between *meanings* and *facts*. For the sake of a preliminary designation, which we will have to refine as we proceed, let us understand by *facts*: 'empirical data.' Let us understand by *meanings*: 'the way in which such data *matters* to us.' An *interpretation*, we will say, provides an account of *meaning*.

For much human history, especially pre-modern history, the category of fact was simply subsumed in the category of meaning. To state a fact was almost always to state it within the context of some interpretation of that fact, i.e., some account of the way that fact *matters*. We see this most clearly in the mythopoetic traditions of so-called 'primitive' cultures: the crops grow due to the beneficent care of the fertility goddess; calamity befalls due to the wrath of the gods – more generally, the world is ordered and has its meanings in terms of the cares and concerns of caring beings. We see a formalized version of this in the Aristotelian concept of "entelechy": things move and develop for the sake of achieving an inner fulfillment. This struggle for fulfilled actualization gives the world its *meaning*.

With the onset of modernism, and related to the subject-object, mind-matter division associated with the philosophy of Descartes (*Cartesianism*), an effort has been made to subsume the category of meaning under the category of fact; i.e., to see the meaning of things in terms of what is available to strictly 'objective' observation, without reference to the concerns of the observing subject or the observed object. This tendency reaches its apex in the twentieth century philosophical movement called "logical positivism." The logical positivists claimed that language is meaningful only to the extent that it refers to what can be empirically observed.

This positivist criterion of meaning broke down, and had to break down, because it failed to recognize that human language is largely, if not primarily, expressive of *concerns* rather than empirical observations. Language, for the most part, expresses our concernful relations with others and with our world, and such concerns are not as such susceptible to empirical observation and verification, but are nevertheless meaningful; indeed, lie at the very core of what meaning is. Such meanings are not grounded in the empirical.

Where are they grounded? Phenomenology has shown them to be grounded in the intentional structure of human subjectivity. Heidegger has dubbed this structure, 'Care.'

In other words, meanings express the perceived relevance of a fact or nexus of facts to the concernful dynamic of human Being – 'Care.' Or, to put this more simply, meanings express our caring about things, and the relevance of things *to* our caring in general. It is Heidegger's contention that our primordial experience of the world is not as a world of bare facts (*Vorhandenheit*) but as a world of meaning (*Zuhandenheit*). The awareness of things as mere facts (i.e., 'present-at-hand,' '*vorhanden*'), itself arises only as an abstraction from our prior awareness of things in their meaning. Reflection is able to step back and isolate the purely factual, i.e., purely empirical, element in those things that we more ordinarily perceive in terms of their meanings. But this is only possible through just such an active 'stepping back' *away from* or *out of* our more usual immersion in the world *as* a world of meaning. The empirical scientist takes off her lab coat and, with it, the detached attitude demanded by empirical investigation, and goes home to her kids, husband, etc., i.e., goes home to her world of meanings.

The priority of meanings over facts in our basic apprehension of the world should not surprise us, given that meanings express the way the world matters to us. What is perhaps more surprising is that this natural priority seems, until recently, to have been contravened in modern scientific thought; where the 'true' has become virtually synonymous with the 'factual,' and the ontological status of meaning has been denied or marginalized. And yet, upon realizing that this reversal is *itself* a specific and historically-bound interpretation, we see that the original priority of meaning over fact hasn't really been effaced. It has just, so to speak, gone underground. The belief that facts are ontologically prior to meanings, which is a correlate of the belief that matter is metaphysically prior to mind, is *itself* an interpretation; i.e., a 'meaning,' with vast implications for human self-understanding.

Some meanings are of greater import than others. The meaning of this fork, for instance, is as an implement serving my desire/need to eat. The fork has meaning strictly as a utensil, and any one fork is easily replaced by another. The meanings of 'mother,' 'father,' 'sister,' or 'lover,' pertain to aspects of my world of far greater moment to me.

Religion is concerned with ultimate meanings; i.e., meanings of supreme import.[1] To the extent that the modern mind is confused over the ontological status of meanings, it will be confused, as well, in its understanding of religion; a point confirmed for us by the positivist designation of virtually all religious language as meaningless. Heidegger's enduring relevance for religious thought is that he has given us a phenomenologically grounded analysis of what may be called the 'ontology of meaning.' He has shown thereby that the tendency to live in terms of meanings is a primordial and unavoidable feature of human Being. Thus, the positivist project of reducing all meanings

1 Tillich characterizes religion as an expression of 'ultimate concern'. He writes: "The object of theology is what concerns us ultimately. Only those propositions are theological which deal with their object in so far as it can become a matter of ultimate concern for us." Paul Tillich, *Systematic Theology, vol. I* (Chicago: University of Chicago Press, 1951). This understanding of religion, Tillich maintains, is biblically based: "Ultimate concern is the abstract translation of the great commandment: 'The Lord your God, the Lord is one; and you shall love the Lord your God with all your heart, and with all your soul and with all your mind, and with all your strength.'" Ibid., 11.

to facts proves to be a futile one. We *will* live in terms of meanings. The only question is *which* meanings we will live in terms of, and how aware of those meanings we will be. The endeavor to escape meaning is itself meaningful: The philosopher Kierkegaard diagnoses it as a symptom of despair.

With Heidegger's *Being and Time*, then, we have the beginnings of what might be called 'the reversal of the reversal' of the Western recognition of meaning as ontologically fundamental. This restitution of meaning to the center stage of philosophical reflection has its ethical or '*geistlich*' roots in the thought of Kierkegaard and Nietzsche, and its methodological and epistemological roots in the work of Kant and Husserl. It takes the form, in *Being and Time*, of an explicit repudiation of Cartesian dualism. In the next section, we will look at how this overcoming of Cartesianism proceeds.

II. Cartesian Dualism

Heidegger's *Being and Time* begins with the statement that we have, "today," forgotten the question of the meaning of Being. And, of course, it is no wonder that we have forgotten this question since we seem to have forgotten, or never to have properly posed, the question of the meaning of *meaning* itself. *Being and Time* endeavors to explore the question of the meaning of Being through an examination of that being for whom Being *has* meaning; i.e., the human being, whom Heidegger calls "*Dasein*" (for reasons we will make clear as we proceed).

In order to do this, Heidegger employs a modified form of the phenomenological method developed by his philosophical mentor, Edmund Husserl. This methodology itself bears a significant relationship to the methodology employed by Rene Descartes, whom some have called the "father of modern philosophy." Indeed, Husserl writes of Descartes that "he stands on the threshold of the greatest of all discoveries – in a certain manner, has already made it – yet he does not grasp its proper sense."[2]

2 Edmund Husserl, *Cartesian Meditations: An Introduction to Phenomenology*, trans. Dorion Cairns, (Dordrecht, The Netherlands: Kluwer Academic Publishers, 1995), 24.

The discovery to which Husserl refers is that of the 'transcendental subject'; the subject *in* whom the world is manifest as intended object. Descartes approaches this discovery, according to Husserl, through his quest for apodictic certainty; his endeavor, in his words, to rid himself of "false beliefs that I had from my earliest youth admitted as true."[3] This desire leads Descartes to his famous procedure of radical doubt in which "I suppose ... that all the things I see are false...I consider that I possess no senses; I imagine that body, figure, extension, movement and place are but the fictions of my mind."[4] But however false the things of experience may be, that there is an *I* who both thinks about and experiences them cannot itself be doubted, thus Descartes concludes: "I am, I exist, that is certain."[5] But what is the nature of this 'I am' that I am certain of? It is, Descartes asserts, "A thing which thinks ... a thing which doubts, understands, [conceives], affirms, denies, wills, refuses."[6] But not only that, *I* am also a thing who "imagines and feels ... that is to say, who perceives certain things ... I see light, I hear noise, I feel heat. But it will be said that these phenomena are false and that I am dreaming. Let it be so; still it is at least quite certain that it seems to me that I see light, that I hear noise and that I feel heat. That cannot be false."[7]

We have arrived, thus, at the domain of apodictic certainty. I cannot doubt that I exist and that I perceive certain things, even if these things have no standing beyond the 'I am' who perceives them. Descartes' error, according to both Husserl and Heidegger, was in not dwelling reflectively with this 'I am' and the world revealed to it, but rather in employing it as the first premise in a deductive argument with which to establish the *independent* existence of that world.

And yet, this 'error,' if it is to be called that, might more properly be recognized as a function of Descartes' very project; which was not to establish a procedure whereby we might grasp the ultimate *meaning* of things, but rather to clear the way for a systematic examination of just this 'objective world' in its *factual* character. Indeed, Descartes

3 René Descartes, "Meditations on First Philosophy" in *The Philosophical Works of Descartes, vol. I*, trans. Elizabeth S. Haldane and G.R.T. Ross (Cambridge: Cambridge University Press, 1911), 144.

4 Ibid., 149.

5 Ibid., 151.

6 Ibid., 153.

7 Ibid.

writes: "We shall not stop to consider the ends which God has set before Himself in the creation of the world and we shall entirely set aside from our philosophy the search for final causes; for we should not take so much upon ourselves as to believe that God could take us into His counsels. But regarding Him as the efficient cause of all things, we shall merely try to discover ... what must be concluded regarding the effects that we perceive by the senses."[8]

Descartes, situated at the dawn of modern science and the twilight of Scholasticism, has had enough of 'meanings' for the time being. God is not to be considered in his aspect of providing a *telos*, i.e., a purpose or meaning, for human life, but merely as the primary *efficient* cause of the world. Descartes is pleased to relegate considerations of purpose to theology so as to liberate his thought for the investigation of that which can be known with mathematical certainty, free from the vagaries of faith. Thus, Descartes quite explicitly bars from consideration any contemplation of what he calls "*final* causality," i.e., the *meaning* or *purpose* of things, not because he doesn't believe such meaning is real,[9] but in order to clear the way for an unprejudiced examination of "*efficient* causality," i.e., the causal basis of things, which is his primary concern. With this we have, so to speak, the birth of the category of pure 'fact.'

What has come to be called "Cartesian dualism" – the sharp distinction Descartes makes between mind and matter – may thus be recognized as having a *strategic* function for Descartes. By looking upon the existence of matter as *independent* of mind and its concerns, Descartes provides the conceptual framework from which the material world can be examined with the detachment and disinterest demanded by the modern sciences. Of course, Descartes is aware

---

8 Descartes, "Principles of Philosophy," in *The Philosophical Works of Descartes*, 230-231.

9 There has been debate over the sincerity of Descartes' religious convictions, some claiming that his allusions to the authority of religion are merely ploys designed to keep him from suffering the fate of Galileo. It has even been claimed that the *Meditations* is not offered seriously but as "a satiric *reductio* of metaphysics showing the delinquency of the idea that conceptual analysis can remedy any shortage of certainty from which science might suffer." Hiram Caton, "Tory History of Ideas" in *Independent Journal of Philosophy VI*, 1985. This seems to me, however, to be an extreme view. More likely is that Descartes' belief in God is real enough but of secondary concern to him. He has envisioned the possibility of establishing a science grounded upon human, rather than divine, assurances, and it is to this work that he dedicates himself.

that this division between mind and matter cannot be absolute; he asserts that, though substantively distinct from *our* perspective, they have an ultimate ontological relation through God. He writes: "By substance, we can understand nothing else than a thing which so exists that it needs no other thing in order to exist. And in fact, only one single substance can be understood which clearly needs nothing else, namely, God. We perceive that all other things can exist only by the help of the concourse of God."[10] Created substances, then, are called substances only by way of a kind of analogy with God, insofar as "they are things which need only the concurrence of God to exist."[11] A created substance, then, is one whose existence depends upon no other *created* thing, analogously to God's substance, which depends upon nothing else whatsoever.

Thus, even from Descartes' perspective, the 'Cartesian dualism' of mind and matter is not absolute. Presumably, if we wished to consider questions of *final* causality – questions of *meaning* or *purpose* – we would need to think beyond such dualism to that supreme Mind[12] in whom all dualities converge. *Meta*-physically, then, Descartes is a monist and *idealist* – there is only one absolute substance and it is of the nature of *mind*; all proceeds from and depends upon the mind of God.

We might say, then, that Descartes hasn't so much *forgotten* the question of the meaning of Being as shelved it in order to ask a different question: the question of the *mechanics* of beings. The question of *meaning* is the province of the Church, and Descartes is content to leave it there. The question of the mechanics of beings is best addressed through a conceptual differentiation between *res cogitans* (mind) and *res extensa* (matter), a differentiation that is possible because they do not depend upon one another *mechanically*; i.e., one is not the efficient cause of the other, rather *God* is the efficient cause of both.

For Descartes, then, the meaning of Being is simply not *in* question, at least not overtly. The only thing in question is the 'how' of Being or, better, of 'beings.' In order to investigate this question, Descartes,

---

10 Descartes, "Principles of Philosophy," 240.

11 Ibid.

12 God, for Descartes, is "an uncreated and independent *thinking* substance..." (my emphasis). Ibid., 241.

along with all modern science after him, has found it convenient to distinguish sharply between that about the object that can be recognized as relative to the subject, and that which seems to stand in a certain independence of the subject; namely, its mathematical properties. It is just such a distinction that allows for detached analysis and manipulation of the material world. This procedure has been hugely successful in providing the modern world with instrumental mastery over physical processes, and to this extent Descartes' project must be deemed a grand success.[13] But it is not, and if we take Descartes' pronouncements about God seriously, is not intended to be, a *radical* ontology. Such could only proceed from a consideration of the Being of *God*.

Husserl's project, then, is dramatically different from Descartes'. Husserl writes: "Epistemological reflection first brings to light that the sciences of a natural sort are not yet the ultimate science of being. We need a science of being in the absolute sense."[14] To secure this "a new science, the critique of cognition, is called for. Its job is to resolve confusions and to clarify the essence of cognition. Upon the success of this science depends the possibility of metaphysics, a science of being in the absolute and fundamental sense."[15]

But *why* do we need "a science of being in the absolute sense"? We certainly don't need it in order to 'ground' empirical science, as Husserl sometimes suggests. Empirical science is able to get along quite nicely without such a grounding, and there is every reason to think that it will continue to do so.

But, in fact, the question has changed. Husserl is implicitly, and Heidegger explicitly, asking a question that Descartes had explicitly set aside. The question of "being in the absolute and fundamental sense" is just what Aristotle dubbed 'theology.' This is a study that seeks, not the 'how' of beings, but *the good* of Being. Aristotle, considering what

---

13 "I will say simply that I have resolved to devote the time left to me to live to no other occupation than that of trying to acquire some knowledge of Nature, which may be such as to enable us to deduce from it rules of medicine which are more assured than those we have had up to now..." Descartes, "Discourse on Method," in *Discourse on Method and The Meditations*, trans. F.E. Sutcliffe (Middlesex, Penguin Books, 1968), 91.

14 Edmund Husserl, *The Idea of Phenomenology*, trans. Alston & Nakhnikian (Martinus Nijoff, 1964), 25.

15 Ibid., 25.

should count as '*first* philosophy' writes: "The science which knows to what end [*telos*] each thing must be done is the most authoritative of the sciences, and more authoritative than any ancillary science; and this end is the good of that thing, and in general the supreme good in the whole of nature."[16] For both Aristotle and Plato, philosophy is defined and motivated by the search for 'the good.' But this is just what Descartes is *not* seeking, on the grounds that it is presumptuous to search for God's ultimate purposes, since "we should not take so much upon ourselves as to believe that God could take us into His counsels." The Greek pursuit of 'the good,' i.e., the *telos* or *meaning* of Being, has, for Descartes, been satisfied (at least ostensibly) by the Church. Descartes' pursuit is of another sort.

Somewhere between Descartes and Husserl something has happened such that the question of meaning has come again to the fore. The distinction between *res cogitans* and *res extensa*, perfectly serviceable when the question is one of mechanics, is no longer serviceable when the question is one of *meaning*. For this we need another vocabulary, which Heidegger sets out to provide in *Being and Time*.

III. The Existentialist Protest

What has led to the resurgence of the question of meaning? The answer to this is historically complex and here we can provide only the briefest suggestion. But it seems clear that Cartesianism itself, in its failure to provide terms in which traditional expressions of meaning could be integrated with the mechanical-empirical conception of the world it has fostered, has led to an increasing inability to appropriate, and be nurtured by, such traditional expressions of meaning. This, in turn, has led to what we might call a 'crisis of meaning' (or, in religious terms, a 'crisis of faith'). In their own ways, the philosophies of both Kierkegaard and Nietzsche may be seen as expressions of, and responses to, this crisis. Nietzsche's famous pronouncement that 'God is dead' is perhaps the most striking expression of this. Although Nietzsche is famous for his strident atheism, he is perspicacious

16 Aristotle, "Metaphysica" trans. W.D. Ross, in *The Basic Works of Aristotle*, ed. Richard Mckeon (New York: Random House, 1941), 982b, p. 692.

enough to realize that the death of God leaves a gaping hole in human life; on what are we now to hang human *strivings* and *values*: "Are we not now plunging continually? Backward, sideward, forward, in all directions? Is there still any up or down?"[17] Previously God, as the supreme *telos*, was that from which human value and meaning could be derived. But no more. Nietzsche's solution is that the individual must take up responsibility for creating her own values; a responsibility that had previously been the province of religion and God.

It is neglect of the question of meaning, neglect of even the basic attitude that would permit the question to be asked, that may also be seen to underlie Kierkegaard's protest against modern rationalism:

> Two ways, in general, are open for an existing person: *Either* he can do his utmost to forget that he is an existing individual, by which he becomes a comic figure, since existence has the remarkable trait of compelling an existing individual to exist whether he wills it or not...*Or* he can concentrate his entire energy upon the fact that he is an existing individual. It is from this side, in the first instance, that objection must be made to modern philosophy; not that it has a mistaken presupposition, but that it has a comical presupposition, occasioned by its having forgotten, in a sort of world-historical absent-mindedness, what it is to be a human being.[18]

The 'modern philosophy' Kierkegaard has in mind in this passage is Hegel's, but the attitude he critiques has its roots in Cartesianism, as we have seen. With the Cartesian disregard of *purpose* (final causality) the question of what a human life is *for* has been cast aside. For Kierkegaard, the existing individual is, as such, concerned to achieve some resolution to the issues pertaining to his or her existence. To disregard this concern, to divert one's attention to merely 'objective' matters, is tragi-comic. Such disregard is named by Kierkegaard 'objective reflection,' to which he contrasts 'subjective reflection':

17 Friedrich Nietzsche, *The Gay Science*, trans. Walter Kaufman (New York: Random House, 1974), sec. 125, p. 181.

18 Søren Kierkegaard (alias Johannes Climacus), *Concluding Unscientific Postscript to the Philosophical Fragments*, trans. David F. Swenson and Walter Lowrie (Princeton: Princeton University Press, 1941), 109.

> The way of objective reflection leads to abstract thought, to mathematics, to historical knowledge of different kinds; and it always leads away from the subject, whose existence or non-existence, and from the objective point of view quite rightly, becomes infinitely indifferent. [19]

On the other hand;

> Subjective reflection turns its attention inwardly to the subject, and desires in this intensification of inwardness to realize the truth. And it proceeds in such a fashion that...the subjectivity of the subject becomes the final stage, and objectivity a vanishing factor. [20]

Kierkegaard's statement that the 'subjectivity of the subject' is the final stage of 'truth' is reminiscent of Christ's proclamation: 'I *am* the Truth.' Truth here is not a matter of abstract cognition, but refers to a state of the subject. Truth is, in other words, a way of Being, the 'right' way of Being, and is related to what the Hebrew Bible calls 'righteousness.' This is, we might say, a religious understanding of the meaning of truth, in which the True and the Good are considered coincident.

But this conception of truth is not confined to the religious tradition. It is also, it may be noted, in close conformity to that of classical philosophy as well.

For both Plato and Aristotle, the goal of philosophy is knowledge of the Good. This supreme Good, for Aristotle, is the 'final cause' toward which all things are drawn: "The *final cause* is an end, and that sort of end which is not for the sake of something else, but for whose sake everything else is."[21] Those who maintain that there is no final cause, Aristotle continues; "eliminate the Good without knowing it."[22] And in eliminating the Good they also eliminate *reason*: " ... nor would there be reason in the world; the reasonable man, at least, always acts for a purpose."[23] The Good, thus, is the proper *goal* of reason.

19 Kierkegaard (alias Johannes Climacus), *Concluding Unscientific Postscript to the Philosophical Fragments*, 173.

20 Ibid., 175-176.

21 Aristotle, "Metaphysica," 994b, p. 714.

22 Ibid.

23 Ibid.

The ideal of knowledge and reason that we find in the ancients, then, is quite other than, even opposed to, the attitude of detached reflection that Kierkegaard critiques.[24] And we can trace this difference, again, to Descartes' renunciation of concern for final causality (a kind of *ir*rationalism, according to Aristotle) and the consequent divorce of subject and object (mind and matter) which it permits. Of course, there is something gained from such detachment: technical mastery of the physical world.

The existentialist protest *against* rationalism, then, is a protest in the name of what, prior to Descartes, had hitherto counted as *reason* itself; it is a protest in the name of the *meaning* of Being (even if, at times, it expresses itself as the despair of finding such meaning). Such meaning is not to be found apart from consideration of the subject; indeed, apart from consideration of the subject's *relation* to the object; and if we do not find explicit discussion of the subject *as such* in the ancients, it is because they did not yet separate out subject from object so as to allow the former to stand in stark relief.

In this respect Kierkegaard's insistence upon subjectivity, freedom, and absurdity in *opposition* to objectivity, mediation, and reason is, in its own way, but another legacy of Cartesian dualism; it appears, indeed, to be its negative image. Kierkegaard, or at least his pseudonym Climacus, remains something of a Cartesian despite himself. He never seems to fully understand *what* the nature of the 'subjective truth' is, as desperately as he longs to find it. As a consequence, he appears to glamorize subjectivity *per se*; where 'subjectivity' is itself understood to be in essential *discord* with objectivity and reason, a point of view in sharp contrast to the classical conception. Thus 'faith,' which might best be characterized as commitment to the Good, becomes, for Kierkegaard, commitment to the 'objective uncertainty' of existence for the purpose, apparently, of intensifying feeling. He writes: "Faith is the objective uncertainty due to the repulsion of the absurd held fast by the passion of inwardness, which in this instance

---

24 Kierkegaard, it might be noted, is aware that his approach bears some affinity to the approach of the ancient Greeks. He writes: "It is therefore an existing spirit who is now conceived as raising the question of truth, presumably in order that he may exist in it ... In this way I believe I can render myself intelligible to every Greek, as well as to every reasonable human being." Ibid., 170-171.

is intensified to the utmost degree."[25] This is a strange understanding of Christian faith, where the affirmation of 'absurdity' (rather than love) is elevated to a supreme principle, and 'intensity' is heralded as a good in itself.[26]

As a result of his radical subjectivism, itself a legacy of Cartesian dualism, Kierkegaard also fails to provide any real entry into the question of *meaning*, and the existentialist movement, reaching a crescendo with the stark dualism of Sartre's *Being and Nothingness* – in which human existence is called a "futile passion" – seems to dissolve in pure pessimism.

IV. OVERCOMING CARTESIANISM

We must now endeavor to get clearer about the problem that Cartesian dualism presents for the question of meaning, how this is related to the question of 'final causality,' and what all of this may have to do with the religious perspective and with Heidegger's philosophy.

If we say there is a difference of *substance* between subject and object what exactly are we saying? Husserl's investigations have revealed that consciousness always presents itself as consciousness *of* something that is also present within consciousness. This suggests a duality in the very nature of consciousness that we will do well to consider. Ordinarily I identify myself with 'my' consciousness. I *am* my consciousness.[27] But if my consciousness is always consciousness *of* something, something 'other' (say, this desk), then my consciousness always contains within it something that is, in some sense, alien to

25 Kierkegaard (alias Johannes Climacus), *Concluding Unscientific Postscript to the Philosophical Fragments*, 540.

26 Tillich, *apropos* Kierkegaard's call for a reason-abandoning 'leap of faith,' writes: "The danger in this concept is asking someone to jump without showing him the direction. Then we have more than subjectivity and paradox; we have willfulness and arbitrariness; we have complete contingency. But if you already know in which direction to jump, in the direction of Christ, for example, then you must have a reason for this. This reason may be some experience with him, some historical knowledge, some image of him from church tradition, etc., but in any case, you have some content. And if you have these things ... it is not a sheer leap anymore. This is a problem which we have to say Kierkegaard left completely unsolved." Paul Tillich, *A History of Christian Thought: From its Judaic and Hellenistic Origins to Existentialism*, ed. Carl E. Braaten (New York: Simon & Schuster, 1967), 471.

27 This identification, of course, is the basis of Descartes' *cogito ergo sum*.

me, or, at least, *other* than me. I am not the desk, nor is the desk me. But the desk is presented to me 'by' my consciousness and, in some sense, appears *in* my consciousness. So there seems to be an ambiguity inherent to the very reality of consciousness as such; *my* consciousness is, at once, *me* and *not me*; it contains 'within it' both that which *is* me and that which is *other* than me. Consciousness is divided between a subject-pole (the *me*-pole) and an object-pole (the *other*-pole). This ambiguity, it might be pointed out, is also the precondition for a non-solipsistic universe. If there is to be more than just me in 'my' universe, then I must be presented with an other.

Husserl acknowledges this ambiguity in his distinction between the 'transcendental ego' and the 'empirical ego.' The 'transcendental ego' is my conscious self as comprehensive of all that my consciousness is directly conscious *of* (including otherness, e.g., the desk), whereas my 'empirical ego' is, so to speak, that part of my transcendental ego that I take to be just 'me.' But even the *transcendental* ego is not inclusive of all Being, and I know this because the other *person's* consciousness does not, and cannot, appear within my own, not even within my *transcendental* ego. Husserl discusses the problem of coming to know the other person, *qua* subjective being, in his fifth *Cartesian Meditation*. He concludes, interestingly, that it is only through recognizing the otherness of the other person that I truly come to recognize the otherness of the material world; for I recognize it as, in some sense, *shared* with one who is other than me, and thereby realize that it too must be other than me.

Thus, my conscious life presents itself to me as a complex of relations in which 'I' am only one element. The question may now be asked: how are we to represent this complex of relations in thought? Descartes divides it in two, distinguishing radically between *res cogitans* and *res extensa* as two distinct 'substances.' How have these two substances come into relation? What is the medium of their relation? Descartes nowhere tells us; he, quite literally, leaves the matter to God – and God, for Descartes, seems to serve no other function than to permit Descartes to set the problem aside. Descartes is not interested in this problem, he is interested in exploring the laws of efficient causality, which are most easily examined when the object is considered as wholly passive, wholly independent of the subject's spontaneity, and, thereby, wholly calculable. Indeed, we see Descartes' passion for the calculable in his denial of any kind of spontaneity to animals. Whatever Descartes can even *conceivably* reduce to the mechanical he does. This allows him to focus his exclusive attention on the question of efficient causality.

But if I now ask another question – if I ask: What does this desk *mean* to me? What does this sun *mean* to me? What does this sky *mean* to me? I am now asking a question that cannot be answered except through consideration of the *relation* between subject and object, for I am, in effect, asking a question pertaining to the relation itself. The question of how I represent this relation now becomes critical. I can try – and Western thought has tried – to continue to represent it in Cartesian terms. The physicalist can give an account of how the light bounces from the object to the retina, resulting in neurological impulses delivered to the brain, which then – somehow – turn into consciousness of the object. (In this account, it will be noted, 'somehow' replaces Descartes' God, who was never very much more than a 'somehow' to begin with.) The problem with this account, besides its very questionable 'somehow,' is that it provides (to use Wilhelm Dilthey's distinction) an explanation with no understanding. I am not now asking about the mechanics of the relation but about the *meaning*.

Meaning pertains to the way in which I care about things, the way in which they *matter* to me. Try as we might, we cannot give a strictly mechanical account of meaning. There is that about meaning that is simply not reducible to some version of 'discrete nodes in spatio-temporal relation' (which is what a mechanical account basically amounts to). Meaning pertains to what we may call the 'axiological' dimension of Being. The Greek word *axios* means 'worth.' Things have 'worth' to me to the extent that they impact upon that which I *care* about. The axiological dimension, then, is the dimension of 'care.' This dimension is not *reducible* to any other and must be seen in its own terms. But it is seen easily enough when we stop to consider it. I prick my finger and it *hurts*. How are we to represent this *hurt* to ourselves? The biologist, of course, can give us a very detailed account of the mechanics of the body's reaction to the prick. But this does not express the *hurt* as such. I think it is safe to say that a being incapable of simply *feeling* such hurt would never be able to understand it, however elaborate a mechanical account she is given of the hurt body. The hurt is not *reducible* to the mechanics of the body; it is something in itself, it exists within its own dimension of Being.

I use the phrase 'dimension' advisedly. A three-dimensional object exists in all three spatial dimensions at once; it does not exist sometimes in this dimension and sometimes in that. It is defined, spatially, by its extension in all three dimensions. Nevertheless, the three spatial dimensions are distinguishable from one another, and we can, if we like, consider any one of them in isolation from the others. Likewise, phenomenological reflection reveals a world in which the axiological dimension is ontologically integrated with, but also distinguishable from, the other, spatio-temporal, dimensions. The desk can be described in terms of its spatio-temporal attributes *as well as* in terms of its meaning or 'value' as a desk. We can neglect the axiological dimension through a discipline of thought, and if our conceptual representations of the world are such as to systematically direct us away from consideration of it, we can all but forget it.

Meaning pertains, then, to the axiological dimension of Being, and this dimension, whether we thematize it or not, pervades our experience of the world. The words we use for things express, by and large, their *meaning*, that is, the way in which the things *matter* to us, not their empirical characteristics; and it is for just this reason that the positivist criterion of meaning was a non-starter. Cartesianism, by conceptually severing the relation between subject and object, eliminates, for thought, the 'space' (or, as Heidegger might say, the 'time') of relation in which meaning abides. We must now assign meaning to *either* the subject *or* the object. But the idea of the object, as *res extensa*, has been *created* for thought as precisely that from which the axiological dimension has been excluded. Thus, we assign the axiological to the subject. Assigned to the subject, meaning is now understood as a *projection* of the subject upon the inherently alien object. Meaning is thus privatized, relativized, and marginalized. The 'atomic subject' now lives in an inherently 'meaningless' world. If we now go further and represent the subject as *itself* just another *kind* of object, we exclude the axiological dimension from our formal conception of Being altogether.[28]

Of course, this is a possible way of looking at things. Metaphysical materialism, which corresponds to this way, is an intellectually viable metaphysic (if we are willing to accept its inability to account for consciousness). But it is not the only way of looking at things, nor, if we can judge from ancient and medieval philosophy and religion, is it the way human beings have looked at things for most of human history. Nor, if we are persuaded by Husserl's and Heidegger's investigations, is it the way in which the world actually presents itself to us.

This severing of subject from object, which eliminates the space of relation in which meaning abides, is only possible through a dismissal of the classical concern for 'final causality.' Let us recall Aristotle's definition of 'final cause': "The *final cause* is an end, and that sort of end which is not for the sake of something else, but for whose sake everything else is."[29] The key phrase here is 'for the sake of.' Heidegger uses just this phrase to express a similar idea in *Being and Time*. But Heidegger never makes the axiological implications of this phrase explicit, which, as I will contend in the next chapter, is a defect in his account – one which must be resolved if we are to advance Heidegger's *own* project. Aristotle, in this respect, is clearer: "It [the Prime Mover, i.e., the universal 'final cause'] is a life such as the best which we enjoy ... since its actuality is also pleasure."[30]

For Aristotle, pleasure is a correlate of actuality; it has ontological status, and beings, defined in terms of 'final causality,' are ontologically oriented toward it. Thus, the 'final cause' of anything, that 'for the sake of which' something is, which is its actualization *and* its 'pleasure,' is also its *good*. The word 'good' implies more than that *toward which* a thing tends. It is that which *satisfies* it. It is its happiness and joy. But such words, 'happiness,' 'joy,' 'satisfaction,' cannot be understood except by reference to an axiological (i.e., caring) subject. Their meanings are not representable in mechanical terms; i.e., in terms of 'discrete nodes in spatio-temporal relation.' They must be charted, so to speak, on another diagonal of the ontological map; an *axiological* diagonal.

28 And we live duplicitously, since no one actually *lives* as if she herself does not matter.

29 Aristotle, "Metaphysica," 994b, p. 714.

30 Ibid., 1072b, p. 880.

Thus, if the Cosmos ('world') is to be construed in terms of *meaning*, it must be construed in terms of an ontological relation between subject and object. Traditionally, of course, God has been understood as 'Spirit.'[31] 'Spirit' here cannot be thought of as merely the subject side of the subject-object polarity, for such would divorce it from the objective Cosmos itself. Spirit must be thought of along the lines of Husserl's 'transcendental subjectivity,' which *comprehends* both subject-pole and object-pole.

Our aim here is not to indulge in a speculative metaphysic. We wish merely to indicate how the Cartesian dismissal of final causality, and its correlate divorce of subject from object, has impacted our capacity to understand Being in terms of *meaning*, and to understand deeply the *meaning* of meaning. Classically, the subject is impelled toward its object in pursuit of its *telos*, its good. The *meaning* of the object is tied up with this pursuit. In denying the ontological primordiality of the subject-object relation, Cartesianism impacts the way we can understand such meaning. As a *strategy* for isolating questions of efficient causality there is nothing inherently wrong with this. But as a fundamental ontological orientation it has vast ethical and spiritual consequences. In effect, any ontological integration of self and other is denied. The universe comes to be viewed as a radical plurality of inherently isolated and disconnected beings, with every individual human being a little ethical fiefdom unto itself.

This view, of course, is inherently at odds with Monotheism. Nor is the problem corrected by imagining God to be the 'most powerful' little ethical fiefdom in the universe. God must be the supreme *good*, which means, ultimately, the supreme *well-being* and *joy* for *all*. It is *as* the supreme good that God is able to provide moral and spiritual direction to human life. Thus, implicit to the religious perspective is the belief that Being *as such* has an axiological dimension, a dimension that must be respected by human beings if they are to fare well – but this requires envisioning the universe as ontologically *integrated* along the axiological dimension. We cannot do this so long as we

31 Aristotle, accordingly, attributes 'life' to God: "Life also belongs to God; for the actuality of thought is life, and God is that actuality ... We say therefore that God is a living being, eternal, most good, so that life and duration continuous and eternal belong to God; for this *is* God." Ibid.

continue to conceive of mind and matter – subject and object – as radically distinct.

It is in this context that Heidegger makes one of his most significant contributions. When we carefully examine the ways we actually experience reality, says Heidegger, we notice that we do not in fact experience ourselves as radically divorced from the 'objective' world in which we live. Rather, the things and people of our world are always *there-with-us*; they are there as aspects of our Being and as matters of our concern. We do not first have to put ourselves into relation with the world. Rather we are always already *in* relation; such relation is of the essence of our Being. This characteristic of our Being as always already in relation to a world with which we are concerned is what Heidegger dubs "Being-in-the-world."

Being-in-the-World can be analyzed into two components that must, nevertheless, always be thought together. There is the *world* that is there before me, and there is the *me* to whom the world is there before. I am what I am *as* involved in the world, and the world is what it is *as* the field of my concernful involvements. In this way Heidegger, taking his cue from Husserl, rethinks the subject-object relation. The subject, the *me*, is concernfully related to the object, the *world*. And the object, the *world*, is there, precisely, *as* the object of my concerns. Thus, *contra* Descartes, *subject and object ('mind and matter') cannot properly be conceived in isolation from one another*.

Heidegger dubs the human being re-envisioned in this way, "*Dasein*." Dasein is a German world which literally means "there (*da*) Being (*Sein*)." The human being, as Being-in-the-world, is *Dasein*, where 'da' refers to the world that is *there* for us, and 'Sein' to the Being (the *us*) for whom the world is *there*.

This re-integration of subject and object allows us to see the *axiological* dimension of Being as ontologically fundamental; i.e. as rooted in the very nature of *what-is*. Thus, with Heidegger's concept of Being-in-the-world we are able to *resume* a perspective lost to us in Cartesianism - the perspective from which religion speaks.

And yet Heidegger's concept of Being-in-the-world is not without its problems. Specifically, it does not seem to deal adequately with the problem of the *other* subject. Although the world may present itself to me, phenomenally, as integrated with *my* Being, I must recognize, if I am not a solipsist, that its actual structure transcends me, insofar as I share it with others. The *same* desk, which is here for me and has meaning for me, is also there for you and has meaning for you. And yet your subjectivity is not present to me as such, nor mine to you. I cannot conceptually integrate the 'subject-object' reality immediately present to me without also considering the 'subject-object-subject' reality inclusive of you, and hence *transcendent* of me. It is this subject-object-subject reality that must ultimately be integrated if we are to finally overcome Cartesian dualism.

Any attempt to integrate this subject-object-subject reality, furthermore, must appeal to some principle of integration *transcendent* of any *one* of its terms, and yet, somehow, *inclusive* of all of them.[32] We will explore, in following chapters, how the Judeo-Christian conception of God – whose essence is 'love' – may be understood as just such an *axio-ontological* principle of integration, connecting not only the individual Dasein with its world, but each individual Dasein with every other.

First, however, we must clarify our understanding of what we have been calling the *axiological dimension* of Being. It is to this we will turn in the next chapter.

32 Heidegger accomplishes this integration in his later work with his notion of the *Ereignis*, which bears certain similarities, but also important dissimilarities, to the Christian idea of God.

II

The Axiological Dimension

I. Meanings and Facts

Our aim is to provide an interpretation of the Judeo-Christian mythos in terms presented us by Heidegger in *Being and Time*. By the 'Judeo-Christian mythos' we refer to the story the Bible tells about Creation, Fall, Law, Christ, and Redemption. We will look at this story as an integral unit that must be dealt with as such; it constitutes one interpretation of the *meaning* of human existence. In calling it a *mythos* we suggest that its primary significance lies in the sphere of *meaning* rather than in the sphere of *fact*.[1] But to get clear about what this itself means we must explore more fully the relation of *meaning* to *fact*, and this itself will require deeper insight into what we have called the axiological – i.e., value-laden – dimension of being.

In distinguishing meaning from fact, we must be careful not to imagine an over simple dichotomy between the two. Rather, fact may be regarded as a *species* of meaning. In stating the meaning of a thing, as we have said, we state the way in which that thing *matters* to us. Something can matter to me, however, only insofar as I am a being who exists as a self-relation; i.e., a self-aware subject. But

1 Both Rudolf Bultmann and Paul Tillich, colleagues of Heidegger at the University of Marburgh in the 1920s, have played significant roles in developing the modern theological understanding of religious language as 'mythological.' In both cases, there is a recognition that language, whether abstract or concrete, cannot express the holy directly. Bultmann's primary statement about this can be found in his *Jesus Christ and Mythology*, (New York: Charles Scribner's Sons, 1958). For Paul Tillich's discussion, see *The Dynamics of Faith*, ed. Ruth Nanda Anshan (New York, Harper, 1956). In chapter six we discuss more fully the challenges involved in interpreting religious language in specific relation to Heidegger's hermeneutical-phenomenological methodology.

merely to say that I am a being who exists as a self-relation, i.e., as a being *aware* of itself or *present* to itself, does not yet express what is critical in respect to the phenomenon of *mattering*. For the meaning of *mattering* is not captured in the idea of awareness alone, but only in the idea of a certain *kind* of awareness, an *axiological* awareness.

Heidegger makes a great advance over previous elaborations of the nature of subjectivity when he describes the human being, 'Dasein,' as a being who is – not a mere *presence* to itself – but an *issue* to itself. "Dasein," writes Heidegger, "is an entity which does not just occur among other entities. Rather, it is ontically distinguished by the fact that, in its very Being, that Being is an *issue* for it."[2] In this word *issue* is expressed the axiological dimension of Being.

In saying that Dasein is an *issue* to itself, Heidegger suggests that Dasein's self-relation is also a self-concern. Something is to be *worked out*, and it can go well or poorly. The terms 'well' and 'poorly' are themselves axiological terms and not reducible to value-neutral terms. For something to go 'well' is for it to promote well-being. For something to go 'poorly' is for it to detract from well-being. Well-being is inherently desirable, that which detracts from it to be avoided. That Being presents us with the possibility of well-being and its opposite indicates that it is inherently axiological. It is our contention that *meaning* itself is rooted in the axiological character of Being.

This is a crucial point, and it reveals a significant shortcoming in Heidegger's account. Heidegger takes pains to distance himself from previous value theories that treat values as mere attributes of things, as if the value of a thing were to belong to that thing as its property. But, having rejected such an interpretation of value, Heidegger never explicitly considers what should replace it. If values are not to be understood as attributes of things, how are they to be understood? Heidegger's answer is to reject value language altogether and replace it with an account of Dasein's temporal relations. What had previously been spoken of in terms of discrete values is now to be spoken of in terms of what Heidegger calls Dasein's "futurity"; i.e., Dasein's projection upon its future for the sake of actualizing its potentialities. Heidegger replaces the idea of 'value' with an analysis of temporal projection.

2 Martin Heidegger, *Being and Time*, trans. John Macquarrie and Edward Robinson (New York: Harper & Row Publishers, 1962), p. 32, H.12.

I believe there is some merit to this insofar as it reveals how value operates in human life, but I also believe that in reducing the idea of value to the idea of temporal projection something important gets lost. Indeed, this replacement of axiological with temporal language may itself be seen as another legacy of the mechanistic-empirical worldview fostered by Cartesianism. In having made space and time the only ontologically respectable categories, it has all but forced Heidegger to slip the axiological into one of them in order to indicate its reality at all. Heidegger makes a great advance in restoring the axiological to the ontological picture (regardless of his failure to name it as such), but now we must endeavor to give it its proper status. *Axiology is not reducible to temporality.*

Let's take an example. I am playing a game of tennis. In order to do so, I employ certain items of equipment (*Zeug*): a tennis racket, a net, a tennis ball, tennis shoes, etc. These items of equipment have, as Heidegger indicates, an 'in-order-to' relation to one another. The tennis racket is in-order-to hit the tennis ball. The tennis ball is in-order-to volley with my tennis partner, etc. All of this equipment, and all of these relations, are *for the sake of* playing the game of tennis. The game has a *super*ordinate relation to the items of equipment, which have a *sub*ordinate relation to it. But in what 'dimension' of Being are these relations so ordered? Heidegger, who has taken most of his examples from the workshop, maintains that these relations are best understood through a modification of our understanding of temporality. Temporality, according to Heidegger, gives us the primary meaning of Being as such, and everything, presumably, can be rendered in its terms. The *for-the-sake-of-which*, then, is best thought of as *to the future* of the in-order-to. The in-order-to activities have their meaning in the *future* actualization of that 'for the sake of which' they are performed.

This, of course, is true as far as the workshop goes, where the aim of the activity is to produce a product whose actualization stands to the future of the activity itself. But this way of describing things breaks down when we consider a tennis game; where the in-order-to activities are really *simultaneous* with *that-for-the-sake-of-which* they are done. True, we hit the ball for-the-sake-of playing the game, we do not play the game for-the-sake-of (just) hitting the ball. The playing of the game is *superordinate* to the hitting of the ball, and the hitting of the ball is *subordinate* to playing the game, but these ordered relations are *axiological*, not temporal. We *enjoy* the game, and we play the game for the sake of this enjoyment. Joy has meaning in the axiological dimension of Being. It is a *good*, it is a species of well-being, and it is not reducible to, nor fully expressible in terms of, mere temporal relations.

This, of course, is not to deny that the joy of playing the game (which, in this case, is the good) takes place *through* time. The joy itself has a temporal structure. The satisfaction of hitting the ball on any given volley is a moment in the enjoyment of the overall game. This, in turn, can be analyzed into its constituent moments: I see the ball coming toward me over the net. I run to where I calculate the ball will land. I swing my racket and connect with the ball, which glides over the net toward my opponent. This sequence of moments has, in turn, a sequence of states-of-mind associated with it: anticipation, attentiveness, excitement, finally, satisfaction upon feeling my racket strike the ball. The satisfaction is not independent of the anticipation, attentiveness, excitement, but their fulfillment. These prior moods are not mere means to the end of the satisfaction, but elements within it, bearing a certain order in relation to it. Had I not undergone the anticipation, attentiveness, excitement, I would not have had the same quality of satisfaction.

On the other hand, I might miss the ball. Then the experience is one of frustration. The possibility of such frustration, and its overcoming in the satisfaction of striking the ball, is *also* a constituent element in the satisfaction. The satisfaction 'knows' itself as having overcome the possibility of frustration and this knowledge is a factor in the satisfaction itself. It too, like the anticipation, attentiveness, excitement, contributes to the quality of the satisfaction. Moreover, the possibility of both frustration *and* satisfaction are present as axiological qualities of my volleying. The excitement is not merely excitement *at* the prospect of satisfaction, but is also excitement *over* the possibility of frustration. The play is characterized by *both* the good it seeks to attain *and* the bad it seeks to avoid. How could we make this clear without language that makes an axiological distinction? The satisfaction is a 'positive' outcome, the frustration a 'negative' outcome. But positive and negative with respect to what? *Not* with respect to mere *futurity*. Temporally, the frustration is *realized* just as positively as the satisfaction; it is its own, positive, state-of-mind, and any careful reflection reveals that the temporal activity takes its character from *both* the possibility of satisfaction *and* the possibility of frustration, as two distinct possibilities that may be realized. These possibilities bear a meaningful relation to one another, but it is not a *temporal* relation.

One might say – and Heidegger sometimes uses this kind of language – that the frustration is a *deficient mode* of the satisfaction. But deficient in *what*? It is not as if the frustration is a weaker, paler, or less intensive *form* of satisfaction – indeed, the experience of frustration can often be *more intensive* than the experience of satisfaction; one can hate losing more than one enjoys winning. Thus, the frustration is very much 'there,' positively, just as surely as the satisfaction. Then in respect to *what* is the frustration 'negative' and the satisfaction 'positive'? It seems that only value-language will do here. The satisfaction is the positive realization of *what is valued*, i.e., a *good*. The frustration is the (temporally positive) realization of the *failure* to realize this good. It is indeed negative as an *absence*, but the absence *of a good*. It is the positive (temporally realized) *presence* of this absence. The *not* here is axiological, not temporal. It is the good that is *not* realized. But this *failure* to realize the good *is* realized. The failure to realize the good is itself a *mode* of Being. For sure, this all occurs temporally. But *what* occurs temporally is a drama that can only be adequately expressed in axiological terms.

This implies that temporal language cannot substitute for axiological language; in fact, the attempt to make it do so will obstruct our understanding of the key existential phenomena with which we are concerned.

But when we say that the axiological is to be distinguished from the temporal, we do not mean to challenge Heidegger's important insight that *all* the dimensions of Being constitute an interdependent, articulated, *unity*. The various dimensions of Dasein's Being are, to use Heidegger's expression, *equiprimordial*. Human Being is, at once, axio-spatio-temporal, and a full description of the Being of anything that appears as meaningful to Dasein involves giving an account of its status in *all* of these dimensions. Nor can these dimensions be properly conceived in isolation from one another (except, perhaps, for special purposes; e.g., to isolate questions of efficient causality). Thus, Heidegger's conflation of the axiological with the temporal, as well as his overt conflation of the spatial with the temporal, is not illegitimate. Ultimately, all the dimensions *are* 'conflatable' insofar as they constitute an interdependent unity. But in failing to name and conceptually distinguish the axiological from the other dimensions, Heidegger misses something of critical importance: for we would say that it is not *temporality* that gives us the *primary* meaning of Being, and in terms of which all else is best understood, but *axiology*. Axiology is, so to speak, the *governing* dimension of Being, in terms of which all the other dimensions receive their fullest meaning.

This insight is an old one. Plato suggests as much when he says that all beings 'participate' in the Good and that their true form, their *meaning*, is in some sense predicated on this participation. Aristotle's concept of final causality is, in many respects, a more elaborated expression of the same. Indeed, when Heidegger asks after the 'meaning' of a being 'in its Being' he seems to be appealing to a conception of Being first elaborated in Aristotle's theory of causes.

Aristotle's 'causes' are not to be understood as causes in the modern sense, but as *ontological determinants*. Aristotle asks what we need to know in order to fully determine a being *as* what it *is* (i.e., in its *Being*), and answers that we need to know how it is constituted with respect to four ontological determinants: the material, the efficient, the formal, and the final. The final cause is the *good* of the thing, which, for Aristotle, corresponds to its full actuality. But this final cause must not be thought of as something a thing realizes only at some temporally *final* moment. On the contrary, for Aristotle the *supreme* final cause is also eternal, and temporally *prior* to much else. To the extent that we speak of it as 'final' in a temporal sense, we are using temporality as a metaphor for its *axiological* status. The final cause is the *fulfillment* of the thing, its finality is *axiological* not temporal. It is the good.

A proper recognition of the axiological dimension of Being is also critical to an understanding of religion. From the religious perspective God is not merely an entity with certain 'objective' attributes. God is the supreme *good*; right relation to God is the 'final cause' of human life.

Without a recognition and appreciation of the axiological dimension of Being the very idea of God loses its meaning.

These considerations will allow us to better understand the relation of *fact* to *meaning*. To give an account of the *full* meaning of a thing, we will now say, is to define it in terms of *all* the ontological dimensions pertaining to it, including the axiological. But the axiological dimension cannot be considered, literally does not *exist*, apart from the caring subject. This is just why it is illegitimate to treat values as if they are attributes of things. Value, and hence meaning, exists in the *relation* between a caring subject and its world, as an expression of the caring subject's caring. And yet there is not just *one* caring subject to whom things have meaning, but a multiplicity of subjects who differ in significant ways from one another. Communication among caring subjects requires a common language. 'Facts' emerge as an expression of this common language.

Let's take another example. I am eating dinner and using a fork. The fork has meaning for me as an implement I use for conducting the food to my mouth. You are sitting across from me. Let's say (to employ a somewhat gruesome example) that you have previously seen someone stabbed to death with just such a fork as I am using. The fork will have a cluster of meanings for you that it will not have for me. You will associate the fork with violence and loss. You may become fearful upon seeing the fork, or angry, or begin to weep. I will make none of these associations. There is, thus, a certain variability in the sphere of meaning having to do with the specific relations pertaining between a given person and the meaningful object. But you and I do not exist in wholly isolated worlds. The fork is there for me as it is for you. You also understand the fork as an implement for eating, and the fork has a shared, culturally established, meaning in this respect (although someone from another culture might not be able to participate in this, *our*, shared meaning). And beyond this, the fork has certain spatio-temporal characteristics that are fixed. These spatio-temporal characteristics also, so to speak, have meanings (or *are* meanings). Given this or that spatio-temporal characteristic of the fork there are things I can do with the fork and things I cannot do with it. But these spatio-temporal characteristics are universal; that is, *everyone* who encounters the fork encounters (or can be brought to encounter) *at least* these spatio-temporal characteristics. These spatio-temporal characteristics constitute, in other words, a *lowest common denominator* of meaning. These, we say, are *facts*. When we isolate the *factual*, we abstract out the *lowest common denominator* of meaning, which is universal for all.

The 'factual,' then, is that meaning of the phenomenon that is available to all observers. In stating the factual I seek to remove from my account anything about the phenomenon that might be relative to someone in particular. But the factual is a cognitive construction out of a more primordial relation to beings, and it is a construction that itself has a meaning and use. To see this, let's consider an example that Heidegger himself employs.[3] Heidegger gives the example of picking up a hammer and finding it to be *too* heavy for a given task. Of course, what is too heavy for me may not be too heavy for you. In stating that the hammer is *too* heavy (for me) I do not provide you with useful information concerning whether or not the hammer will be too heavy for you. But if I say that the hammer weighs 'a pound,' and define 'a pound' in terms of the extent to which the hammer will depress a spring-scale built to a common standard, you are now able to assess how the hammer's weight will be for you – so long as you have had experience with other things weighing 'a pound.'

I have now given the hammer's weight as an objective measure, i.e., in factual terms. Insofar as the aim of the factual account is to say what is so about the phenomenon for *all* observers, I no longer express the fact in terms of its relativity to *any* observer. I say that the hammer *itself* has the 'property' of weighing a pound. We have now removed the *subject* from our picture altogether.

But we have still done so *for the sake of* the potential user of the hammer. The factual account has enormous practical value. It allows human beings to effectively communicate about features of our common spatio-temporal environment across cultures and across generations. It allows for the amassing of great quantities of 'empirical data' which can then be put to use in a huge variety of ways. The 'fact,' thus, is an enormously potent *cognitive construction* from a more primordial relation to beings.

3 Ibid., p. 412, H. 360.

But it is not itself expressive of this primordial relation; indeed, it tends to obscure it, and, thus, provides us with an ontologically limited, even distorted, representation of Being. Indeed, it is of the essence of the factual account to minimize the relational as far as possible, so as to maximize the usability of the information proffered. But it is to the relational that the *fullness* of meaning belongs. The *significance* of the hammer's weight is not expressed in the statement that it weighs a pound, but in the statement that it may, therefore, be *too* heavy to use. The factual is a construction in service to the relational.

Heidegger expresses the relational nature of Dasein's Being through his analysis of temporality. If the hammer is too heavy, it is too heavy *for* some project I am engaged in. If I am engaged in a project I am so *for the sake of* actualizing some potentiality of my Being. Let us say I am using the hammer to build a house. I do not build the house for no reason, nor am I mechanically impelled to build it. Rather, I build the house because I desire a home. I seek to actualize my potentiality for 'being-homed.' Being-homed is not just 'having a house,' but is a potential state of my Being with a wide variety of implications for how I may live. My project of being-homed is what renders the hammer meaningful to me. It is serviceable (or not) for this project. Ultimately, then, my relation to the hammer (and nails, and wood, etc.) is part of a relational complex (a complex of 'involvements,' as Heidegger puts it) through which I am related to *myself*; i.e., to my own potentiality for, in this case, being-homed.

Heidegger understands this self-relation in terms of temporality, and he understands authentic temporality as primarily *futural*. But his understanding of the futural is not the conventional one. He writes, "By the term 'futural,' we do not here have in view a 'now' which has not yet become 'actual' and which sometime *will be* for the first time. We have in view the coming [Kunft] in which Dasein, in its ownmost potentiality-for-Being, comes toward itself."[4]

In other words, the futural is inherent in the potentiality that Dasein *already is*. Hence, Dasein 'comes to itself' in realizing it. This understanding of temporality, we note, bears a close relation to Aristotle's notion of the *precedence* of act over potency. Aristotle writes: "From the potentially existing the actually existing is always

4 Ibid., p. 373, H. 325.

produced by an actually existing thing ... there is always a first mover, and the first mover *already* exists actually" (my emphasis). [5] The *future* actuality, for Aristotle, is inherent to the *present* potency, and can be so because it has been put there by a *prior* actuality. Thus, the future is, in some sense, *already there*, just not yet fully realized. The future actuality is implicit in (folded within) the present potency. The present contains the *seed* of the future.[6]

Heidegger does not engage in Aristotle's speculative metaphysics, but he seems to be functioning from a similar intuition.[7] Dasein's *future* actuality (being-homed) is implicit in its *present* potency, and, hence, is *already there* rendering Dasein's activity meaningful. Dasein, thus, in seeking to actualize this potential of its Being, is 'coming toward itself.' My potentiality for being-homed is *drawing me* toward its actualization.

But again, Heidegger neglects to make explicit the *axiological* significance of these temporal relations. True, I am drawn toward being-homed. But I am not drawn toward being-homed as a piece of iron is drawn toward a magnet (a mechanistic relation), but as a *free agent* is drawn toward a *good*. I *choose* to actualize this, rather than other, potentialities, and I choose to do so on an axiological basis; i.e., because I consider it to be the greater good. Temporality, here, is the medium through which the *axiological* is, so to speak, expressed. But the primary *meaning* of the relation, of the *self*-relation, of my 'coming towards myself,' is obscured in a strictly temporal account. I *value* the state of being-homed, and this is why I work for it. It is the *value* of being-homed that is drawing me towards it, and rendering my activity, and the world in which it occurs, *meaningful*. The relation is *axiological*, not simply temporal. This is something Aristotle understands when he calls the final cause the *good*. Heidegger, for the most part, also seems to understand it, but he shies away from making

5 Aristotle, "Metaphysica," p. 829, 1049b.

6 Note the echo of this in Heidegger's definition of temporality: "The character of 'having been' arises from the future, and in such a way that the future which 'has been' (or better, which is 'in the process of having been') releases from itself a Present. This phenomenon has the unity of a future which makes present in the process of having been; we designate it as 'temporality'." Heidegger, *Being and Time*, p. 374, H. 326.

7 There is also indication that Heidegger was reading Aristotle rather closely at the time he formulated his ideas; see Theodore Kiesiel, *The Genesis of Heidegger's Being and Time* (Berkeley: University of California Press, 1993).

it explicit. He imports the axiological into his account almost on the sly – through such terms as 'care,' and 'concern,' and 'issue' – but he refuses to name the *axiological* as such, and thereby presents us with a distorted picture.

This understanding of 'fact' as the 'lowest common denominator' of meaning will also allow us to distinguish between a mere *explanation* of something and full *understanding* of it. The German philosopher Wilhelm Dilthy first made this distinction. Simply put, a Diltheyan 'explanation' is a factual, mechanical account. Sometimes that is all the *understanding* we are interested in. If the toaster is broken and we wish to make toast, we need a factual explanation as to what is wrong with it and how to fix it. We wish to understand the toaster mechanically, not axiologically (although, of course, we wish to do so because the toaster *matters* to us; the axiological dimension is never altogether missing from our concern). An explanation of the mechanics of the toaster, then, constitutes *one aspect* of a *full understanding* of the toaster. A *full* understanding of the toaster would require a complete account of how the toaster *matters* to us, an account of the toaster's meaning along the axiological dimension. A person who had never seen a toaster would not *understand* the toaster through a mere mechanical account of how it works; she would need to know what it is *good for*.

It is, then, the *axiological* dimension of Being that lies at the core of meaning in its *fullness*. It can do so only because Dasein is an *axiological* self-relation, a being who *cares* about itself, a being who experiences its Being as *of worth*, a being whose Being is therefore, as Heidegger says, an *issue* to itself. Dasein's caring about itself renders the world meaningful. The world is meaningful *in relation* to Dasein's caring and in terms of it. Even the 'factual,' as we have seen, is derivative of the wider category of meaning and has axiological import. But the world is not only meaningful in respect to practical concerns. It is meaningful as *beauty*. It is meaningful as *love*. These are relational states of supreme, intrinsic, worth. Their value is not *reducible* to anything else; we cannot express the value of beauty as a mere temporal or mechanical relation. There are non-utilitarian vistas of value that are simply not expressible in any other than axiological terms.

II. SUBJECTS, OBJECTS, AND SUBJECTS

But if the axiological pertains to the relation between subject and object, and if, therefore, meaning is only fully given through an account of that relation, is it even possible to speak of *the* meaning of Being? Must we not rather speak of the *meanings* of Being, and recognize that Being will have as many meanings as there are subjects to whom it has such meanings? Our pursuit of meaning drives us beyond the subject-object schism of Descartes (Cartesianism), but does it do so only to present us with a new schism, a subject-subject schism? It is to this question we will now turn.

As we have noted, Heidegger's primary ontological designation for the human being is 'Being-in-the-world.' In saying that Dasein is Being-in-the-world Heidegger indicates that Dasein is related to itself *through* its relation to the world. The self-relation of Dasein is not closed in on itself; it *includes* its relation to its world and cannot properly be thought without it. For this very reason a *factual* account of Being, i.e., one which endeavors to minimize or discount the world's relation to Dasein, provides us with a distorted representation of Being, one in which the *issue* that Dasein is to itself cannot be adequately expressed or addressed.

The connection of Dasein to its world forces us to inquire into the ontological basis of this connection. *How* does Dasein come to be connected to its world? When we approach this question with Cartesian assumptions we find that we run into difficulties.

If mind and matter are two distinct substances, the question becomes: what is the *medium* of their relation? To say that they are in physical contact with one another will not work because only physical things can be in physical contact; such an answer subsumes the mental under the material. To say that they are in 'mental' contact with one another will not work for only mental things can be mentally related (e.g., one thought to another); such an answer subsumes the material under the mental. We might suggest that there is some *third* substance, of which they are both, in some sense, *species*, and through which they are related. Descartes suggests as much when he attributes their relatedness to God. But, then, what is this third substance and how does it relate the two?

This problem is pressing because we live in the midst of, indeed, in some sense, we *are*, their relation. But in this very fact, Heidegger sees a solution. Descartes, according to Heidegger, has *imposed* an interpretation upon the world that is not consonant with our actual experience of it, and this is what has produced our problem: "The kind of Being which belongs to entities within-the-world is something which they themselves might have been permitted to present; but Descartes does not let them do so. Instead he prescribes for the world its 'real' Being, as it were, on the basis of an idea of Being whose source has not yet been unveiled and which has not been demonstrated in its own right ..."[8]

Heidegger's phenomenology reveals that our 'minds' are *always already* 'in touch' with the 'material' world. We do not need to reconcile the one with the other because our primordial experience is that they are already reconciled: "The world is disclosed essentially *along with* the Being of Dasein," writes Heidegger.[9] The problem itself is an artificial one, which emerges only because we have misinterpreted, or really just neglected, our primordial experience of the world as always already *there for us*. We have, in reflection, conceptually divorced ourselves from the world and then puzzled over how to relate ourselves to it again, while being all the time always related to it.

For Heidegger, then, the problem is not in answering how we have come to be related to the world, but in answering how we have come to think of ourselves as detached from it. The problem is that we suppose there to be a problem. But this – that we mistakenly suppose ourselves to be detached from the world – is itself a real problem, which Heidegger takes some pains to address.

We will, as our work proceeds, consider Heidegger's treatment of this second problem. But for now, I would like to remain with Heidegger's solution to the first, and consider whether it really works.

"The world," Heidegger writes, "is disclosed essentially *along with* the Being of Dasein."[10] This is certainly true. The question, however, is: what is the ontological status of the '*along with*'? *Whose* 'Being' does the 'along with' belong to? Heidegger's answer would seem to be that the 'along with' belongs to the Being of Dasein itself. "*Dasein*

8 Heidegger, *Being and Time*, p. 129, H. 96.

9 Ibid., p. 247, H. 203.

10 Ibid.

is its disclosedness."[11] If Dasein *is* its disclosedness, and the world is disclosed in this disclosedness, and there is no need to question *how* the world comes to be disclosed in this disclosedness, then this implies that the world, somehow, is inseparable from this disclosedness. Thus, Dasein's Being and the Being of the world disclosed to it are, in some sense, *one*. But what about the *other person* to whom the world is also disclosed? The implication seems to be that *my* world, the world disclosed through me, is identical with *my* Being. That's fine so long as I am sitting alone in my room. But what about when I go out to meet you? You are also disclosed in 'my' world. Are you, then, also identical with my Being? Certainly, we would not wish to say so. But if I except you from identity with my Being, what of the world *between* us? W*hose* world is this? These problems are not as easily dispensed with as Heidegger seems to suggest.

Let us consider: You and I sit across the table from one another. I see the table from one perspective, you from another. Nevertheless, we see the *same* table. Not only must we assume that we see the same table in order to meaningfully communicate with one another, but, if we should ever doubt it, we could amass overwhelming evidence to the effect that we do, indeed, see the same table. I push the salt shaker from my side of the table to your side of the table. You pick it up. Clearly, we are in the same world and dealing with the same things. The saltshaker that *I* see is the saltshaker that *you* pick up. But you do not see it as I see it. You see it from your perspective, I from mine.

Clearly, then, the *Being* of the table cannot be simply identical with our perspectives on it, since these perspectives are not themselves identical. The Being of the table *exceeds*, in some sense, our perspectives on it. It *transcends* us.

So, then, *where* is it? What is the ontological 'space' of its Being? The Being of the table is not identical with *my* disclosedness of it, nor with yours. It is, thus, not simply identical with *our* Beings. It is *transcendent* of us. Its Being abides in an ontological 'space' that is not simply identical with ours. And yet it is certainly *related* to ours. We each have a perspective on it. It coincides with us to some degree but *exceeds* us. The only alternative to this conclusion is solipsism.

11 Ibid., p. 171, H. 133.

Does this drive us back to Cartesian dualism? Must we return to the notion that the table and saltshaker are essentially 'material' entities abiding in an 'objective' space which our 'minds,' somehow, consciously 'respond' to – with all the problems of relating mind to matter that we've considered?

Perhaps.

And yet even Descartes, as we have seen, was not a 'Cartesian dualist' in quite the sense we've been using the term. Descartes never posited an *absolute* dichotomy between mind and matter, between *res extensa* and *res cogitans*. Rather, they are resolved, for Descartes, in the mind of God. In the *mind* of God. Ultimately, for Descartes, *res cogitans* and *res extensa* derive from something that is far more like mind than matter.

The view that reality is essentially mind-like is called 'idealism.' Heidegger is aware of the idealist implications of his work. He writes: "If what the term 'idealism' says amounts to the understanding that Being can never be explained by entities but is already that which is 'transcendental' for every entity, then idealism affords the only correct possibility for a philosophical problematic."[12] His objection to the label *idealist* involves his feeling that it implies a choice for mind-substance over matter-substance, when, as he maintains, the whole problematic of mind vs. matter as distinct *substances* has been ill-conceived.

The 'modern-empiricist' solution to this problem tends toward materialism. What materialism basically does is to take the *factual* account of the world as ontologically fundamental. How human beings with *minds* fit into this factual account is something materialism hasn't yet worked out. But regardless of our assessment of materialism's capacity to solve this problem, it is important for us to see the *axiological* implications of materialism. The *factual*, as we have seen, is constructed by reducing the meaningful to its *least common denominator*. This has *practical* value, for it allows us to decontextualize features of our experience of the world so as to make them useable in other contexts. But as a *fundamental* ontology, it effectively renders the world meaningless.

12 Ibid., p. 251, H. 208.

What do we mean by 'meaningless'? If meaning expresses the way in which something matters to us, then the statement that the world is meaningless might be thought to be the assertion that the world does *not* matter to us. But this, of course, is not true. The world *does* matter to us. *We* matter to us and we are indissolubly implicated in the world which, therefore, also matters to us. To say, then, that the world is meaningless is really to say that the world *resists* our mattering to us, it *defeats* our mattering to us. And, certainly, it often does. But does it do so *essentially*? These are the issues that are at stake.

Our concerns here are not metaphysical, but axiological. We are wrestling with the question of what hermeneutic of existence will be possible for us. Heidegger never provides us a way of modeling the world that would allow for the transcendence of the table and the saltshaker without a reversion to Cartesian dualism. If we are to make fast Heidegger's insights concerning Being-in-the-world, if we are to make them available to us in our actual living, we must try to find one. Such a model will also help us address ethical and religious issues concerning Dasein's relations with others, by helping us see that such relations are not incidental to Dasein's Being, but essential.

I am by no means going to give – nor am I capable of giving – a fundamental metaphysic of Being. The best we can do is *gesture* to that which is, admittedly, beyond us. We are looking for a workable model that will accommodate the possibility of *meaning* in its fullness; we are not looking for apodictic certainty. The *standard* of certainty is inappropriate to the kinds of truths we are now seeking: truths of *meaning*.[13] Still, this is not to say that some accounts are not *better* than others.[14]

You and I sit across the table from one another. I have a perspective on the table and so do you. The table itself, we must concede, is

13 "It is the mark of the educated man to look for precision in each class of things just so far as the nature of the subject permits..." Aristotle, "Nicomachean Ethics," trans. W.D. Ross, in *The Basic Works of Aristotle*, p. 936, 1094b.

14 David Carr considers many of the paradoxes involving the world's 'immanence in' and 'transcendence of' the subject in his book *The Paradox of Subjectivity: The Self in the Transcendental Tradition* (New York: Oxford University Press, 1999). He writes: "The relation between the transcendental subject and world is not a part-whole relation but exclusively an intentional relation. Thus the world is not a part of the subject and the subject not part of the world. But this does not make the transcendental subject worldless, since its only function is to give meaning to the world." (p. 134) Carr sees no resolution to the paradox: "These two descriptions of the subject—subject for the world and object in the world—are equally necessary and essentially incompatible."

transcendent of our perspectives on it. And yet they are perspectives on just this table. They are not perspectives on some *other* table. Thus, though the table is transcendent of our perspectives it is also *immanent* to our perspectives. The table is immanent to our perspectives but not reducible to these perspectives. The table 'in itself' *exceeds* our perspectives. *Where* is this excess?

The 18th century thinker George Berkeley, considering this problem, answered, 'the mind of God.' We make no pretense to being able to work out the metaphysics of this, any more than the materialist can work out the mechanics of how matter turns into mind. But our concern is with the implication this has for the question of *meaning*. For the materialist, the table is essentially *meaningless*. It is *matter* upon which I *project* a meaning. The materialist is not troubled by the thought that this interpretation of the table is *already* a projection. But we now say that the table is 'in the mind of God.' It is, in other words, an item in *God's* 'Being-in-the-world.' It is a *creation* of God's. This suggests that it already *has* a meaning, *transcendent* of me and my projections.

What is this meaning? Certainly, I cannot simply identify *my* meaning for the table with *God's*. Much of the reaction against monotheism in the modern world is a response to the cultural hegemony involved in identifying one's *own* meanings with *God's*. I am aware, then, that *your* meaning for the table may differ from mine. Beyond this, I myself can put the table to a variety of uses. What the table means for me today it may not mean for me tomorrow. Today it may be a dinner table, tomorrow a desk. Perhaps after that, we will chop it up for firewood. We can do so because the table, the *matter* of the table, has a certain plasticity to it. It is not confined to just one meaning. It can accommodate multiple meanings. But in this very openness to divergent meanings, may we not, indeed, see a meaning? Is not one of the meanings of matter just this plasticity? Matter has meaning, among other things, as the capacity to *embody* meanings that we invent. In this 'mind of God,' then, there is the opportunity

(p. 135). A question remains, however, as to whether some way of thinking about the metaphysical 'substratum' of the self-world relation, through which the paradox would be resolved (if we only understood it), may be necessary for meaning-constitution itself. To the extent that it is, metaphysical materialism and metaphysical idealism become significant, not as possible solutions to the conceptual paradox, but as having different implications for the self's understanding of its relations to self, world, and other.

for human *inventiveness*. There is the opportunity for human *differentness*. The table may mean one thing to me and another to you. And just because of this, just because of this openness to difference, there is the opportunity for human *freedom*. Matter's plasticity is not its meaninglessness, rather its *meaning* is its plasticity.

When we look at the table in this light, then, we see a plurality of meanings. There is the plasticity of the matter, whose meaning is just this plasticity, and there is the meaning of the table *as* a table; i.e., *as* a cultural artifact. This matter, in this case, has been made into something culturally meaningful, it has been joined to a human meaning; it is a *table* – a table around which we eat and drink, a table around which we commune, a table upon which we work. We cannot look up the meaning of *this particular table* in the dictionary. Here is the place where we carved our initials as children. Here is the corner around which we sat through the night conversing.[15] Even when the *matter* of this table is gone, the *meaning* of this table will endure for as long as we remember it. But, of course, one who has not had these experiences with the table will not be able to share in these, *our*, meanings for the table. Thus, the 'table' will have a variety of meanings in relation to the variety of people who encounter it.

And this is a point we must note and whose implications we must come to understand. The same item is susceptible to a variety of meanings, a variety of interpretations. The variability of meaning, in this regard, is a function of the *relationality* of meaning together with the *diversity* and *creativity* of human beings. Given the relational nature of meaning, and the diversity of human beings, meaning *must*, necessarily, manifest itself variously for different individuals, different cultures, and different historical epochs. This variability of meaning is not to be confused with randomness or meaninglessness. On the contrary, what we see in the pluralistic world is not *meaninglessness*, but, if anything, a daunting abundance of meaning. We are overwhelmed by the vast variety of meanings we encounter and daunted by the task of reconciling them.

---

15 See Martin Heidegger, *Ontology—The Hermeneutics of Facticity*, trans. John Van Buren (Bloomington: Indiana University Press, 1998), sec. 19-20, where Heidegger gives a description of the 'meanings' to be found in his drawing room at home in similar terms.

Consider: I enter the Church. I stand under the vaulted archway and gaze at the tinted light streaming through the stained-glass window. A girl sits in the front pew, praying. I hear the echo of my shoes upon the stone floor. I enter the *schul.* Old men with gray beards davening, whispering. A man in a prayer shawl cries out a prayer in an ancient language. I enter the carnival grounds. My ears are accosted by a cacophony of piped music, shrill laughter, boisterous voices. Visions of hot dogs and cotton candy and running children flash by me. It is all *meaningful*, although not all *clear*. Indeed, the confusion is itself meaningful.[16] The world is a *flood* of meanings.

Where do these meanings come from? We might say, not that they emerge *from* human beings, but that they emerge *through* human beings (who, after all, do not emerge *from* themselves). They emerge *through* the collective efforts of creative (and inspired) individuals whose creativity is never a sheer *creatio ex nihilo* but always an ex-pressing of that which they discover in themselves and in the depths of their world. And, of course, even the most creative (and inspired) human beings always exist far more as receivers of, and responders to, meanings already inherent in their cultures than as creators of new ones. Indeed, the problem we find with Cartesianism – and to which Heidegger's entire philosophy may be seen as a response – is that it entails a certain impoverishment of meaning: the Cartesian *Weltanschauung*, taken as a fundamental ontology, no longer presents the human being with meanings that speak to, or call forth, the most profound human aspirations.

From this perspective, the Monotheist's proclamation that 'God is One' is not to be taken to mean that some *one* of these many meanings should dominate and quash the others, but that *each* of these meanings has its place in the life of God, and are therefore due respect. God's Oneness bespeaks an *inclusivity*; *all* is included in the Oneness of God. Also suggested, of course, is the possibility of an

16 The confusion is meaningful in just this way: Meaning expresses the way in which things matter to me, the way in which I am related to them. In not understanding the meaning of something I do not know how I am related to it; hence, I do not know how to relate to it. The confusion signifies a breakdown in relation. Thus I become isolated and alienated. This is why 'meaninglessness' is so often correlated with alienation. This is also why the Cartesian 'ethos,' if we may call it that, contributes to alienation.

ultimate reconciliation of meanings at the highest level. This possibility of reconciliation drives the need for *interpretation*, which renders meanings *meaningful*, i.e., understandable, across persons and cultures. Such reconciliation does not imply a reduction to cultural uniformity, any more than God's Oneness implies the organic uniformity of all natural life forms. Rather, God's Oneness is manifest in the creation as *relation*, *comm*-unity, in which difference thrives through relation and relation is not broken by difference. In Christianity, the name for such healthful relationality, in which difference and comm-unity support and reinforce one another, is *agapic love*.

But the transcendence of God, as the universal foundation of meaning, also implies certain hermeneutical limits. We cannot make anything at all out of the matter of the table. The matter of the table is something I encounter, it is not something I create. It is not simply *one* with my Being such that I can dispose of it however I like. It has its own character that I must respect. It has a certain spatio-temporal constitution that I cannot violate. These are the *facts* pertaining to it. But, also, given that its ontology is not determined at the *lowest* common denominator of meaning but, ultimately, at the *highest*, there are other limits to observe: aesthetic limits, ethical limits, and spiritual limits. At each of these levels there is a price to pay for violating these limits, and this price varies depending upon the nature and extent of the violation. Our failure to fully observe these higher-order limits in the modern world is bringing us to the edge of environmental catastrophe.

There is a price to pay because we live in a world whose contours are axiological. This axiology is not imposed upon us but inherent within us. If we did not *care*, there could be no price. If it did not *matter* to us, it would make no difference. But, of course, it *does* matter to us. We cannot shake off this mattering because we are, intrinsically, axiological beings. It is just because of this, and only because of this, that we seek to understand the *meaning* of Being, which itself can only mean: to work out the terms of our axiological ontology.

III. Meaning and Truth

We are working our way toward an interpretation of the Judeo-Christian mythos *through* an interpretation of Heidegger's *Being and Time*. We call the Judeo-Christian mythos a *mythos* in order to indicate that it expresses, or seeks to express, high-level meanings rather than mere empirical facts. The Judeo-Christian mythos professes to tell us something of what is *true* about the meaning of human existence. We are, of course, familiar with assessing the truth-value of statements of fact: If I say it is raining out and it is not, I am speaking a factual falsity. But can we say something similar about meaning? Are some statements of meaning more *true* than others?

Heidegger investigates the meaning of the word 'truth' through an etymological analysis of its Greek counterpart, *aletheia*. *Lethe*, in Greek, can mean 'hidden' or 'forgotten,' hence *a-letheia* suggests 'unhiddenness' or 'unforgottenness.' This bears, at least, a semantic resemblance to the Platonic notion of *anamnesis*, which might also be rendered 'unforgottenness.' The implication of both these terms is that the search for truth is an attempt to uncover something that has been concealed, to find again something previously lost. Finally, we note that the Christian term 'revelation' has a similar etymological implication: to re-veal is to 'remove the veil.'

One can only wish to *remove* a veil to the extent that one experiences something *as* veiled; i.e., recognizes that what one presently encounters is, in some measure, distorted or incomplete, in a word, concealed. Concealment as such is a *privative* concept. Concealment must first of all be experienced as privation, as lack, in order for one to see it *as* concealment and wish to overcome it. Hence, the primitive idea of truth, if we accept these etymological clues, always implies a *search* for truth, a *seeking* of truth. Such a search implies a longing and such longing suggests an essential *be*-longing to that which one experiences as somehow missing.

Heidegger begins his discussion of truth by noting its traditional definition as '*adaequatio intellectus et rei*': the adequation of thought to thing. In *Being and Time*, he considers this strictly in its modern sense, as referring to a correlation of human thought to material reality.[17] In a later essay, *On the Essence of Truth,* he notes that this formula is itself the inversion of a more original one referring to the correspondence of a thing to its idea, not in the human intellect, but in the *divine* intellect: "*Veritas* as *adaequatio rei ad intellectum* does not imply the later transcendental conception of Kant ... that 'objects conform to our knowledge.' Rather, it implies the Christian theological belief that, with respect to what it is and whether it is, a matter, as created (*ens creatum*), *is* only insofar as it corresponds to the idea preconceived in the *intellectus divinus*, i.e., in the mind of God, and thus measures up to the idea (is correct) and in this sense is 'true.'"[18]

It is odd that Heidegger never connects this theological notion of truth with the one that he himself develops, but there seems to be a clear connection which we will attempt to draw out. 'Truth,' for Heidegger, means, as we have seen, *unconcealment. Un*concealment has meaning only vis-à-vis concealment; i.e., if Being did not present itself as to some extent 'concealed' there would be no need for 'unconcealment' and hence no explicit concept of truth. The concept of 'truth,' then, stands always in relation to the concept of 'untruth.' The truth is that which has been brought out of the untruth; that which has been unconcealed, disclosed, after having been concealed: "To say that an assertion '*is true*' signifies that it uncovers the entity as it is in itself. Such an assertion asserts, points out, 'lets' the entity 'be seen' (*apophansis*) in its uncoveredness."[19]

This must be understood in relation to Dasein as Being-in-the-world. To say that Dasein is Being-in-the-world, as we have said, is to say that Dasein relates to itself *through* its relation to its world. The quality of its relation to the world, then, is part and parcel of the quality of its relation to itself. If the meaning of beings in the world are in some sense concealed from Dasein, this is as much as to say that Dasein is concealed from itself. In order for Dasein to disclose the true meaning of beings, then, it must first of all come to the truth of itself. Thus, Heidegger writes: "The most primordial, and indeed the most authentic, disclosedness in which Dasein, as a

17 Heidegger, *Being and Tim*e, sec. 44.

18 Martin Heidegger, "On the Essence of Truth," trans. John Sallis, in Martin Heidegger: Basic Writings, 118.

19 Heidegger, *Being and Time*, p. 261, H. 218.

potentiality-for-Being, can be, is the *truth of existence.*"[20] By 'existence' Heidegger refers to Dasein's own Being-in-the-world. Thus truth is realized, i.e., Being is disclosed, when and *as* Dasein comes into the truth of itself: "Truth, understood in the most primordial sense, belongs to the basic constitution of Dasein."[21]

This, it will be noted, bears some resemblance to the Kierkegaardian notion of 'subjective truth' that we reviewed in the last chapter. Truth is a standard to which Dasein's Being may or may not conform. If we were to translate this into theological terms, we might say that it is Dasein itself whose existence can conform to its idea in the *intellectus divines* – the mind of God – or fail to. If it does, when it does, *then* beings are disclosed in their own truth; i.e., in their proper relationship to each other and to Dasein, otherwise all is *awry, disordered*, in *falsity*.

The concept of truth, then, suggests a polarity between two *ways* of Being for Dasein: the way of truth and the way of untruth. It refers to what we have been calling *meaning*, but with a qualification. It suggests that some expressions and/or disclosures of meaning are axiologically *sound* and some are not, some are genuine expressions of the actual thrust of our caring, and some distortions and misrepresentations of our caring. Dasein can live in terms of genuinely disclosed meanings, or can live in self-distortion, in self-concealment. When it does the former it lives 'in the truth,' when it does the latter it 'lives in untruth.' For the most part, Heidegger tells us, Dasein lives in untruth: "*Because Dasein is essentially falling,*" writes Heidegger, *"its state of Being is such that it is in 'untruth'*."[22]

Heidegger insists that his use of the term 'untruth' does not bespeak a value judgment. "This term ... is here used ontologically. If we are to use it in existential analysis, we must avoid giving it any ontically negative 'evaluation'."[23] But this leads to the question of what *criteria* may be brought to bear for discerning truth from untruth. Since truths concern meanings, and not mere empirical facts, we cannot apply a simple empirical criterion. If there is also no distinction to be drawn concerning *value*, if one interpretation of Being is not

20 Ibid., p. 264, H. 221.
21 Ibid., p. 269, H. 226.
22 Ibid., p. 264, H. 222.
23 Ibid., pp. 264-265, H. 222.

ultimately *better* than another, i.e., more expressive of or conducive to *the good*, it is hard to say in what sense one might be said to be 'true' and the other 'false.'

We can take an example from the sphere of physical health. In what sense is it ever true to say that a person is sick? We can describe the state of the body in empirical terms, but to then add the qualification that this state constitutes 'sickness' is to apply a normative standard whose justification is axiological. We suppose it to be better for the body to be in one state than another, and suppose the standard by which we judge this to be inherent to the nature of the body itself, not a mere prejudice we project upon it. There is a healthful state of the body, and when the body conforms to this state it is as it *should* be. Except for some such axiological criterion it is hard to see how there can be truth or untruth in the sphere of health, or, more generally, human Being.

Of course, the Medieval Scholastics, who first articulated the definition of truth as '*adaequatio rei ad intellectum*,' where the *intellectum* in question was that of God, had no problem in this regard. To live truly was to live in conformity with the Divine will and mind; it was to actualize oneself as the 'image of God.' Such an understanding of truth may be called ontological, but only so long as we recognize that, for the Scholastics, ontology was always, implicitly, *axio*-ontology. God is goodness itself. God is, at once, supreme Being *and* supreme Good.[24] That which conforms to its idea in the mind of God actualizes, by that very conformity, its supreme good.

But Heidegger does not speak in terms of God. The distinction between Dasein 'in the truth' and Dasein 'not in the truth' is rendered as the distinction between 'authenticity' and 'inauthenticity.' Authentic Dasein, as Heidegger presents it, is one who "resolutely" pursues its "ownmost potentiality-for-Being." Heidegger's notion of potentiality, as we have seen, seems to draw upon the Aristotelian distinction between actuality and potency. The actuality is *implicit* in the potency. The potency is not a bare openness to any and all possibility; it is an impetus to its *own* actualization. The potency

24 "Goodness and being are really the same, and differ only in idea... The essence of goodness consists in this, that it is in some way desirable." Thomas Aquinas, The Summa Theologica, vol. 1, trans. Fathers of the English Dominican Province (Westminster, Maryland: Christian Classics, 1948), P1, Q5, A1, p. 23.

is driven to actualize itself. Thus, Dasein lives 'in the truth' when it resolves to live according to its *own* potentialities rather than in accord with random schemes that have been thrust upon it through its interaction with the world. Such authentic commitment to the realization of one's own potentialities, Heidegger calls "resoluteness."

In a sense, Dasein's "ownmost potentiality-for-Being" serves the role, for Heidegger, that God serves for the Scholastics. It provides a standard of existential *truth* to which Dasein may or may not conform, and upon which it may or may not resolve. In resolving upon it, Dasein *chooses* to actualize its authentic self, but it does not thereby *create* itself; on the contrary, Dasein must resolve upon what it *already inherently is*.

But what is it? If we are to distinguish between Dasein's truth and untruth we must know something of Dasein's essential potentialities, since it is in relation to these that Dasein may or may not be 'in the truth.' What is authentic Dasein to resolve *upon*? At this point, Heidegger's work takes an odd turn: "What if resoluteness, in accordance with its own meaning, should bring itself into its authenticity only when it projects itself not upon any random possibilities which just lie closest, but upon that uttermost possibility which lies ahead of every factical potentiality-for-Being of Dasein, and, as such, enters more or less undisguisedly into every potentiality-for-Being of which Dasein factically takes hold? What if it is only in the anticipation of [*zum*] death that resoluteness, as Dasein's *authentic* truth, has reached the *authentic certainty* which *belongs* to it?"[25]

Dasein, Heidegger tells us, is "Being-towards-death." Death, in some sense, expresses the *truth* under which Dasein must live if it is to live authentically. Indeed, it is because Dasein is in *flight* from this truth that the genuine *meaning* of Dasein and its world has been concealed from it. Thus, it is Dasein's flight from death, which is also its flight from itself, that produces the polarity of truth and untruth. Dasein hides the meaning of itself from itself because it finds this meaning repellent. We will find that the Judeo-Christian interpretation of human existence both agrees, and disagrees, with Heidegger's assessment. But if we are to understand how Heidegger has arrived at this conclusion, we must first follow the argument of

25 Heidegger, Being and Time, p. 348, H. 302.

Being and Time as Heidegger himself presents it to this point. It is to this we turn in the next chapter.

III

Dasein

When Heidegger writes that Dasein is "Being-towards-death," he does not simply mean that Dasein is destined to die. He means something more like: Dasein lives under the specter of death. 'Specter' is my word and Heidegger might avoid one with so negative a connotation. Nevertheless, Being-towards-death is a *way* of Being for Dasein, a *mode* of Being realized through a specific *understanding* of Being. It is a way of Being that is *native* to Dasein as such. It is, in Heidegger's phrase, Dasein's "uttermost possibility," i.e., the possibility that in some sense qualifies every other possibility.

Dasein can live in acknowledgment or disacknowledgment of Being-towards-death, but in neither case can Dasein escape it. To live in acknowledgement of it is what first allows Dasein to live in *truth*. To live in disacknowledgement of it is to live in distortion, concealment, flight. This distinction, then, corresponds to the distinction between authenticity and inauthenticity, truth and untruth. Authentic Dasein lives in acknowledgement of Being-towards-death, and therefore in the truth of itself, inauthentic Dasein lives in some form of denial or flight from this, and hence in untruth.

Being-towards-death has a specific character, which Heidegger spends some time laying out in detail. We will also spend some time considering it. But the task of this chapter is to set the discussion in context by reviewing how Heidegger has arrived at this notion. The concepts we have already developed in the last two chapters will aid us in this.

I. THE QUESTION OF THE MEANING OF BEING

Being and Time begins as an investigation into the question of the meaning of Being, a question which, Heidegger tells us, "has today been forgotten."[1] The brief preface to *Being and Time* begins with a quote from Plato's *Sophist*: "'For manifestly you have long been aware of what you mean when you use the expression 'being.' We, however, who used to think we understood it, have now become perplexed.'"[2]

We might suppose, upon reading this, that we are about to enter into an investigation into grammar or semantics; we wish to clarify the meaning of this word '*being*.' But it is not so much the meaning of the word that Heidegger wishes to direct our attention to, as the impetus that drives us to ask about it. Or, to put this perhaps a better way, it is only through understanding the impetus that drives us to ask this question that we can hope to approach an understanding of that to which the word refers. "Are we nowadays even perplexed at our inability to understand the expression 'Being'? Not at all. So first of all we must reawaken an understanding for the meaning of this question."[3]

We must first understand the meaning of the *question*. "Every inquiry," Heidegger writes, "is a seeking."[4] Every seeking is the seeking of someone who seeks. To properly understand the question, we must understand the seeking that asks about it, and, thus, the being who seeks. The being who asks this question, of course, is *we ourselves*, whom Heidegger calls 'Dasein.' *We* are the being who asks this question. And yet it is a question, Heidegger tells us, that "has today been forgotten." The suggestion, of course – a suggestion which will later be made explicit – is that in having forgotten the question we are asking, we have, in some manner, forgotten ourselves.

Thus, *Being and Time* quickly turns from an investigation into the meaning of the word 'being' to an analysis of the being who investigates this meaning, Dasein. And yet, in this turn, Heidegger by no means abandons his initial interest in the question of the meaning of Being. On the contrary, Heidegger sees clearly, and from the very beginning,

1 Heidegger, *Being and Time*, p. 21, H. 2.
2 Plato, *Sophist*, 244a, as quoted in Heidegger, *Being and Time*, p. 19, H. 1.
3 Heidegger, *Being and Time*, p. 19, H. 1.
4 Ibid., p. 24, H. 5.

that this question is not one that Dasein puts *indifferently*; in asking the question of Being, Dasein is asking the question of *itself*, it is inquiring into the meaning of its *own* Being, it is struggling to learn what it is for *itself to be*, and it is doing so because, for Dasein, *Being* is an *issue*, a matter of concern: "Dasein is an entity which does not just occur among other entities. Rather it is ontically distinguished by the fact that, in its very Being, that Being is an *issue* for it."[5]

In some sense, then, a sense that is not yet altogether clear, Dasein's Being is *at stake*. Dasein's struggle to discover the meaning of Being is also its struggle to resolve the issue that it is to itself. But all of this, at this point, is 'seen through a glass darkly.' Dasein has 'today' *forgotten* this question, and *Being and Time* takes its stance from the standpoint of this forgottenness. In Heidegger's later writings he will approach the question of Being from a new standpoint, presumably from the standpoint of the *recollection* of the question. But *Being and Time* is only on the way to that transition. Dasein has 'today' forgotten the issue that it is to itself and it is from within this forgottenness that it must begin, again, to inquire – and it *must* begin because, however oblivious it is to itself, it continues to be motivated by *just this issue*.

We recall that it is just such obliviousness that Kierkegaard found so 'comical' about Hegelian philosophy. The 'Herr Professor' (as Kierkegaard calls Hegel) churns out paragraph upon paragraph about the 'meaning of Being' while never showing the least evidence of being personally engaged; as if the whole thing concerned someone else. In this respect, it is part of the strange genius of *Being and Time* that Heidegger manages to find a language that opens up the passionate interestedness of Dasein while remaining, all the time, descriptive and detached. Is Heidegger also displaying 'Hegelian' aloofness? It seems there is a difference. Heidegger manages to present us with a work that is, at once, written in the mode of 'objective reflection' while being, at the same time, an exposé of it. He presents what might otherwise be dismissed as 'subjective musings' in a mode that gives it the seriousness and status of a 'scientific' inquiry. He writes in a later work that the language of *Being and Time* "even falsifies itself, for it does not yet succeed in retaining the essential help of phenomenological seeing while dispensing with the inappropriate

5 Ibid., p. 32, H. 12.

concern with 'science' and 'research.' But in order to make the attempt at thinking recognizable and at the same time understandable for existing philosophy, it could at first be expressed only within the horizon of that existing philosophy and its use of current terms."[6]

And yet this very need to falsify language helps to make Heidegger's point. The objective inquiries of science and research are never *just* 'objective inquiries,' because there is no domain of 'objectivity' that is untouched by Dasein's self-concern. To the extent that they pose as such they reveal, through their very attempt to conceal, Dasein's discomfort with itself. The question of Being, then, as a seeking, proves to have a deeply ambiguous quality. It is, in fact, a *hiding and* a seeking. This very questioning, which arises out of Dasein's fundamental interest in itself, seeks to hide from itself the very interest that motivates it.

II. The *Mineness* of Dasein

Dasein, says Heidegger, "is in each case *mine*."[7] In naming the human being, 'Dasein,' Heidegger means to indicate, among other things, that Dasein is to be considered, not as an anthropological specimen, a member of the genus 'Homo Sapien,' but as the 'I' who is named in every first person reference. It is *I* who am concerned with myself, and it is only *as me* that I am concerned. The one who is being investigated *is also* the one who is investigating, and this is not an odd coincidence that just happens to be true in this case, it is essential to the nature of *all* investigation. There is no investigation that is not instigated by some *I* for the sake of some *I*; the scientific ideal of objective reflection, in which the *I* is disregarded, involves a kind of falsification. Dasein is in each case *mine* and there is no Dasein

6 Heidegger, "Letter on Humanism," in *Basic Writings*, 258.

7 "That Being which is an *issue* for this entity in its very Being, is in each case mine. Thus Dasein is never to be taken ontologically as an instance or special case of some genus of entities as things that are present-at-hand. To entities such as these, their Being is 'a matter of indifference'; or more precisely, they 'are' such that their Being can be neither a matter of indifference to them, nor the opposite. Because Dasein has *in each case mineness* [*Jemeinigkeit*], one must always use a personal pronoun when one addresses it: 'I am,' 'you are.'" Heidegger, *Being and Time*, pp. 67-68, H. 42.

who is not some *me*; i.e., some self-concerned being whose Being is an issue to itself.

Thus, Dasein is a self-concerned self-relation. The very notion of self-relation suggests the circularity of going forth and coming back; a self-separation that resolves itself (or tries to) in a self-reunion. This process is what Heidegger calls '*existence*.' In later writings Heidegger will make explicit what is implicit in his choice of this word by spelling it *Ek-sistence,* and thereby emphasizing its etymology, which means 'to stand (*sistere*) out (*ek*).' Dasein is existent insofar as Dasein, as a concernful self-relation, *stands out* beyond itself into its possibilities. But insofar as these possibilities are indeed *its* possibilities, in standing out beyond itself it also stands out *toward* itself. Thus, Dasein *is* itself *as* standing out beyond-itself-toward-itself. It is this structure of concernful-standing-out-beyond-itself-toward-itself that Heidegger means by *existence*. *Being and Time*, thus, as an exploration of the Being of Dasein's existence, is an existential-ontology.

III. Being-in-the-World

Dasein stands out beyond itself *toward* its possibilities *through* its world. As ek-sistent, Dasein does not simply happen to be involved in a world; it is of the very nature of ek-sistence that it must stand out beyond itself and have that *wherein* it stands out. This '*wherein*' is Dasein's world. As we said earlier, Dasein, as a self-relation, relates to itself *through* its relation to its world. Heidegger's term for this is 'Being-in-the-world.' The hyphens express the idea that Dasein is not, just incidentally, in touch with its world, but that relation to a world is essential to the Being of Dasein. Dasein cannot *be* without its world. Relation to a world is *constitutive* for Dasein's Being.

And it is in the context of this idea that we are able to understand Heidegger's choice of the word 'Dasein' to name the human being. Etymologically, the German word *Dasein* means 'being-there' or 'to-be-there,' and is often used to express existence in the ordinary sense of the term; i.e., in the sense of something's just 'being there' (on the table, in the room, etc.). Heidegger exploits the etymology of this word in order to suggest, once again, a being who stands out from itself into some 'there.' Thus, the term 'Dasein' may be thought of as an abbreviated version of the phrase 'Being-in-the-world.' Both endeavor to say the same thing: that Dasein is a being whose very Being is a standing out from itself into some 'there,' some 'world,' which is also to be understood as an essential aspect of this being's *Being.*

IV. Significance and Meaning

The world that Dasein stands out into is not, primordially, a world of indifferent *things*, although Dasein, in its self-forgetfulness, may take it to be so. *Just* insofar as Dasein is a *concernful* self-relation, Dasein's world presents itself to it as a world of concern; a world, thus, that has *meaning*. 'Proximally and for the most part' (a phrase Heidegger employs throughout to refer to Dasein's customary way of Being) the kinds of meanings Dasein is concerned with are practical. I am writing to a friend. I sit at a desk with a pad and pen, perhaps a cup of coffee. The pad, the pen, the desk are items that have meaning to me in relation to my project of writing. The pad is in-order-to write on, the pen in-order-to write. The pen requires the pad and the pad the pen. The pad, the pen, and the desk are not bare *things* merely 'present-at-hand' in their sensory manifestness, but are related to each other in what Heidegger calls a 'significance-structure' which derives its meaning from my projects; in this case, my project of writing.

My project of writing, of course, is *my* project. It is expressive of my own concernful self-relation – ultimately, of the *issue* that I am to myself. It is my project of writing that renders the pad and the pen and the desk, etc., meaningful. The significance-structure whereby things acquire their meaning is *for-the-sake-of* my project. Language itself is functionally related to such projects. Ultimately the meaning of words – including, of course, the meaning of the word '*Being*,' whose investigation began our inquiry – derive from, and express, my own Being as concernful self-relation.

V. Temporality

The ontological mode of Dasein's relation to its world, and, hence, itself, is *temporality*. Dasein does not only stand out of itself into its world but also into its *future*; and these two 'standing outs' are really one: Dasein stands out into its future *through* its standing out into its world. But Dasein's standing out into its future, which Heidegger calls *projection*, is also Dasein's relationship with itself. Dasein stands out into its future *for-the-sake-of* actualizing its potentialities. Thus, the future is not to be thought of as just a later now which simply comes along as time passes. Rather, future, past, and present are organically connected as the modes of Dasein's self-relation; each requiring the others and implicated in the others.

Insofar as Dasein is concerned with its future, it is (in Heidegger's phrase) "ahead-of-itself," and, indeed, this phenomenon of 'ahead-of-itselfness' is Dasein's primordial access to anything like a future; i.e., Dasein only knows of anything like a future through its standing out *toward* its future, i.e., its 'ahead-of-itselfness.' Something similar is true of past and present. The phenomenal present, says Heidegger, is really a "*making*-present," in which Dasein actively engages with its world for the sake of its project. It is Dasein's project that 'makes' the present what it is – i.e., gives the present its meaningful character. Finally, Dasein is engaged in a world that it finds already there at the time of its engagement. This 'already-there-ness' of the world, Heidegger calls its "having-been." The way in which Dasein experiences the 'having-been-ness' of the world will depend upon the way in which it seeks to make-present, which, in turn, depends upon the character of its 'ahead-of-itselfness,' i.e., its projection upon its future. Once again, it is only due to its experience of the 'having-been-ness' of the world that Dasein is able to form anything like a concept of past. Thus, our customary concepts of past, present, and future are actually abstract derivations from our more primordial immersion in the *phenomena* of the 'ahead-of-itself,' the 'making-present,' and the 'having-been.' These phenomena themselves gain their character from Dasein as *existent*, i.e., as a *concernful* self-relation standing out beyond itself *toward* the actualization of its potentialities. This entire existential structure is an expression of the way in which Dasein is an *issue* to itself, or *cares* about itself. Heidegger, thus, labels the entire structure *Care*.

As we have noted from the start, it is Heidegger's recognition that human Being – and, by implication, Being as such – is permeated through and through by *care* or *concern* that makes his work so significant for the study of religion.

VI. *WHO* IS DASEIN?

Heidegger's inquiry began as an endeavor to understand the meaning of the word *Being*. In order to understand the meaning of this word, Heidegger told us, we had first to understand the meaning of the question that asks about it, and, in turn, the nature of the Being who asks this question: ourselves. We have made some progress. Dasein is a concernful self-relation who projects itself toward the realization of its potentialities through its dealings with its world. It is just this self-projection that renders the world meaningful, including the words it uses to express and represent this world, including, therefore, the word *Being*.

But thus far we have given only the bare ontological structure of Dasein. We have said nothing of what Dasein's projects *portend*. Dasein's projects are for the sake of itself, but *who* is the self to whom these projects refer? Dasein's projects are for the sake of Dasein, who is in each case *mine*, but *who* is the *me* expressed through these projects? Or, to put this another way, what is the fundamental concern that motivates me, and projects me into my future? Clearly, it is only in answering this question that I will then be able to understand the nature of the concern that asks the question of *Being*.

We might suppose we could gain insight into this by looking at the ways in which Dasein, who, after all, *is* itself, understands itself. But now Heidegger entertains a suspicion, a suspicion that has been lurking there from the beginning: "Dasein is in each case mine, and this is its constitution; but what if this should be the very reason why, proximally and for the most part, Dasein is *not itself*? What if the aforementioned approach, starting with the givenness of the 'I' to Dasein itself, and with a rather patent self-interpretation of Dasein, should lead the existential analytic, as it were, into a pitfall?"[8] In other words: what if Dasein's most customary self-interpretations constitute, in fact, a *mis*interpretation of itself? What if Dasein's most ordinary

8 Ibid., p. 151, H. 115-116.

ways of Being are not attestations of who Dasein is 'in truth'? What if Dasein, to put it most simply, is living a lie?

These suspicions are not without their ground. The very fact that we have, thus far, failed to understand the meaning of the most fundamental questions we ask is already some indication that we live in a state of concealment from ourselves. The fact that we have, thus far, represented Dasein as a 'thinking substance' in essential separation from a world characterized as an 'extended substance' shows that our self-conceptualization is at a far remove from the actuality of our existence as concernful Being-in-the-world. The fact that the idea of 'meaning' has been reduced to 'verbal reference,' with no recognition that such references ultimately spring from our projects, which themselves arise from our concerns and circle back upon them, suggests that we live in some disacknowledgment of the thrust of these projects and the nature of these concerns. The fact that we speak of 'past,' 'present,' and 'future' with no recognition of the *care* that is integral to the phenomena that have given rise to these concepts, suggests a drive toward objectification that is itself a concealed drive toward self-concealment. "Perhaps," then, Heidegger writes, "when Dasein addresses itself in the manner which is closest to it, it always says, 'I am this entity,' and in the long run says this loudest when it is 'not' this entity."[9]

VII. DAS MAN

Indeed, Heidegger concludes, 'proximally and for the most part,' the projects that Dasein involves itself in are not expressive of what Dasein is in truth. Rather than living out of its own potentialities, Dasein has, for the most part, had its identity assigned to it by the world, and lives in accordance with this assignment. Dasein comes to understand itself, not in terms who it truly is and what it truly seeks, but in terms of alien meanings and values thrust upon it by the world.

This might at first seem a paradoxical conclusion, since we have already established that Dasein's world gains *its* meaning, *its* identity, from Dasein's potentialities. But this paradox is resolved by taking into consideration something previously neglected: that Dasein lives

9 Ibid.

in a world of *other* people, *other* Daseins. Heidegger writes: "In our previous analyses, the range of what is encountered within-the-word was, in the first instance, narrowed down to equipment ready-to-hand or Nature present-at-hand, and thus to entities with a character other than that of Dasein. This restriction was necessary not only for the purpose of simplifying our explication but above all because the kind of Being which belongs to the Dasein of Others, as we encounter it within-the-world, differs from readiness-to-hand and presence-at-hand."[10]

Just as Dasein, as Being-in-the-world, is essentially and primordially related to its world, so Dasein is essentially and primordially related to other Daseins. This relation Heidegger calls *MitDasein* (Dasein-with). MitDasein is not something in addition to Being-in-the-world but is a component of it; Dasein exists in, *as*, an essential relation to others: "Being with Others belongs to the Being of Dasein ..."[11]

This statement, of course, is not to be read as stating that *others themselves* belong to the Being of Dasein (who is in each case *mine*), but it does raise a series of questions that problematize the way in which Dasein may be thought to be 'with' its world and others. What exactly is the ontological status of the 'with'? We explored some of these questions in the previous chapter, and will have much more to say about them as we proceed. For now, however, we will continue following Heidegger's footsteps.

Insofar as Dasein is also Mitsein (i.e., being-with-others), it is possible for Dasein to get its projects, not from itself, but from just this world of others, and 'proximally and for the most part,' this is indeed what happens, and it characterizes Dasein's everyday life. Rather than being drawn to its future from its own potentialities, its life is driven by the 'alreadyness' of what it encounters in its world. As we might say, Dasein lives *reactively* rather than *proactively*. But, then, *who* is doing the driving? Is there some one person or group of people whose projects are driving this vast human machine?

Heidegger's answer is no. The machine is, in effect, being driven by the unwillingness of anyone to drive. No one wishes to be responsible. Everyone absolves herself of responsibility by taking upon herself the

10 Ibid., p. 154, H. 118.
11 Ibid., p. 160, H. 123.

self-identity foisted upon her by a standard that has itself grown out of no one's setting a standard. This Heidegger calls *das Man*. The word *Man* in German is used somewhat as the English word 'one,' to indicate an anonymous, but also normative, 'anyone,' as in the phrase '*One* does not do that sort of thing.' It is translated (somewhat awkwardly) as "the they" in the Macquarrie-Robinson translation of *Being and Time* that we have been using. This anonymous 'anyone' becomes the standard against which all compare themselves, and from which all take their self-identity. For just this reason the *who* of Dasein is, for the most part, "not itself." Dasein's identity is characterized by a flight from its identity. This Heidegger calls, the "dictatorship of *das Man*," an ironic phrase since das Man is really no one. No one is piloting the human ship. And it is just for this reason that Dasein does not experience the *meanings* of its world as its own.

Although Heidegger has a great deal to say about the way the individual Dasein becomes lost in the world of das Man, he is less clear about how this world itself gets constituted. The world of das Man, after all, is not a chaos. It is full of projects and activities, values, and norms. If it is indeed a result of Dasein's flight from itself, then this flight proves to have its own logic and form and to be remarkably capable of sustaining itself. This suggests that the world of das Man, to the extent that it is a distortion, is a distortion, not merely of authentic Dasein in its individuality, but of authentic *Mitsein*, i.e., social relations. But what would constitute authentic *Mitsein*? This is a question Heidegger tends to neglect, but one at the core of the Bible's concerns. It is a question we will need to consider more carefully as we proceed.

VIII. Anxiety and Thrownness

Why is Dasein in flight from itself? Our search for the question of the meaning of Being has taken a curious turn. This question arises out of Dasein and we will understand it only by understanding Dasein. But Dasein is in hiding from itself. We cannot read the meaning of this question off from Dasein as Dasein presents itself 'proximally and for the most part,' for Dasein is 'proximally and for the most part' *not* true to itself. Heidegger writes: "Thus by exhibiting the positive phenomenon of the closest everyday Being-in-the-world, we have made it possible to get an insight into the reason that an ontological interpretation of this state of Being has been missing. *This very state of Being, in its everyday kind of Being, is what proximally misses itself and covers itself up.*"[12]

But why? In order to understand this, we must bring another aspect of Dasein's Being to light. Dasein is not only projected into its future, it is *affected* by its circumstances. Indeed, Dasein is always already in some mode of *having been* affected. This affective state Heidegger calls 'state-of-mind' (*Befindlichkeit*).[13] It is only because Dasein can be affected that it can be *troubled* by the difficulties it encounters in its world. Dasein's state-of-mind is the most immediate manifestation of the way in which the world *matters* to it.[14]

Dasein always already encounters the world from the perspective of some affective mode, some 'state-of-mind,' which is manifest as some specific 'mood' (*Stimmung*). Such moods are not arbitrary feelings, but are disclosive of Dasein's relationship to its world: "*Existentially, a state-of-mind implies a disclosive submission to the world, out of which we can encounter something that matters to us*. Indeed, from the ontological point of view, we must as a general principle leave the primary discovery of the world to 'bare mood.' Pure beholding [*sans* mood] ...could never discover anything like that which is threatening."[15]

The etymology of Heidegger's term '*Befindlichkeit*' expresses the idea that Dasein always (already) *finds itself* in some state-of-mind, some affective mode. Dasein does not, first of all, *choose* its state-of-mind. And this reveals a basic fact about Dasein as existent: Dasein is not a product of itself. When Dasein first becomes aware of itself, it finds itself *already* in a world – some particular world with its

---

12 Ibid., p. 168, H. 130.

13 The English phrase 'state-of-mind,' as Macqurrie and Robinson point out, is a very loose and approximate translation of Heidegger's '*Befindlichkeit*,' which might be more fully rendered: 'the (affective) state in which one finds oneself.'

14 Ibid., p. 176, H. 137.

15 Ibid., p. 177, H. 137-138. It will be noted that what Heidegger is here calling state-of-mind and mood is the ground for what we have previously labeled the 'axiological dimension of being.' Heidegger, in effect, acknowledges the axiological implications of 'state-of-mind' in the quoted passage. Heidegger, though, never explores the relation of states-of-mind to the formation of values and, thus, leaves a very important domain of human concern – even of his own concerns – unconsidered.

particular characteristics to which Dasein has, in some way or other, *already* responded. Dasein finds itself as *already* having-been. Nor does it know the *whence* of its having-been. This Heidegger calls Dasein's *thrownness*. Dasein experiences itself as *thrown* into a world not of its own making: "In thrownness is revealed that in each case Dasein, as my Dasein and this Dasein, is already in a definite world and alongside a definite range of definite entities within-the-world."[16]

Such thrownness is accompanied by *anxiety*. Anxiety, Heidegger tells us, is a basic state of Dasein's Being, and it is from such anxiety that Dasein endeavors to escape through its flight into das Man, which Heidegger also expresses as a 'falling' into the world (of das Man) out of authenticity. Again, we see the strange ambiguity of Dasein. Dasein's anxiety is an expression of the issue that it is to itself. *That* Dasein is an issue to itself is the very thing that makes Dasein uncomfortable with itself. The issue Dasein is to itself leads it to avoid the issue it is to itself. And yet it is just this issue that must be addressed.

Dasein's 'falling' into das Man disburdens Dasein of its having to be responsible for itself, presents Dasein with the illusion that all is well, and thereby soothes Dasein's anxious self-concern: "The supposition of the 'they' [das Man] that one is leading and sustaining a full and genuine 'life,' brings Dasein a tranquility ..."[17]

But it is, decidedly, a false tranquility, and, thus: "falling Being-in-the-world is not only tempting and tranquilizing; it is at the same time *alienating*."[18]

IX. AUTHENTICITY AND WHOLENESS

We are still in search of the meaning of the question of Being. This question arises out of Dasein and we must understand Dasein if we are to understand what the question itself means, but Dasein has proven an unreliable witness to itself. We must endeavor to gain some insight into what Dasein is 'in its truth,' i.e., in its 'authenticity.' We have laid out the existential-ontological structure of Dasein as 'concernful self-relation projected toward the future realization of

16 Ibid., p. 264, H. 222.
17 Ibid., p. 222., H. 177.
18 Ibid., p. 222, H. 178.

its potentialities through its dealings with the world.'[19] This structure Heidegger labels '*Care*.'[20] Care, as we have seen, is 'fallen' into its world and, thus, its self-projective character has become distorted. It no longer projects itself toward its authentic potentialities, but is driven hither and thither by its immersion in das Man. If we are to gain a clear view of what Dasein *authentically* is, then we must consider Dasein's authentic potentialities.

But now Heidegger notes a paradox. In order to know concretely what Dasein is (i.e., the *meaning* of Dasein's Being), we must know something of Dasein's *ultimate* potentialities. True enough, any given project is for the sake of actualizing some potentiality, which renders that project meaningful, and that project, in turn, is for the sake of something further, and so on. But if we are ever to get Dasein's meaning into our view as a *whole*, we must discover the *ultimate* potentiality from which all its more preliminary potentialities acquire their meaning. What is the ultimate '*for which*' of Dasein's Being? What is Dasein, finally, *after*? If we could answer this question we would have Dasein in our view 'as a whole,' which seems essential to knowing *who* Dasein is (authentically).

But given the essential temporality of Dasein this matter turns out to be highly paradoxical: "It is essential to the basic constitution of Dasein that there is constantly something still to be settled ... Such a lack of totality signifies that there is something still outstanding in one's potentiality-for-Being. But as soon as Dasein 'exists' in such a way that absolutely nothing is still outstanding in it, then it has already for this very reason become 'no-longer-Being-there' [Nicht-mer-dasein]."[21] Thus, "As long as Dasein is as an entity, it has never reached

19 Or, as Heidegger puts it: "ahead-of-itself-Being-already-in (the world) as Being-alongside entities which we encounter (within-the-world)" Ibid., p. 293, H. 249.

20 Heidegger distinguishes terminologically between 'Care' (*Sorge*) and its modes of 'concern' with things in the world (*Besorgen*) and 'solicitude' toward people (*Fursorge*). For our purposes it is not necessary to observe these terminological distinctions and we will, generally, use the terms care and concern more or less interchangeably. Care, as the primary signification of Dasein, is, as such, always *self*-concern: "If one were to construct the expression 'care for oneself' [Selbstsorge], following the analogy of 'concern' [Besorgen] and 'solicitude' [Fursorge], this would be a tautology." But *self*-concern, for Dasein as Being-in-the-world-(with-others), is always, also, *world* concern (Besorgen) and *other* concern (Fursorge). Ibid., p. 237, H. 193.

21 Ibid., p. 279-280, H. 236.

its 'wholeness.' But if it gains such 'wholeness,' this gain becomes the utter loss of Being-in-the-world."[22]

It would seem that Dasein, as futurally projective, can only reach 'wholeness' when it has ceased to be projective, for otherwise there is something 'still outstanding.' But given that projectivity is essential to existence itself, Dasein can only cease to be projective when it has ceased to exist; i.e., in death. By this reasoning, it would seem that Dasein can only be "whole' after it has died. But this seems absurd. Dasein does not become "whole" in death, it ceases to exist altogether.

Is it then impossible to speak of Dasein as *whole*? But perhaps this very paradox – that Dasein cannot be regarded as whole in life *or* death – is a function of the fact that we have not yet really grasped the way in which the end of Dasein – death – figures in the *existence* of Dasein: "Have we, in our argument, taken 'Being-not-yet' and the 'ahead' in a sense that is genuinely *existential*? Has our talk of the 'end' and 'totality' been phenomenally appropriate to Dasein? Has the expression 'death' had a biological signification or one that is existential-ontological, or indeed any signification that has been adequately and surely delimited? Have we indeed exhausted all the possibilities for making Dasein accessible in its wholeness?"[23]

The answer, of course, is that we have not.

22 Ibid.

23 Ibid. p. 280, H. 237.

IV

Being-Towards-Death

I. Telos

It may appear that Heidegger has subtly changed the nature of the discussion. We have been involved, up until now, in laying bare the ontological structure of Dasein. Heidegger has emphasized throughout the importance of maintaining an ontic/ontological distinction in these analyses. An *ontological* inquiry seeks to uncover the fundamental structures of Dasein's Being. An *ontic* inquiry is concerned with the particular traits and activities that may arise from these fundamental structures. Thus, *ontologically*, Dasein is "Being-in-the-world." *Ontically*, Dasein's Being-in-the-world may take any number of particular forms: Dasein may be a doctor, a carpenter, a teacher, etc. *Being and Time* is not interested in the *ontic* choices Dasein may make, but in the *ontological* basis upon which it makes any choice.

To this end, Heidegger has arrived at an ontological designation of Dasein's basic structure as (to express it briefly) 'self-projective concern.' Of course, we can expound upon the traits of this basic structure almost indefinitely, and Heidegger goes into great detail enumerating many of its interrelated features. Why are we not now done? Why, with the designation of Dasein as 'self-projective concern,' is our project not complete?

The answer, of course, is that the aim of *Being and Time* was never simply to provide an ontological analysis of Dasein, but to achieve insight into the question of the meaning of Being. The ontological analysis is for this purpose. It is a presupposition of the work that this question is not one that Dasein puts *casually*; it expresses something essential to the nature of Dasein itself, insofar as Dasein's Being is an *issue* to itself. So, we must now ask: having identified Dasein as 'self-projective concern' have we answered our initial question? Have we resolved the perplexity that launched our inquiry? It does not appear that we have, or at least not fully. Why not?

It can only be that the meaning of this question is not fully given in Dasein's purely *formal* structure. It seems that we need to inquire into the *character* of Dasein's concern in order to make further progress. Does this violate the ontic/ontological distinction? Is investigation into the *character* of Dasein's concern an *ontic* investigation? We need to consider this more carefully.

Heidegger himself does not explicitly discuss this, but perhaps we can gain some insight by putting the matter in Aristotelian terms. In the designation of Dasein as 'self-projective concern,' we have, in effect, given an ontological account of Dasein in respect to what Aristotle would call *formal causality*. And yet, in this very form is revealed the fact that Dasein's ontology is not fully specified through its *form* alone. For Aristotle, the most important ontological determinant of a Being is not its formal but its final, or *telic*, cause – i.e., that *toward which* it aims. Indeed, for Aristotle, who was not a mechanistic thinker, the telic cause is ultimately the efficient cause as well, in that every entity is propelled toward the fulfillment of its *telos*. As we have seen, Heidegger draws upon this insight, or seems to, in developing his concept of temporality as primarily *futural*.

What is Dasein's ultimate *telos*? What does its Being aim to become? That is the question we must now consider. Our formal reflection on Dasein has revealed it to be a telic being; i.e., a being oriented toward goals or *teloi*. Thus, to complete our investigation into the ontology of Dasein we must consider the question of Dasein's *telic* thrust. Indeed, to ask the meaning of Dasein's questioning, which is what we do when we ask after the meaning of Dasein's question about Being, is itself to inquire into the character of Dasein's *telos*: What is it that Dasein seeks *such that* this question arises?

What Heidegger's inquiry has made clear is that the telic is just as ontologically basic as the formal, and, indeed, must take hermeneutical priority in our understanding of Dasein. It is just for this reason that the recognition of Dasein's lostness in das Man is not of mere sociological interest, but is a factor in the ontological problematic; for it signifies (if we accept Heidegger's analysis) that, in its ordinary living, Dasein is not properly oriented toward its *telos*. Indeed, it is the possibility of such an improper telic orientation that lies behind the distinction between 'authenticity' and 'inauthenticity,' living 'in the truth' and living 'in untruth.' There is something in Dasein's ontology – something inherent to the fundamental nature of Dasein's Being – that *throws it off* and causes it to become alienated from its own true goals.

Heidegger's discussion of Being-towards-death is his attempt to identify this something. In this chapter we will consider Heidegger's treatment of this topic closely. To help make the distinction between the ontic and the ontological clear in this regard, however, and to help shed light on another aspect of Heidegger's analysis that is critical to our discussion, we will first look at Heidegger's comparison of the ontic mood of fear with its ontological basis, anxiety.

II. Fear and Anxiety

The distinction between fear and anxiety, Heidegger will maintain, is not simply that between an ontic mood and its ontological ground but, also, that between an inauthentic and authentic orientation to that ground: "Fear is anxiety, fallen into the 'world,' inauthentic, and, as such, hidden from itself," writes Heidegger.[1] We will consider this claim as we proceed, but for now we are interested in considering in what sense anxiety may be said to be the ontological 'ground' of fear.[2]

In every instance of fear, says Heidegger, there are three elements that may be distinguished: that "in the face of which" we fear (what frightens us), the "mood" of fear itself, and that "about which" we fear (what we fear *for*).[3] What frightens us is one or another thing in the world that we take to be detrimental and, thus, threatening. What we fear *for* is always ourselves. Ordinarily, we take the fear itself to issue from the thing that is fearsome. It is because this or that thing in the world is threatening that I am afraid, and if I could only rid

1 Ibid., p. 234, H. 189.

2 "*Anxiety...is what first makes fear possible.*" Ibid., p. 230, H. 186.

3 Ibid., p. 179, H. 140.

my world of it and things like it, I would cease to be afraid. The fear is taken to be a function of that which threatens.

But, as Heidegger points out, it is only because, in our basic constitution, we can first of all feel threatened, that we can then experience any particular thing as threatening: "Only an entity for which in its Being this very Being is an issue, can be afraid."[4] If we did not first of all care for ourselves, if we were not first of all concerned for our well-being, not only would we not fear, but it would not be possible to experience anything as threatening. That which is threatening is only threatening in relation to our ontological constitution as *care*. But for this, it would be meaningless to speak of the threatening at all.

This signifies that fear does not first come to us from that which is threatening, but that, on the contrary, that which is threatening is threatening only because we are first subject to fear. In this or that particular (ontic) instance of fear, we are revealed, ontologically, as a kind of being who *can* fear; i.e., a being whose Being is an issue to itself, a being who is concerned for its well-being.

This basic self-concern, considered ontologically, is manifest in *anxiety*. The experience of authentic anxiety, according to Heidegger, is a relative rarity.[5] Mostly, even what we call anxiety is experienced as a response to this or that life circumstance. But when anxiety is experienced authentically, it reveals the way in which *we* are an issue to *ourselves*. That is, it reveals that *we* are the issue, not this or that life circumstance. Anxiety is the manifestation of our self-concern *as such*. Thus, whereas the experience of fear drives us away from that which we fear, the authentic experience of anxiety calls us back to ourselves. Fear, in effect, points to something 'out there' as the issue, whereas anxiety indicates that it is I myself, my very Being-in-the-world, that is the issue. It is not this or that life circumstance that *makes me* anxious, rather, Being-in-the-world is anxious as such, and, as such, *makes* this or that life circumstance relevant and/or meaningful.

And yet this raises a question: Granted that I am an issue to myself, and that anxiety, in its ontological character, reveals that it is *I* who am the issue, and not this or that life circumstance—do not

4 Ibid., p. 180, H. 141.

5 "Under the ascendancy of falling and publicness, 'real' anxiety is rare." Ibid., p. 234, H. 190.

these circumstances, and the way in which they excite my anxiety, reveal something of the *character* of the issue that I am to myself? Granted that I am a caring being, *what*, then, do I care *about*? What is the ultimate *telos* of my caring?

III. The Telos of Dasein

The endeavor to identify an *ultimate* telos for Dasein is, as Heidegger notes, paradoxical. How can a being whose very essence is self-projection ever have anything like an *ultimate* telos, given that the realization of such a telos would, presumably, then put an end to just those self-projections?: "If [Dasein's] essence is constituted in part by potentiality-for-Being, then, as long as Dasein exists, it must in each case, as such potentiality, *not yet be* something."[6] But this, Heidegger notes, seems to imply that Dasein's telic ontology resists the possibility of achieving anything like wholeness or completeness: Dasein, as *essentially* self-projective, must be always seeking something beyond itself, seeking to transcend itself. How then can it have an *ultimate* telos or project? But if we cannot identify an ultimate project for Dasein, how can we understand the meaning of its more preliminary projects? Is there no *telic principle* that connects Dasein's projects to one another such that we can understand Dasein as *one* and *whole*? Might the endeavor to understand Dasein as one and whole be futile, given the self-projective nature of Dasein's Being?

And yet, as Heidegger considers this, it occurs to him that Dasein does indeed have the consciousness of coming to a *kind of* completion, namely in death: "As long as Dasein is, there is in every case something still outstanding, which Dasein can be and will be. But to that which is thus outstanding, the 'end' itself belongs. The 'end' of Being-in-the-world is death. This end, which belongs to the potentiality-for-Being – that is to say, to existence – limits and determines in every case whatever totality is possible for Dasein."[7] Certainly, the factor of death must be figured into any account of Dasein's possible 'wholeness.' But this requires that we come to understand just what death *means*, existentially, to Dasein: "If, however, Dasein's

6 Ibid., p. 276., H. 233.
7 Ibid., pp. 276-277, H. 233-234.

Being-at-an-end in death, and therewith its *Being-a-whole*, are to be included in the discussion of its possibly Being-a-whole, and if this is to be done in a way which is appropriate to the phenomena, then we must have obtained an ontologically adequate conception of death – that is to say an *existential* conception of it."[8]

If we are to attain insight into the way death may figure into Dasein's 'wholeness,' we must arrive at an adequate understanding of how Dasein's subjection to death affects it. Let us, then, turn to Heidegger's treatment of this issue.

IV. DEATH

Heidegger asks how we know of death. None of us has yet died, of course. Still, death is a factor in our lives and culture. We experience the dying of others, attend their funerals, grieve their loss, etc. Is this the primary source of our knowledge of death? Do we know of death because we know of others having died? When we think of our own death, do we think of it primarily by way of analogy with the deaths of others? Do we imagine experiencing death in whatever way we observe them to have experienced death?

But, of course, we cannot, for we do not in fact observe their experience of death. Though we can witness the termination of another's biological life, we cannot witness another's death as it is for that person. If we do not get our idea of death from observing the death of others, nor from having experienced death ourselves, whence comes our understanding of the meaning of death? "The only remaining possibility for the analysis of death as dying," writes Heidegger, "is either to form a purely *existential* conception of this phenomenon, or else to forgo altogether any ontological understanding of it."[9]

When we consider our own death, we consider it as the prospect of our coming to an end. But surely, says Heidegger, we do not mean by this end a 'coming to completion,' in the sense of finally having 'together' what had hitherto been lacking: "That Dasein should *be* together only when its 'not-yet' has been filled up is so far from the

8 Ibid., p. 277, H. 234.
9 Ibid., p. 284, H. 240.

case that it is precisely then that Dasein is no longer."[10] Nor may we think of life's culmination in death as like the ripening of a fruit: "With ripeness, the fruit fulfills itself. But is the death at which Dasein arrives, a fulfillment in this sense?"[11] Certainly not, on the contrary, "for the most part, Dasein ends in unfulfillment, or else by having disintegrated and been used up."[12]

So, again, in what sense is death an 'end' for Dasein? We might, of course, think that death is an end simply in the sense of a stopping. When Dasein dies, the process of its life simply stops. This certainly seems to be true, but, nevertheless, we have never thus far experienced such stopping. Such stopping can have meaning for us only as the *prospect of stopping*: "Just as Dasein *is* already its 'not-yet,' and is its 'not-yet' constantly as long as it is, it *is* already its end too. The 'ending' which we have in view when we speak of death, does not signify Dasein's Being-at-an-end [Zu-Ende-sein], but a *Being-towards-the-end* [*Sein zum Ende*] of this entity. Death is a way to be, which Dasein takes over as soon as it is."[13]

In other words, this *prospect of stopping*, this '*being-towards-death*,' is something we already *are*, i.e., it is something that characterizes us now and throughout life. Death has existential meaning just as this pervasive prospect. We live in the awareness (often the denial) of having to die. But even in our denial we manifest our awareness, for the denial is really a *mode* of the awareness itself. Death, the prospect of death, is not merely something we encounter at the *end* of our lives, it is something that characterizes our lives throughout.

Existentially, then, death is construed as Being-*towards*-death, and such Being-towards-death is recognized as, in some manner, characterizing life; i.e., as rendering life meaningful in a distinctive way. Our next question, then, is: in what way? What is the character of Being-towards-death?

---

10 Ibid., p. 287, H. 243.
11 Ibid., p. 288, H. 244.
12 Ibid.
13 Ibid., p. 289, H. 245.

V. THE CHARACTER OF BEING-TOWARDS-DEATH

Heidegger divides the character of Being-towards-death into five primary elements: Death is Dasein's 'ownmost,' it is 'non-relational,' it is 'not to be outstripped,' it is 'certain,' and it is 'indefinite.' Let us consider each of these in turn.

1. DEATH AS DASEIN'S 'OWNMOST'

Dasein, as existent, is a being who is essentially projected toward possibilities. Insofar as Dasein is 'towards-death,' then, death too may be regarded as a possibility toward which Dasein is projected, although certainly a distinctive one. What, then, is death the possibility of? It is, says Heidegger, "the possibility of no-longer-being-able-to-be-there."[14] This possibility does not confront Dasein from elsewhere, like the possibility of winning the lottery, or the possibility of encountering a storm, rather it is an essential feature of Dasein's very Being. But even as an essential feature of Dasein's Being, it is utterly distinctive. Death is the possibility of im-possibility, i.e., of no further possibility. The prospect of death, thus, pertains to me in a way that no other prospect does. Grammatically, I can construct the sentence 'I will die' along the same lines as 'I will go to the market,' but this grammatical similarity conceals a profound dissimilarity, for whereas it is *I* who will experience the market when I go, I will not experience 'my' death. Death is the end of experience. Thus, to state it more precisely, it is not I *who* dies, it is the I *that* dies.

Death threatens the very *mineness* of my Being. It is not something that happens *to* me, but is the end of the 'me' that I am. Thus, death touches *me* in a way that nothing else does or can. Nothing in my Being-in-the-world but *I myself* touches me as intimately as my death. But this sentence itself fails to capture just what is meant. Indeed, the very subject-predicate structure of language makes it all but impossible to adequately express the intimacy of death. Death is not something I do, nor something done to me. It is the elimination of the I that I am.

Thus, the prospect of death, Being-towards-death, when confronted forthrightly, highlights the *I* that I am in a way that nothing

14 Ibid., p. 294, H. 250.

else can. In highlighting the I it highlights the issue that I am to myself. My death, thus, is distinctively ***mine***, distinctively ***my own***. For this very reason I cannot flee from the prospect of my death without fleeing from *I* myself. This is what Heidegger means when he says that, as das Man, Dasein is ***not itself***. He does not mean that Dasein flees from some characteristic of itself, but from the very *I* that it is. It flees from the I that it is by evading its very ***I-ness***.

Being-towards-death, then, is one's ownmost in an altogether *distinctive* way, indeed, in the way that *I myself* am my own.

2. Death is 'non-relational'

It is for this reason that death is also 'non-relational.' Of course, Heidegger has made clear that Dasein's Being, as Being-in-the-world, is essentially related to the things and people encountered in its world. The 'non-relationality' of which Heidegger here speaks is, again, a distinctive one.

What death reveals to Dasein is that nothing in its world does, or can, provide for it an ultimate support. Thus, through Being-towards-death Dasein sees that its Being cannot, and, hence, does not, finally depend upon the world of things and others. In this respect, 'non-dependent' might better capture what Heidegger intends here than non-relational. Dasein's Being, in its ultimate status, is independent of the world, hence it need not be in thrall to the world. Being-towards-death, writes Heidegger, "makes manifest that all Being-alongside the things with which we concern ourselves, and all Being-with Others, will fail us when our ownmost potentiality-for-Being is the issue."[15]

3. Death is 'not to be outstripped'

Death is Dasein's 'uttermost possibility'; i.e., it is not on the way to anything and thus does not have its meaning in terms of something else. Resolved upon authentically, it allows Dasein to take ownership of itself as a whole, and to order its priorities accordingly: "Since anticipation of the possibility that is not to be outstripped discloses also all the possibilities which lie ahead of [i.e., before] that possibility, this anticipation includes the possibility of taking the whole of Dasein

15 Ibid., p. 308, H. 263.

in advance in an existentiell manner; that is to say, it includes the possibility of existing as a *whole potentiality-for-Being*."[16]

4. Death is 'Certain'

The certainty that pertains to death is not inductive and statistical, although everyday Dasein tends to represent it as such and thereby objectify death as, essentially, something that happens to others. But the certainty of death is revealed in our ineluctable anxiety with respect to it: "In evading its death, even everyday Being-towards-the-end is indeed certain of its death in another way than it might itself like to have true on purely theoretical considerations. This 'other way' is what everydayness for the most part veils from itself."[17] The certainty of death presents Dasein with the choice of either 'holding it for true' or living in evasion of it.

5. Death is 'Indefinite'

Finally, death's certainty is indefinite. Dasein does not know when it will come, and this 'not knowing' keeps Being-towards-death *alive* as a constant factor in Dasein's existence.

VI. Death and das Man

We return again to the question we asked above: How does Dasein know of its death? Whence does the understanding of death that Heidegger has sketched above arise? Our knowledge of death, Heidegger insists, is neither empirical nor theoretical: "Dasein does not, proximally and for the most part, have any explicit or even theoretical knowledge of the fact that it has been delivered over to its death, and that death thus belongs to Being-in-the-world. Thrownness into death reveals itself to Dasein in a more primordial and impressive manner in that state-of-mind which we have called 'anxiety'."[18] "Being-towards-death," writes Heidegger, "is essentially anxiety."[19]

---

16 Ibid., p. 309, H. 264.
17 Ibid., p. 302, H. 257-258.
18 Ibid., p. 295, H. 251.
19 Ibid., p. 310, H. 266.

We can become clearer about this by considering what it is that one who fears death may be said to fear. If death is essentially 'no longer being there,' then, presumably, the dead are no longer there to suffer from it. There is, then, quite literally, ***nothing*** to fear. And yet this realization does not relieve the fear of death. The fear of death is a feature not of death as such, but of death as *impending*. Death's meaning is exhausted, so to speak, in the ***prospect of death***. The existential concept of death is, ultimately, nothing but this prospect itself. Whereas death as an event may lie in the future, the meaning of death, i.e., the prospect of death, is ever-present throughout life. It is, to express it in the terms we explored in chapter two, a distinctive feature of Dasein as *futural*.

The character of death as impending is revealed, says Heidegger, in ***anxiety***: "In anxiety," Heidegger writes, "one feels '***uncanny***'."[20] The word that Macquarrie and Robinson translate as 'uncanny' is the German word '***unheimlich***' which literally means 'unhomelike.' This literal meaning is important to Heidegger's sense. Being-in-the-world, ***as such***, feels not at home with itself. Such not-at-homeness is revealed to it in, ***as***, anxiety. Such anxiety does not arise from this or that life circumstance. It is an essential feature of Dasein: "That ***about which*** anxiety is anxious reveals itself as that ***in the face of which*** it is anxious – Being-in-the-world."[21] Such anxiety has all the characteristics of Being-towards-death we have enumerated: It is one's 'ownmost' – arising essentially from oneself and not conditioned by something else; it is 'non-relational' – it is not finally ***relative*** to this or that life-circumstance and, thus, reveals Dasein's ultimate, ontological, independence of its world; it is 'not to be outstripped' – i.e., not to be finally escaped through some modification of circumstances; it is 'certain' in an even more primordial sense than Descartes' *cogito*, for it reveals the truth of Dasein in a more authentic way than does the *cogito*[22]; and it is 'indefinite,' in the sense that it is not specific to one thing or another but is a pervasive presence.

20 Ibid., 233, H. 188.

21 Ibid.

22 "The evidential character which belongs to the immediate givenness of Experiences, of the 'I,' or of consciousness, must necessarily lag behind the certainty which anticipation includes. Yet this is not because the way in which these are grasped would not be a rigorous one, but because in principle such a way of grasping them cannot hold *for true* (disclosed) something which at bottom it insists upon as 'having there' as

In anxiety, then, Dasein experiences a sense of being *not-at-home* in itself: *Unheimlichkeit*. This sense of not-at-homeness induces Dasein to flee from itself into its world, a flight which Heidegger calls 'falling into the world': "By this time we can see phenomenally what falling, as fleeing, flees in the face of. It does not flee in the face of entities within-the-world; these are precisely what it flees *towards* ... When in falling we flee *into* the 'at-home' of publicness, we flee in the face of the 'not-at-home'; that is, we flee in the face of the uncanniness which lies in Dasein."[23] We now see the source of Dasein's flight from the truth of itself into what Heidegger has called "das Man." Dasein seeks to escape the uncanniness of Being-towards-death experienced in anxiety, which it can only do through escaping *itself*, through self-forgetfulness, since this uncanniness is a feature of Dasein's own Being as such.

This flight into das Man, while robbing Dasein of its authenticity and its capacity to pursue its authentic potentialities, has a *tranquilizing* effect upon Dasein. It soothes the anxiety inherent in Being-towards-death by, in effect, denying the characteristics of Being-towards-death. First, it denies that Dasein's life is essentially its *own*. As das Man, Dasein takes itself to be merely 'one of the crowd,' adopts the opinions of the crowd, and pursues goals dictated to it by the values of the crowd. Next, das Man denies the *non-relationality*, or, as we have expressed it, *non-dependency*, revealed in Being-towards-death. Dasein *as* das Man persuades itself that the world of things and others can indeed provide it with ultimate, ontological, support, and that, therefore, success in this world is all important. Das Man (i.e., Dasein *as* das Man) also denies the inevitability of death – its *non-outstripability* – by, in effect, allowing Dasein to identify itself with the crowd that endures. Death is always something that has happened to someone else, something that Dasein has *survived*. Also, the *certainty* of death, although acknowledged, is only acknowledged as something that 'happens' to 'everyone,' and, thus, is of no specific concern to oneself. Finally, das Man denies the pervasive impendingness of death, its *indefiniteness*. Death is put off as something that will happen later, at the end of life, which is

true: namely, Dasein itself, which I myself *am*, and which, as potentiality-for-Being, I can be authentically only as anticipation." Ibid., p. 310, H. 265.

23 Ibid., pp. 233-234, H. 189.

always *not yet*, and, therefore, of no immediate concern: "One says, 'Death certainly comes, but not right away.' With this 'but ...,' the 'they' denies that death is certain...Death is deferred to 'sometime later.'"[24]

In all these ways Dasein seeks to escape the anxiety of Being-towards-death and thereby achieve a certain tranquility. Das Man, writes Heidegger, "provides a *constant tranquilization about death*."[25] But such tranquility is gained only at a price, the price of authenticity. Thus, such tranquility is also, at the same time, a self-alienation. The fall into das Man is a fall *from oneself*: "Dasein has, in the first instance, fallen away from itself as an authentic potentiality for Being its Self, and has fallen into the 'world.'"[26] Dasein is tempted to this fall from self by the tranquilization it offers. But such a fall from self is also an alienation from self: "Falling Being-in-the-world is not only tempting and tranquilizing; it is at the same time *alienating*."[27] Such alienation "closes off from Dasein its authenticity and possibility, even if only the possibility of genuinely foundering."[28]

The tranquilization provided by das Man, however, is never complete, and cannot be complete just because it is essentially false. Thus Dasein's "uncanniness pursues Dasein constantly, and is a threat to its everyday lostness in the 'they'."[29] Anxiety is forever 'breaking out' upon Dasein in its lostness, and Dasein is forever employing strategies to manage this break out, but can never succeed once and for all, because, as said, anxiety is essential to the Being of Dasein as such. Thus, Dasein's fleeing from itself is also a *struggle* to flee from itself. Dasein is 'haunted' by the call of its own authenticity; which Heidegger dubs 'the call of conscience.' We will discuss this call in the next chapter.

---

24 Ibid., p. 302, H. 258.
25 Ibid., p. 298, H 253.
26 Ibid., p. 220, H. 175.
27 Ibid., p. 222, H. 178.
28 Ibid.
29 Ibid., p. 234, H. 189.

VII. DEATH AND WHOLENESS

We must now consider in what sense Heidegger's treatment of Being-towards-death resolves the paradox of Dasein's telos, which must be resolved if we are ever to grasp Dasein as an ontological *whole*. This, remember, is necessary in order to finally understand the question of the meaning of Being, which is, as well, the question of the *issue* that Dasein is to itself.

The paradox may be stated, again, as follows: Dasein, as existent, is essentially self-projective. Dasein is always projected upon its own potentialities. It is from the 'upon which' of Dasein's projections that Dasein's world, and its life, acquire meaning. To understand Dasein as a whole, then, it would seem we must understand the *ultimate* 'upon which' of its projection, for this is what would provide final meaning to the entirety of Dasein's life. But it would seem that Dasein, as *essentially* self-projective, cannot have an *ultimate* upon-which, for were it ever to reach such an ultimate state this very reaching would be Dasein's undoing as the self-projective being it is. Does this signify, then, that Dasein's life cannot *have* coherent meaning, or that Dasein, for as long as it lives, is essentially fragmentary?

On the contrary, says Heidegger, Dasein is able to come to itself as a *whole* through adopting an *authentic* orientation towards death. Through such an authentic orientation, writes Heidegger, "the possibility of Dasein's having an authentic potentiality-for-Being-a-whole emerges."[30] Thus, according to Heidegger, Being-towards-death is able to provide for Dasein something of the 'ultimate telos' we have been asking about.

But how? Death, of course, cannot be construed as a *telos* in the ordinary sense. It is not something Dasein seeks to actualize. Indeed, it *cannot* be actualized. The moment one 'actualizes' death one ceases to be actual. In this respect, says Heidegger, death is *pure possibility*: "In accordance with its essence, this possibility offers no support for becoming intent on something, 'picturing' to oneself the actuality which is possible, and so forgetting its possibility."[31] But this pure possibility nevertheless has *meaning*, in just the ways we have

30 Ibid., p. 311, 266.

31 Ibid., p. 307, H. 262.

cited. It lights up Dasein's self-concern as *its own*, and thereby has the power to draw Dasein out of its lostness in das Man. It constitutes not a specific telos, but what we will call a *telic context*[32] in terms of which Dasein's specific projects may be axio-ontologically oriented and understood.

To get clear on what is meant by 'telic context', let us take an analogy. The mariner navigates his ship *by* the North Star. He does not thereby navigate his ship *to* the North Star. Rather, he navigates his ship from port to port. But he is able to orient himself spatially by reference to the North Star. Through this he is able to know where he is at any given moment, and how to steer his ship so as to get him to where he wants to go. The North Star is a fixed point which allows him to orient himself spatially vis-à-vis his sea voyages. Likewise, Being-towards-death, as Heidegger envisions it, provides an ultimate, axio-ontological *orienting context* that allows one to order one's priorities so as to get one to 'where one wants to go'; i.e., to the fulfillment of one's *ontic* potentialities.

In this respect, Being-towards-death and das Man may be viewed as two opposing *telic contexts*. Each provides Dasein with a certain orientation to life; each makes certain demands and provides Dasein with a certain outlook through which Dasein lives out its specific projects. But, of course, for Heidegger, these two telic contexts are not on a par, nor are they independent of one another. The context of das Man is essentially a reaction to, and a flight from, the context of Being-towards-death which is Dasein's *true* telic context. But, because of the anxiety inherent to Dasein's true telic context, Dasein lives, proximally and for the most part, in flight from itself. The telic context of das Man is essentially a running away from the telic context of Being-towards-death.

To overcome this running away one must reverse it. One must 'run towards' oneself *as* a 'running towards' one's essential Being-towards-death. Such 'running towards' Heidegger calls '*anticipation*.' The word 'anticipation' is the Macquarrie-Robinson translation of *Vorlaufen*, which quite literally means 'running towards.' Such 'running towards' death, of course, does not mean wishing to die or working at dying. On the contrary, according to Heidegger, it is through just

32 This is not Heidegger's term, although it bears some analogies to what Heidegger calls a 'horizon.'

such 'anticipation' of death that one is finally freed to fully *live* as oneself. Anticipation, here, means affirming Being-towards-death as one's ultimate *telic context*; a context that has just the meanings we've seen. This, finally, allows Dasein to wrest itself away from das Man and live as itself. It does not prescribe the specifics of *how* Dasein is to live, but frees Dasein itself to prescribe these specifics from out of its *own* potentialities, rather than have them prescribed for it by das Man. The term Heidegger employs for such self-prescriptivity is *resoluteness*. Authentic Dasein, then, lives as *anticipatory resoluteness*; i.e., as resolved upon the fulfillment of its specific potentialities under the ultimate telic context of Being-towards-death.

There are many questions that arise from this account, however, questions that Heidegger himself never addresses, but which will become important for us in considering the relation of Heidegger's understanding of Dasein to the Judeo-Christian account of human Being. If Being-towards-death is indeed Dasein's true 'telic context' why should it present Dasein with the sense of being 'not-at-home'? One would expect, on the face of it, that Dasein's *truth* would also feel to Dasein like its *home*. Heidegger never gives the kind of thoughtful analysis to the *Befindlichkeit* of *Being-at-home* that he gives to 'not-at-homeness.' And yet, surely, 'not-at-homeness' is only called such because it names what feels like the *privation of being at home.* The state-of-mind of 'not-at-homeness,' then, presupposes a more primordial state of *Being-at-home*. What is the significance of this?

And why should the mood that most essentially characterizes Dasein's authenticity, anxiety, just happen to be associated with a mood whose essential meaning is 'run away!', i.e., *fear*. Heidegger himself has made us aware of the *disclosive* nature of moods, that moods are not arbitrary feelings but are disclosive of meaning. What meaning does anxiety disclose? Is it not *danger*? How is it that so essentially *repellent* a mood as anxiety should be the mood that one must 'run towards' in order to truly realize oneself? Does this not make Dasein the most self-contradictory of beings? A being who is *essentially* repelled by itself?

Next, why should the flight into das Man be *tranquilizing*? One might suppose that the clustering together of a number of essentially anxious beings would result in an *exacerbation* of their anxiety, as each sees her own anxiousness reflected in the others. And yet, on the contrary, it turns out that it is just such clustering that *soothes* Dasein's anxiety, even if incompletely. What is the meaning of this?

Finally, if Dasein is *essentially* self-projective, and in such a manner that the 'upon-which' of its projections is always already implicated in its present self-understanding, would not even the *prospect* of death, i.e., the prospect of no further projections, be an affront to the essential tendency of its Being? Hasn't Heidegger, despite his early cautions, simply conflated the idea of *termination* with the idea of *wholeness*? Wouldn't the wholeness of a self-projective being have to involve the *fulfillment* of its self-projective tendencies rather than their termination, however conceptually vague our idea of such fulfillment might be? Indeed, is not the religious notion of *eternal life*, as the *overcoming* of death, an attempt to convey just such a possibility of fulfillment and wholeness?

Might it be, then, that there is a *third telic context* that Heidegger has not considered? A telic context that is neither Being-towards-death nor das Man, but *through which* the meaning of both may be finally understood? Indeed, we find just such a telic context articulated in the religions of the world, and in the Judeo-Christian mythos in particular, and we name it *Being-towards-life*.

But before we turn to its consideration we must follow Heidegger through his own endeavors to confirm his analyses thus far. Heidegger asks whether there is any indication that Dasein itself feels that it lives, often, in *untruth*. Is Heidegger's claim that everyday Dasein lives in falsity merely an expression of Heidegger's own peculiar prejudices, or can one find something in human culture more generally that suggests Dasein's awareness of such falsity? Does Dasein in general testify to a sense of being 'untrue' to itself? Heidegger believes so, and he believes that we find this testimony in the phenomena associated with what has traditionally been called 'conscience.'

V

The Call of Conscience

I. The Criterion of Truth

Is there an *existential* truth from which Dasein is generally alienated? In the second chapter we considered Heidegger's notion of truth as *aletheia*, i.e., unconcealment. But unconcealment is a metaphor. The metaphorical image is of something once hidden that is now unhidden, something in darkness that has been brought to light. And Heidegger has now delineated two ways of Being that correspond, in his view, to hiddenness and unhiddennness, truth and untruth; i.e., das Man and Being-towards-death.

But even if we grant Heidegger's claim that these two terms name two distinct 'telic contexts' under which Dasein may live, on what grounds does Heidegger maintain that the one constitutes 'truth' and the other 'untruth'? There is a normativity implicit in this claim that requires clarification. This is by no means a minor problem, nor a problem concerning only Heidegger's work. The Judeo-Christian tradition has long advanced a concept of truth with striking similarities to Heidegger's. It has claimed to speak in the name of a truth, not of empirical propositions, but of existence itself. The counterclaim that there is no such truth is characteristic of much modern and post-modern secular thought. Indeed, it is possible to see the epistemological minimalism characteristic of modern thought, beginning with Descartes, as a reaction against the absolutistic, existential truth-claims of the Judeo-Christian tradition.

In his preference for Being-towards-death over das Man, has Heidegger done anything more than reveal his own personal prejudices?

Is there that in Dasein itself which 'calls' it to honor something on the order of 'existential truth'? These are questions that Heidegger himself now entertains: "We must investigate whether to *any* extent and in any way Dasein *gives testimony*, from its ownmost potentiality-for-Being, as to a possible *authenticity* of its existence, so that it not only makes known that in an existentiell manner such authenticity is possible, but *demands* this of itself."[1]

If there is any such thing as *existential* truth, then its *truth* character can only be testified to by existence itself; which is to say, by Dasein. Dasein itself must show some evidence of sometimes feeling 'in truth' and sometimes 'in falsity' with respect to itself. Dasein itself must show signs of being sensitive to some standard of existential *normativity* by which its life 'should' be governed. Heidegger claims that we do indeed see such evidence, and we see it in the phenomenon that has been conventionally called 'conscience.'

II. The Question of Method

Heidegger now begins his investigation into the ontology of conscience. His methodology here, as throughout, is that of hermeneutical phenomenology. That is to say, Heidegger will observe the phenomenon (presumably as he finds it in himself) and then interpret the significance of this phenomenon in relation to others he has previously observed and interpreted. The question of method is of particular moment at this point because Heidegger is now examining that very phenomenon that is to serve, to some degree, as confirmation of his previous findings and, by implication, of his methodology itself.

But are we not now in the tightest methodological loop? The same Martin Heidegger who has employed his method of hermeneutical phenomenology to arrive at the distinction between das Man and Being-towards-death will now employ this same method to investigate the phenomenon that, he claims, will vindicate his findings. This problem becomes all the more pressing when we see, as we shall, that Heidegger's interpretation of conscience departs, sometimes radically, from the conventional one. Have we anything more here than one prejudice confirming another? Can we even avoid the

1 Martin Heidegger, *Being and Time*, p. 311, H. 267.

suspicion that Heidegger's analysis of conscience is *guided* by the conclusions he wishes to reach?

This has come to be known as the problem of the hermeneutical circle, and it is a problem that Heidegger himself addresses: "Any interpretation which is to contribute understanding must already have understood what is to be interpreted."[2] Dasein does not and cannot begin its investigation of itself from a neutral place. It must begin with the understanding that it already has. Nor can Dasein retreat to some position outside of itself from which to observe itself 'objectively'; not only because there is no such 'outside,' but, even more to the point, because interpretation itself, the phenomenological-hermeneutical *process* of interpretation, requires the active enlistment of those very features of Dasein that are to be interpreted. 'Presupposition,' of one sort or another, is essential to the project of interpretation itself. Thus, there is no escape from the circle: "What is decisive is not to get out of the circle but to come into it in the right way ... In the circle is hidden a positive possibility of the most primordial kind of knowing. To be sure, we genuinely take hold of this possibility only when, in our interpretation, we have understood that our first, last, and constant task is never to allow our fore-having, fore-sight, and fore-conception [our presuppositions] to be presented to us by fancies and popular conceptions, but rather to make the scientific theme secure by working out these fore-structures by the things themselves."[3]

But how are we to do this? Does not the endeavor to 'purify' our presuppositions itself entail the enlistment of these presuppositions? Are we not motivated by these very presuppositions when we initiate our hermeneutical investigation? Heidegger himself raises these questions:

> Where does this Interpretation get its clue, if not from an idea of existence in general which has been 'presupposed'? How have the steps in the analysis of inauthentic everydayness been regulated, if not by the concept of existence which we have posited? And if we say that Dasein 'falls,' and that therefore the authenticity of its potentiality-for-Being must be wrested from

2 Ibid., p. 194, H. 152.

3 Ibid., p. 195, H. 153.

> Dasein in spite of this tendency of its Being, from what point of view is this spoken? Is not everything already illuminated by the light of the 'presupposed' idea of existence, even if rather dimly? Where does this idea get its justification?[4]

And he answers as follows:

> When it is objected that the existential Interpretation is 'circular,' it is said that we have 'presupposed' the idea of existence and Being in general, and that Dasein gets Interpreted 'accordingly,' so that the idea of Being may be obtained from it. But what does 'presupposition' signify? In positing the idea of existence, do we also posit some proposition from which we deduce further propositions about the Being of Dasein, in accordance with formal rules of consistency? Or does this pre-supposing have the character of an understanding projection, in such a manner indeed that the Interpretation by which such an understanding gets developed, will let that which is to be interpreted *put itself into words for the very first time, so that it may decide of its own accord whether, as the entity which it is, it has that state of Being for which it has been disclosed in the projection with regard to its formal aspects*? Is there any other way at all by which an entity can put itself into words with regard to its Being?...What common sense wishes to eliminate in avoiding the 'circle,' on the supposition that it is measuring up to the loftiest rigor of scientific investigation, is nothing less than the basic structure of care.[5]

The alternative to the circle is a retreat to the epistemological minimalism of, say, logical positivism, in which only what appears in the public space of the empirical is 'officially' allowed meaning. But this in effect makes philosophy impossible, if what we mean by philosophy is the disciplined endeavor to obey the Socratic dictum: 'Know thyself': "Because understanding, in accordance with its existential meaning, is Dasein's own potentiality-for-Being historiological

4 Ibid., p. 361, H. 313.

5 Ibid., pp. 362-363, H. 314-315.

[or, for that matter, philosophical] knowledge transcends in principle the idea of rigor held in the most exact sciences."[6]

Does this mean we are trapped in a hopeless redundancy? Can a philosopher do nothing more than reiterate what he or she already believes? The practice of philosophy itself proves otherwise. Indeed, the 'circle' is an overly simplistic metaphor for the true hermeneutical process, which involves investigation, examination, dissection, and novel *re*-integration of what has been newly investigated and examined. What guides this process? What criteria can be brought to bear to determine whether these novel interpretations are in any sense sound? What guides it is also what motivates it, and what may simply be called 'fit.' The interpretation must 'fit' the phenomena as they appear to us (as we *live* them), and must fit it along *all* the axio-ontological dimensions by which our existence is bound. To suggest that our assessment of 'fit' will be dictated by our presuppositions, and is therefore an unsound criterion, is a naïve critique – for it is just because we sense that our presuppositions *do not* 'fit' that we have ventured upon the hermeneutical path to begin with.

In the case of *Being and Time*, it is the whole modern self-interpretation that Heidegger has called into question, that Heidegger has claimed does not 'fit.' In a sense, the 'forgotten question' (of the meaning of Being) serves merely as a *token* for this general sense of lack of fit. Heidegger's entire critique of das Man is doubtless an attempt to articulate and clarify his pre-philosophical *intimation* that the common person's self-interpretation is at odds with a more authentic relation to self. Out of this, *Being and Time* endeavors to provide, at a very fundamental level, a reinterpretation of what it is to be a human being. What criteria can we bring to bear in assessing whether or not its reinterpretation is apt? Just this sense of 'aptness' or 'inaptness' itself, which we must struggle to articulate as best we can.

This is, for sure, a sloppy and inexact method. But not only is it the only method available to us, it is the only one remotely possible, given the kind of beings we are. The ideal of apodictic certainty, which launched the Cartesian project and has characterized so much of modern thought, needs itself to be interrogated with respect to its presuppositions, and, even more, its existential implications. What

6 Ibid., p. 195, H. 153.

is it we are trying to achieve through such certainty? And what must we give up to achieve it?

So, we will disagree with Ludwig Wittgenstein's famous dictum: "Whereof one cannot speak [with perfect precision], thereof one must be silent." On the contrary, we assert that those things that cannot be said with perfect precision must, nevertheless, be said as best they can, for they are among ***the most important things to say***. This principle, derived here from Heidegger's work, can serve as both a justification for, and a caution with respect to, any formal articulation of religious faith. Faith entails a commitment to an interpretation of Being (a telic context) that can never achieve apodictic certainty. Faith is not thereby invalidated, given that human beings must, nevertheless, live within the context of some such uncertain interpretation. But this very fact, which serves as faith's justification, also implies its fallibility. Such fallibility does not require that faith be abandoned; it does require that we humbly acknowledge the inevitable imperfection of any human articulation of faith.

We can say the same of Heidegger's treatment of conscience. Certainly, and necessarily, Heidegger's treatment is bound up with his entire analytic of Dasein and, if it is in any way confirmatory of that analytic, it is so only to the extent that we are persuaded by it. On the other hand, even if we are not wholly persuaded, it is not therefore worthless. The interpretation of human existence is and must be a 'work in progress'; contributions to this work are not lost, even when surpassed by more satisfactory ones.

III. SCHULDIGSEIN

Heidegger begins by acknowledging that the very reality of conscience has often been called into question: "That the very 'fact' of conscience has been disputed, that its function as a higher court for Dasein's existence has been variously assessed – all this might only mislead us into dismissing this phenomenon if the very 'doubtfulness' of this Fact – or the way in which it has been interpreted – did not prove that here a *primordial* phenomenon of Dasein lies before us."[7] Heidegger does not elaborate on this point but what he presumably means is that

7 Ibid., p. 313, H. 268.

the very questioning of the phenomenon of conscience indicates that there is *something* to question, even if its customary interpretation is considered dubious. Even for dismissive interpretations, in which what is customarily called conscience is explained away in terms of psychological or sociological factors, some phenomenon must stand as the target of these dismissals. *Something* is being denied a particular meaning. The task of the existential analytic, then, is to identify this something, and state is true meaning.

What conscience is conventionally said to do is to make one aware of one's 'guilt.' Insofar as one has been afflicted by a 'pang' of conscience, one has come to recognize one's guiltiness with respect to something. Heidegger now asks: what are the ontological conditions for the possibility of being *guilty*? What must be true of a being for it to be susceptible to an experience of guiltiness? Heidegger notes that 'guiltiness' always suggests an indebtedness of some kind: "Everyday common sense first takes 'Being-Guilty [*Schuldigsein*] in the sense of 'owing,' of 'having something due on account.' One is to give back to the Other something to which the latter has a claim."[8] This connotation of indebtedness, it must the noted, is far more pronounced in the German word *Schuldigsein*, which can mean simply 'indebted' in the sense of owing money, than in the English word guilt, which does not have the same etymological base. Nevertheless, even in English we speak of a criminal having to 'pay his debt' to society or of justice 'exacting its due.' In the idea of guiltiness, then, as well as in the idea of general indebtedness, is the idea of coming to be *responsible* for the lack of something. To the extent that one has incurred a debt one is responsible for paying it back. To the extent that one has wronged another, one is responsible for making reparations. "These ordinary significations of 'Being-Guilty' [Schuldigsein] as 'having debts to someone' and 'having responsibility for something' can go together and define a kind of behavior which we call '*making oneself responsible*'."[9]

One becomes responsible to another, in this sense, to the extent that one has *deprived* that other of something belonging to them. If one has borrowed money from the other, then one is the source of the other's 'lack' of this money, and one is responsible for making it

8 Ibid., p. 327, H. 281.
9 Ibid., p. 327, H. 282.

up. If one has wronged another and hampered her life in some way, then one is the source of this negativity and, again, responsible for making it up. Through such considerations, Heidegger arrives at a formal conception of Schuldigsein as "*Being-the-basis* for a lack of something in the Dasein of an Other, and in such a manner that this very Being-the-basis determines itself as 'lacking in some way' in terms of that for which it is the basis."[10] In other words, one comes to be *schuldig* (in debt) in relation to another to the extent that one has deprived that other of something belonging to the other, *and* to the extent that one does not *oneself* have the resources for making it up. Of course, if one possessed the resources to cover what one owes, then one might do so and would no longer be in debt. One is essentially *in a state of debt* (schuldig) *just insofar* as one is both responsible for the other's loss and *unable* to make it up.

Thus indebtedness, *Schuldigsein*, has something to do with *lack*, or, more precisely, with the potentiality of a human being to be in a state of lack. Heidegger dubs this state 'nullity.' One becomes indebted to another just to the extent that one has made oneself the basis of a 'nullity' in another: "Hence we define the formally existential idea of the 'Guilty!' as 'Being-the-basis-for-a-Being which has been defined by a 'not' – that is to say, as '*Being-the-basis of a nullity*'."[11]

Yet it is not enough that one *be* the basis of a nullity in another. In order for the phenomenon of guilt to exist, one must be capable of *recognizing* oneself to be such a basis. Thus, *Being*-indebted (Schuldig-*Sein*) is not, first of all, a matter of legal or social convention. There is that in Dasein which is able to *own up* to such Being-indebted, to acknowledge that the other has a *legitimate* claim on one, a claim grounded in an ontological legitimacy that precedes and is the basis for any possible social or legal legitimacy. Indeed, the proof of this is that Dasein can feel itself to be *wrongly* accused and convicted of debt, forced to pay what it does not *really* owe. This is a case in which the exception proves the rule: for if Dasein can feel *wrongly* convicted of debt, it can, by implication, feel *rightly* convicted as well.

What is the ontological condition for the possibility of such *Being*-indebted, such *recognizing oneself* as indebted? Heidegger traces

10 Ibid., p. 328, H. 282.

11 Ibid., p. 329, H. 283.

this possibility to what he calls the ***nothingness*** or ***nullity*** inherent in Dasein's very Being. Dasein's nullity may be seen in three ways, corresponding to the three modes of Dasein's temporal constitution: there is the nullity implicit in Dasein's thrownness (past), the nullity implicit in Dasein's freedom (present), and the nullity implicit in Dasein's Being-towards-death (future). "*Care ...* " writes Heidegger, "***is permeated with nullity through and through.***"[12]

First, Dasein's thrownness entails nullity insofar as it reveals that Dasein is not the basis of its own Being: "As being, Dasein is something that has been thrown; it has been brought into its 'there,' but not of its own accord."[13] Dasein first of all finds itself already 'there' (i.e., in the world). It does not first put itself 'there.' Its ultimate *whence* is veiled from it. Thus, Dasein's Being rests upon, as Heidegger expresses it, 'a null basis.'

Next, Dasein is null in respect to its freedom. Nullity, indeed, is the very condition for the possibility of freedom. To choose to actualize one potentiality is to exclude other potentialities from actualization. This is the sense of freedom's 'nullity' that Heidegger himself notes. But perhaps even more to the point is that freedom, as such, entails a lack of definite determination to ***any one*** possibility. Dasein stands before its possibilities in a place of choice, at a crossroad of options, and, just as long as it stands at this crossroad of options, it is not determined to any ***one*** of them. There is, thus, a certain 'nothingness' implicit in freedom itself. As free, Dasein is determined, so to speak, by a lack of any definite determination.[14]

Finally, Dasein is 'null' insofar as it is Being-towards-death; i.e., Being-towards the possibility of no-further-possibility. This also, like freedom, constitutes a lack of determination; in this case, a lack of *ultimate* determination. So, not only is Dasein, as thrown, null in its basis, but, as Being-towards-death, it is null in its final term. And as free it is null in its present stance.

These three nullities are related to one another and, taken together, constitute a fundamental *lack of determinateness* at the core of Dasein's

12 Ibid., p. 331, H. 285.

13 Ibid., p. 329-330, H. 284.

14 Dasein is, in Jean-Paul Sartre's phrase, 'condemned to be free.' Sartre examines this aspect of freedom's 'nothingness,' with more penetration than Heidegger, in his book *Being and Nothingness.*

Being. Even the apparent determinateness of Dasein's facticity is not a true determinateness for, as thrown, Dasein "has been *released* from its [factical] basis ..."[15]

But what has Dasein's lack of determinateness to do with the phenomenon of Being-indebted? Heidegger's suggestion is that this nullity constitutes Dasein's primordial *indebtedness* to *itself*. This indebtedness, of course, is not something Dasein has incurred through some action it has taken. Rather, it is an implication of Dasein's very Being as projected upon potentialities that draw it forth. Dasein is in debt to itself. This primordial *indebtedness* to self, *responsibility* to self, is what Heidegger calls *Schuldigsein*, translated in the Macquarie-Robinson text as *Being-Guilty*. This translation, I believe, is extremely misleading, for the English word 'guilt' does not have 'debt' as an alternate meaning, as does the German *Schuld*; whereas it is just this sense of debt that I believe is uppermost in Heidegger's mind.[16] Dasein is primordially *responsible* to itself, responsible for making something determinate of its indeterminateness. This responsibility to self is a feature of the *issue* Dasein is to itself. In its flight into das Man, it evades this issue and this responsibility.

It is only because Dasein exists as primordial indebtedness/responsibility to itself that it can incur debts in relation to others. It is the ontological structure of *Schuldigsein* that makes Dasein a creature whose life can be reckoned in terms of 'debts,' 'responsibilities' and 'guilt': "Being-guilty does not first result from indebtedness, but ... on the contrary, indebtedness becomes possible only 'on the basis' of a primordial Being-guilty."[17] Thus what Heidegger is pointing to with his notion of *Schuldigsein* is the ontological *ground*, the condition for the possibility, of *obligation* itself. This ground of obligation constitutes a *normative claim* (i.e., a "should" claim) that Dasein's Being makes upon itself.

15 Ibid., p. 330, H. 285.

16 There is little question, also, that Heidegger is suggesting that this phenomenon constitutes the ontological underpinnings of what, in Christianity, comes to be interpreted as 'original sin.' We will have more to say about this as we proceed.

17 Ibid., p. 324, H. 284.

IV. THE CALL OF CONSCIENCE

We are made aware of this primordial responsibility to ourselves, according to Heidegger, via the 'call of conscience': "Conscience summons Dasein's Self from its lostness in the 'they'."[18] As das Man, Dasein is in flight from an authentic encounter with itself; a flight that leads to an evasion of its responsibility to itself. It is the function of conscience to call Dasein back to itself, back to an acknowledgment of its primordial self-responsibility. In this call there are three elements, says Heidegger: the one who calls, the one who is called, and the content of the call itself. We will consider each of these in turn.

"If the caller is asked about its name, status, origin or repute, it not only refuses to answer, but does not even leave the slightest possibility of one's making it into something with which one can be familiar when one's understanding of Dasein has a 'worldly' orientation."[19] The caller's sole concern, according to Heidegger, is in having us respond to the call itself, it is not interested in having us speculate about the origin of the call and, thereby, divert ourselves once again from what we are being called to. Its "peculiar indefiniteness" about itself, makes "known to us that the caller is solely absorbed in summoning us to something, that it is heard only as such, and furthermore that it will not let itself be coaxed."[20]

Nevertheless, the existential analytic, as such, has an interest in understanding the ontology of the call and therefore the identity of the caller. But the answer to the question of who calls is, in a sense, implicit in the nature of the call itself; for what else can call one to a responsibility to *oneself* but this very responsibility? If one were not *first of all* (primordially, ontologically) responsible to self no call from elsewhere could make one responsible. It is one's own Being *as responsible* that calls one into acknowledgment of one's responsibility: "*In conscience Dasein calls to itself*."[21] Of course, the call does not come from oneself as one currently understands oneself. The call, in effect, is one's own authenticity breaking out upon one's inauthenticity

18 Ibid., p. 319, H. 274.
19 Ibid., p. 319. H. 274.
20 Ibid., p. 319, H. 274-275.
21 Ibid., p. 320, H. 275.

in order to call it to account. Thus: "The call comes *from* me and yet *from beyond me and over me*."[22]

The call, then, is phenomenally experienced as transcendent and 'uncanny,' insofar as it emerges from a more primordial place in oneself than one is customarily aware of. It is this that has led to its being interpreted as a call from God, according to Heidegger: "These phenomenal findings are not to be explained away. After all, they have been taken as a starting-point for explaining the voice of conscience as an alien power by which Dasein is dominated. If the interpretation continues in this direction, one supplies a possessor for the power thus posited, or one takes the power itself as a person who makes himself known – namely God."[23] But this interpretation, says Heidegger, is a function of our proclivity to assign phenomena to something we encounter in the world, a proclivity we must resist: "We must instead hold fast not only to the phenomenal findings that I receive the call as coming both from me and from beyond me, but also the implication that this phenomenon is here delineated ontologically as a phenomenon of *Dasein*."[24]

It is Dasein who calls to itself, Dasein "in its uncanniness: primordial, thrown Being-in-the-world as the 'not-at-home' – the bare 'that-it-is' in the 'nothing' of the world. The caller is unfamiliar to the everyday they-self; it is something like an *alien* voice."[25] Nevertheless it is I myself, my own truth, calling me into self-acknowledgment.

Who then is addressed by the call? It is, of course, Dasein *as* das Man, Dasein *as* flight from itself, as 'fallen' into the world: "Losing itself in the publicness and the idle talk of the 'they,' it fails to hear its own Self in listening to the they-self."[26] The call of conscience is Dasein calling itself back to itself, back to its 'truth' from its lostness in 'falsity.'

And what does the call say? Heidegger answers: "Taken strictly, nothing. The call asserts nothing, gives no information about world-events, has nothing to tell. Least of all does it try to set going a soliloquy in the Self to which it has appealed. Nothing gets called *to*

22 Ibid., p. 320, H. 275.
23 Ibid., p. 320, H. 275.
24 Ibid., p. 320, H. 275.
25 Ibid., p. 321, H. 276-277.
26 Ibid., p. 315, H. 271.

this Self, but it has been *summoned* to itself."[27] The call says nothing that can be put into words, but it gives one to understand: 'In debt!', i.e., '*Responsible!*' Not responsible in the sense of accountable for what one has done, but responsible rather for *taking responsibility* for who one is.

We will entirely fail to understand this if we hear it merely as an expression of *Heidegger's* conviction that people should live responsibly. Rather, Heidegger is here claiming that there is that in each of us which *demands such* of ourselves, and this is revealed in the phenomenon of conscience. That is, it is revealed in the very fact that there can be such a phenomenon as conscience. This phenomenon is only possible to the extent that Dasein is *already* aware of the possibility of something on the order of *responsibility*. Where can Dasein have learned of this possibility? Surely not by observing things in the world. The very *idea* of responsibility is only possible on the basis of an ontological disposition to responsibility that Dasein finds in itself. And it is only on the basis of this that there can be any such thing as *moral* responsibility or *financial* responsibility, etc.

V. RESOLUTENESS

The decision to live one's life *as* responsible (as *Schuldigsein*) is called by Heidegger 'resoluteness.' Heidegger defines resoluteness as the "reticent self-projection upon one's ownmost Being-guilty."[28] Again, 'Being-guilty' is a misleading translation of *Schuldigsein*. What Heidegger means here is 'Being-indebted (to oneself).' When Dasein is resolute about taking responsibility for itself, and *only* when Dasein is resolute, is the world disclosed in its truth, which is also, of course, the *truth* of Dasein. It is through resoluteness, then, that Dasein achieves authenticity.

The German word translated as resoluteness, *Entschlossenheit*, contains an etymological duality that is lost in translation but important to Heidegger's sense. *Schlossenheit* taken by itself might be translated *closedness*, in the sense of something having the quality of being locked up. The prefix *Ent-* can function as either an intensive or a

27 Ibid., p. 318, H. 273.
28 Ibid., p. 343, H. 297.

privative. Thus, *Entschlossenheit* can mean to 'lock in' on something, just as the English word 'resoluteness,' and this is its common meaning in German. But if the privative sense of its prefix is emphasized (as Heidegger sometimes does in writing it *Ent-schlossenheit*), it can connote 'unlocking' something, 'being open' to something. Heidegger's implication is that the authentic person is open to her primordial sense of self-responsibility (*Schuldigsein*), and this openness allows her to then 'lock in' on specific tasks in an authentic manner. Thus, it is impossible to give a general statement as to what an authentic person resolves upon, for this must be revealed to her by her openness to her own self, in each and every situation: "*Only* the resolution itself can give the answer. One would completely misunderstand the phenomenon of resoluteness if one should want to suppose that this consists simply in taking up possibilities which have been proposed and recommended, and seizing hold of them."[29]

Resoluteness, then, is a general life orientation in which one owns up to one's self-responsibility and lives accordingly. It is, so to speak, 'responding responsibly to one's self-responsibility.' Heidegger's assumption seems to be that in 'wanting to have a conscience,' i.e., in wanting to 'respond responsibly to one's self-responsibility' *that which* one is concretely responsible for in any given situation will be made plain.

VI. Anticipatory Resoluteness

We began the discussion of conscience in search of a phenomenon through which Dasein attests to a sense of sometimes being 'in the truth' and sometimes 'in the untruth' in respect to itself. Heidegger's claim is that the call to self-responsibility, to *Schuldigsein*, which is customarily called 'conscience,' is just such an attestation. Of course, commonly understood, conscience is that which convicts one of moral transgression. But Heidegger's point – quite typical of Heidegger – is that such self-conviction as is found in the ordinary experience of conscience is only possible on the ground of a prior ontological disposition to *responsibility* as such. Only a being who is primordially disposed to something like responsibility can be convicted of irre-

29 Ibid., p. 345, H. 298.

sponsibility in some particular case. Thus, the common phenomenon of conscience, even as commonly understood, testifies to Dasein's sense of a normative standard to which it owes allegiance.

The question remains, however, whether this call to responsibility is, indeed, one that calls us *out of* das Man and *into* Being-towards-death. Even if we are persuaded by Heidegger's treatment of an ontological disposition to self-responsibility at the core of Dasein, this in itself does not entail that Being-towards-death, as Heidegger has explicated it, is the proper expression of this disposition. We have two issues here that need to be kept distinct. Heidegger may well argue that the call to self-responsibility is, as such, a call out of das Man, insofar as das Man is *defined* as an evasion of such responsibility. There is a clear connection between the call of conscience (as the call to self-responsibility) and the call *out of* das Man. But it is less clear that the call out of das Man is also a call *into* Being-towards-death.

What is Heidegger's argument for this? We remember that Being-towards-death was first proposed as a way of envisioning Dasein's *wholeness*. Heidegger has enumerated the features of Being-towards-death as Dasein's 'ownmost, uttermost, non-relational, certain and, as such, indefinite' potentiality. The link between resoluteness and Being-towards-death pertains most prominently to the first three of these features. What Being-towards-death reveals to Dasein, according to Heidegger, is that it is responsible to itself *all the way to the end.* In other words, the call of conscience calls Dasein to self-responsibility in the current factical situation; 'resoluteness' is Dasein's appropriate response to this call. But Heidegger's analysis of temporality, in which we see that the three temporal modes (past, present, future) are mutually implicated in one another, implies that any given factical situation is only understandable in terms of that toward which it tends. To act responsibly in the moment I must, at the same time, act responsibly toward the future that gives it meaning. In effect, then, responsibility in the moment entails responsibility to the future. But if there is no terminus to this future, if each future's meaning depends upon some further future's meaning *ad infinitum*, then the meaning of the *present* can never gain closure or wholeness. At best, my life breaks up into a series of discrete projects that don't connect to one another. Under such circumstances I can never come into full ownership of myself *as a whole*, and true resoluteness (responsibility-to-my-(whole)-self) is made impossible.

Thus, for Dasein's call to self-responsibility (resoluteness) to be 'certain of itself' it must be able to project itself to the point of no-further-possibilities (or potentialities), i.e., to the point of death, for only then can it know that its projections will not be overruled (outstripped) by something beyond. Beyond this, Dasein, as Being-in-the-world, is always tempted to lose itself in projects presented to it by its world. Indeed, the others in Dasein's life will tend to encourage this. But a full acknowledgment of Being-towards-death allows Dasein to recognize that, when all is said and done, its ultimate responsibility is to itself. Death – Being-towards-death – makes it clear to Dasein that, ultimately, its life is its own, and that, in the end, it is Dasein, and Dasein alone, that has responsibility for it.

Resoluteness, then, is only 'sure of itself' in the context of Being-towards-death, which is to say, as *anticipatory resoluteness*. Because Dasein's ultimate term is null, this ultimate term constantly directs Dasein back to *itself* in the moment, to its resolute action *for itself*, and frees it for this resolute action. Being-towards-death makes clear to Dasein that its call to responsibility is a call to *self*-responsibility. In circling Dasein back upon itself, it reveals to Dasein that the meaning of its life is its *own*.

When Dasein lives as its own, as responsible to its own truth, it lives authentically. "Anticipatory resoluteness" is Heidegger's term for the existential disposition of the fully authentic human being. The remainder of *Being and Time* is, by and large, Heidegger's attempt to explicate Dasein's *fall* from authenticity in terms of his existential conception of temporality. As for the manner of life of the truly authentic person – about this Heidegger is notoriously vague, at least in *Being and Time*. Nevertheless, if we are to try to grasp Heidegger's argument in its entirety we must now consider his treatment of this question.

VII. HISTORICALITY

> In the existential analysis we cannot, in principle, discuss what [authentic] Dasein factically resolves in any particular case. Our investigation excludes even the existential projection of the factical possibilities of existence. Nevertheless, we must ask whence, in general, Dasein can draw those possibilities upon which it factically projects itself. One's anticipatory projection of oneself on that possibility of existence which is not to be outstripped – on death – guarantees only the totality and authenticity of one's resoluteness. But those possibilities of existence which have been factically disclosed are not to be gathered from death.[30]

Heidegger has, it might be pointed out, painted himself into something of a corner. He has so emphasized Dasein's *nullity* that it has become difficult to say just *where*, in principle, Dasein is to draw its particular projects *from*. If Dasein's ultimate term were *something* rather than nothing, it might draw its projects from the endeavor to realize this something. But as Being-towards-death, as Heidegger himself concedes in the above quote, Dasein is, ultimately, not directed to anything but itself; that is, Dasein's ultimate term does nothing but constantly direct it *back* to itself in the moment. Can Dasein get its projects, then, from its 'thrownness'? But Dasein has been *released* from its thrownness such that it is not determined by it; indeed, this releasement is just what is signified in the expression 'thrownness.' Nor can Dasein get its projects from its freedom, for such freedom is, precisely, the freedom from determination to any particular project. Then *where*? Authentic Dasein, as a call to responsibility, seems to be all dressed up with nowhere to go. What is this difficult call to responsibility *for*?

Heidegger now suggests that Dasein's authentic possibilities are to be found in Dasein's *heritage*. He writes: "The resoluteness in which Dasein comes back to itself, discloses current factical possibilities of authentic existing, and discloses them *in terms of the heritage* which that resoluteness, as thrown, *takes over*."[31] In coming back to oneself,

30 Ibid., p. 434, H. 383.

31 Ibid., p. 435, H. 383.

out of das Man, one becomes aware of the situation one is thrown into *as* that which has been handed down to one and which one, in some manner, must now (responsibly) 'take over.' By 'taking over' the possibilities passed down to one in one's heritage one is linked to one's past. In then projecting these possibilities upon one's for-the-sake-of which, one links one's past to one's future. Such linkage Heidegger calls 'historicality,' and the process of such linkage 'historizing': "Once one has grasped the finitude of one's existence, it snatches one back from the endless multiplicity of possibilities which offer themselves as closest to one – those of comfortableness, shirking, and taking things lightly – and brings Dasein into the simplicity of its fate [*Schicksals*]. This is how we designate Dasein's primordial historizing, which lies in authentic resoluteness and in which Dasein ***hands*** itself ***down*** to itself, free for death, in a possibility which it has inherited and yet has chosen."[32]

Thus, the factical possibilities upon which authentic Dasein may resolve are presented to it by its heritage, which Dasein has first been thrown into but now must responsibly choose: "The resoluteness which comes back to itself and hands itself down, then becomes the ***repetition*** of a possibility of existence that has come down to us. ***Repeating is handing down explicitly*** – that is to say, going back into the possibilities of the Dasein that has-been-there."[33]

But it is hard to avoid the suspicion that we are involved in something of a shell game. If the Dasein of today is not endowed with that wherein it can generate meaningful possibilities for itself, how is it to find these possibilities in the Dasein of yesterday? Was the Dasein of yesterday better endowed with meaning-generating capacity than the Dasein of today? Then where did *it* get it from? Heidegger, it seems, has misconstrued his own question. He himself is now confusing the ontic with the ontological; he is confusing the particular manner in which Dasein is presented with meaningful possibilities with the fundamental ground of meaning within the Being of Dasein. We are seeking the *ontological* ground of meaning. Only so far as we can find it will we gain insight into our original question: the question of the *meaning* of Being. We have sought this ground through an analysis

32 Ibid., p. 435, H. 384.
33 Ibid., p. 437, H. 385.

of Dasein – that being for whom Being *has* meaning – hoping to catch sight of this ground in the course of this analysis. But it has turned out that Dasein, as thrown Being-towards-death, is pervaded with *nullity* through and through. The anxiety associated with such nullity has driven Dasein into a determined self-forgetfulness which has hidden the true ground of meaning from its (our) purview. The call of conscience calls Dasein back to its authenticity, and we have turned to an examination of Dasein's authenticity in the hope, again, of discovering this elusive ground of meaning, hidden from inauthentic Dasein.

So *where is it*? Now Heidegger tells us it is in Dasein's *heritage.* But where has this 'heritage' come from if not from Dasein itself, i.e., from the Dasein of yesterday? Was the Dasein of yesterday equipped with something that the Dasein of today is not? If so, *what*? It is only to the extent that we can identify this *what* that we will come within striking distance of answering our original question. And yet, not only does Heidegger not identify this *what*, he does not even ask about it.

And there is a further, related, problem. Heidegger's analytic gives us no clue as to the *basis* upon which the Dasein of today is to choose between the various options passed down to it by the Dasein of yesterday. It is not enough to say that resolute Dasein must decide this for itself. Certainly this is so *ontically*, but what we are seeking here is some insight into the *ontology* of the choice. A choice bespeaks a *preference*. What is the ontology of *preference*? Heidegger's analytic gives us no clue as to why, or even *how*, one mode of existence might be preferable to another. Heidegger does allude to the issue. The repellent nature of angst gives inauthentic Dasein a preference for the existential disposition of das Man. But what is the relationship between the mood and the preference? What is it about moods and states-of-mind that make some preferable to others, and what are the implications of this? These are questions Heidegger never explores.

And yet, these questions lie at the very core of what concerns us here. Does not one build a house and, thereby, pursue the project of Being-homed, because one *prefers* Being-homed to Being-homeless? Isn't this *preference*, then, an integral part of the project's meaning, indeed, of its *intensity* of meaning? – for some meanings have greater intensity than others, because some projects are more *important* than others. But these distinctions between the important and the unimportant, the crucial and the incidental, are only intelligible within the context of an ontology of preference.

The name for such an ontology, as we have said, is *axiology*. As we have pointed out, Heidegger does not so much ignore axiology as subsume it within his analysis of temporality. It is there but one must dig it out. This is something, however, that Heidegger not only fails to do, but fails to *see*, and this failure leaves questions unasked that are critical to our investigation. Granted that Dasein, as 'thrown,' must live in the context of a pool of possibilities derived from its heritage; still, heritage *as such* can neither constitute the ontological basis of these possibilities nor the ontological basis of Dasein's proclivity to pursue some possibilities as opposed to others. What can? Any full analytic of Dasein must address this question. We can find such an analytic in the religious interpretation of Dasein.

VIII. The Question of God

It is interesting to note that the Bible agrees with Heidegger about the essential nullity of the human being left to itself: "From dust were you made," says God to Adam and Eve, "and unto dust shall you return." Dust, as such, is meaningless and void. It receives meaning only when animated by the spirit of God. According to the Judeo-Christian tradition, the *font* of meaning is not to be found in the human being *per se*, but in God. That phenomenological ontology should find no *ground* of meaning in its strictly secular examination of Dasein is confirmatory of the religious point of view. But this raises a question as to the relationship of philosophy to religion. If philosophy is that pursuit that strives to understand 'the question of the meaning of Being,' and if meaning stems, primordially, not from the finite human being *as such* but from the human being in relation to God, then it would seem that philosophy is driven to theology in the natural course of its investigations.

Granted, this is only the case to the extent that we concede that the font of meaning is indeed trans-human. So long as philosophy denies this claim, it remains free to pursue meaning wherever it may hope to find it, without venturing into the traditional terrain of theology.

But it has long been a belief in theological circles that philosophy, if pursued diligently and earnestly enough, must eventually lead, at least, to the *question* of God. Thomas Aquinas considered philosophy a *prolegomenon* to theology. His famous proofs for the existence of God serve to indicate that any investigation of the natural world, pursued diligently enough, must eventually lead to the question of its ultimate ontological/metaphysical underpinnings; i.e., to the question of God.[34] This suggests that philosophy, in asking the question of fundamental ontology, cannot avoid entering upon the terrain of theology; for theology, after all, is just that discipline that reflects upon Being Itself: *Esse Ipsum*.

Interestingly, in 1927, the year *Being and Time* was first published, Martin Heidegger gave a lecture in Tübingen in which he forcefully denied the above thesis.[35] Theology, according to Heidegger, is a positive, ontic, science, in the same category as, say, physics. It is not the science of Being as such, but of a certain type of being. On the other hand, "*the* science of [B]eing, the ontological science, [is] philosophy."[36]

According to Heidegger, Christian theology is "a positive science," and, hence, absolutely different in kind from philosophy. "A positive science is the founding disclosure of a being that is given and in some way already disclosed."[37] "What is given for theology (its positum) is Christianness."[38] And what is 'Christianness?' "We call faith Christian. The essence of faith can formally be sketched as a way of existence of human Dasein that, according to its own testimony – itself belonging to this way of existence – arises not *from* Dasein nor spontaneously *through* Dasein, but rather from that which is revealed in and with this way of existence, from what is believed."[39] "Theology," thus, "is the science of that which is disclosed in faith, of that which is believed."[40]

34 See Paul Tillich, *A History of Christian Thought*, 195. Also, *Systematic Theology*, vol. 1, (Chicago: University of Chicago Press, 1951), 208.

35 Martin Heidegger, "Phenomenology and Theology" trans. James G. Hart and John C. Maraldo in *Pathmarks*, ed. William McNeill (Cambridge: Cambridge University Press, 1998).

36 Ibid., 41.

37 Ibid., 43.

38 Ibid.

39 Ibid., 43-44.

40 Ibid., 45.

Thus, Christian theology is the science of one particular way of Being, that of Christian faith, whereas philosophy is the science of Being as such. Philosophy, as the science of Being as such, is able to provide theology with ontological ground concepts in terms of which it can formulate its ontic themes: "All theological concepts necessarily contain that understanding of [B]eing that is constitutive of human Dasein as such, insofar as it exists at all."[41] Heidegger considers, as an example, the relation between his own ontological concept of 'guilt' (*Schuld*) and the Christian concept of 'sin': "If sin, which is the counterphenomenon to faith ... is to be interpreted in theological concepts, then the *content* of the concept *itself*, and not just any philosophical preference of the theologian, calls for a return to the concept of guilt."[42] We remember that by 'guilt' (*Schuld*) Heidegger does not mean the state of having transgressed, but, rather, the ontological condition for the possibility of transgression; i.e., the demand for self-responsibility that is ontologically native to Dasein as such. Only a being who is first of all 'called to responsibility' can transgress against that call in a specific way and, thereby, *sin*.

Thus, philosophy can provide theology with its ground concepts but, of course, philosophy is not restricted to this function. On the contrary, "it can be shown that philosophy, as the free questioning of purely self-reliant Dasein, does of its essence have the task of directing all other nontheological, positive sciences with respect to ontological foundations."[43] The relation between theology and philosophy is only incidental to the latter. Theology is only one of many ontic disciplines for which philosophy is to provide an ontological foundation.

But is the matter really as clear-cut as this? Let us return to Heidegger's designation of theology as 'the science of that which is disclosed in faith.' Everything now depends upon what is understood by 'that which is disclosed in faith.' Heidegger writes: "For the 'Christian' faith, that being which is primarily revealed to faith, and only to it, and which, as revelation, first gives rise to faith, is Christ, the crucified God."[44] Christian theology, then, is the study of the revelation of 'the crucified God.' This is as far as Heidegger goes in

41 Ibid., 51.
42 Ibid., 51.
43 Ibid., 53.
44 Ibid., 44.

attempting to explicate the *content* of Christian faith. But it seems that he misses something crucial. The 'crucified God' is not simply revealed to faith as 'crucified God' but as one who claims to be '*the truth*.' And the truth claimed here is not just one truth among many, but, precisely, the *truth of existence*. Understanding truth in just Heidegger's sense of unconcealment (of meaning), this is as much as to say that the 'crucified God' of Christianity claims to be, or to somehow disclose, the very *meaning of Being* for which philosophy looks.

This implies that the relation between philosophy and theology is far tighter than Heidegger suggests, especially if we accept Heidegger's definition of philosophy, as 'that discipline which considers the question of the meaning of Being.' Of course, a distinction can be drawn between the *question* of the meaning of Being and any attempted response to the question. One can explore the nature of the question and the implications of the question, develop the terminology in which the question can be meaningfully put, even explore the conditions for the possibility of the question, without ever entering into consideration of a possible way of responding to the question. At times, this seems to be what *Being and Time* endeavors to do. And yet, in its very entry into the question, as we have seen, it has been forced to consider the way in which Dasein may authentically *respond* to this question. What else, after all, are Heidegger's analyses of 'anticipatory resoluteness,' 'das Man,' and 'Being-towards-death,' but Heidegger's attempt to consider Dasein's authentic (and inauthentic) *responses* to the question of the meaning of Being; responses which entail a particular *way* of Being? Indeed, the fact that the question of Being is not asked indifferently, but as a means of addressing the *issue* that Dasein is to itself, implies that the pursuit of the question cannot be divorced from the pursuit of a satisfactory *response* to the question.

But are das Man and Being-towards-death the *only* responses to the question of the meaning of Being Dasein is familiar with? They are not. Religion, specifically the Judeo-Christian tradition, gives us an account of *another* response, another way of understanding Dasein as authentic and whole. This way may be called 'Being-towards-(eternal)-*life*.' Presumably, this mode of projective life has *also* been revealed ('disclosed') to Dasein – in this case, to *religious* Dasein. Interestingly, though Heidegger has next to nothing to say about the religious experience of Being-towards-life, religion, as we shall see, has a great deal to say about what Heidegger calls 'Being-towards-death.'

Both Being-towards-death and Being-towards-life, then, are projective *interpretations* of the meaning of human Being. Both involve an interpretive projection *from* the here-and-now of finite Dasein *toward* an ultimate 'upon which' that gives the here-and-now meaning in a particular way. Both are ways in which Being may be 'disclosed' for Dasein.

Neither of these interpretations can be *verified* in the finite here-and-now of Dasein. Indeed, given the projective nature of *ek*-sistence, it is questionable just what *verification* would mean in this context. If it means actually dying (in the sense of ceasing to be), then Being-towards-death can never be verified by one who is still alive (nor, obviously, by one who isn't). If it means actually living forever (i.e., *never* ceasing to be), then *eternal life* can just as obviously never be finally verified. But neither Heidegger nor religion understands these to mean mere cessation, on the one hand, or endless continuance, on the other. Rather, these modes of projective life have their significance in the ways in which life is lived under them in the *here-and-now*; i.e., they render the here-and-now *meaningful* in distinctive ways. Meaning, we said, pertains to the way in which things matter to us; i.e., to the way things pertain to the *issue* we are to ourselves. Who but *we ourselves*, then, we who *are* this issue, can judge whether or not the issue is being adequately addressed in these projective interpretations?

In the remainder of this work we will employ Heidegger's existential analytic of Dasein as the philosophical basis for an examination of a Judeo-Christian understanding of the meaning of Being. Our approach remains philosophical throughout, in the sense that we approach the primary texts of the Jewish-Christian tradition, not with a prior commitment to their truth, but with the aim of understanding what they have to say to us as seekers after truth. We stand in the place of the *question* and approach the biblical message from this place. Though this approach is philosophical, it is not without biblical sanction:

"Ask and it will be given to you; seek and you will find, knock and it will be opened to you. For everyone who asks receives, and he who seeks finds, and to him who knocks it will be opened." (Mt 7:7-8)[45]

45 All biblical quotations, unless otherwise noted, are from the *New American Standard Bible*, 1995.

Part Two

VI

Methodological Interlude

At this juncture, it might be helpful to remind ourselves just what we are about. The aim of our work, as we've said, is to employ Heidegger's existential analytic of Dasein as a vehicle for exploring a Judeo-Christian understanding of human Being. The inspiration for our work is twofold: First, we find in Heidegger's hermeneutical phenomenology a way of thinking about human existence that makes possible a new, and more penetrating, rational apprehension of religious faith, insofar as it highlights the concernfulness native to our apprehension of Being. Second, we find in the religious interpretation of human Being one (although perhaps not the only) way of resolving issues left unresolved in Heidegger's work itself (such as what underlies Dasein's anxiety).

In the following chapters we will employ Heidegger's new conceptual framework to present a reading of the biblical understanding of human Being, one that will base itself in the existential analytic of *Being and Time* while suggesting ways in which this analytic might itself be modified and extended in a religious direction. In this chapter, however, I would like to step back and reflect upon the problems encountered in thinking about religion at all. Religion presents rational thought with some of its greatest challenges. Heidegger's work can help us address some of these challenges. In this chapter we will consider how.

I. METAPHYSICS AND RELIGION

In a conversation between Heidegger and a group of German theologians held in 1958, the theologian Hermann Noack remarked that "Heidegger's thinking moves in a dimension which alone makes room for doing genuine theological 'thinking' once again – inasmuch as theology at a very early stage fell under the spell of 'metaphysics,' which is inappropriate for speaking about the truth of revelation."[1] In this and following sections, we will consider what is meant by the "spell of 'metaphysics,'" in what way it is "inappropriate for speaking about the truth of revelation," and how Heidegger's thinking "makes room for doing genuine theological 'thinking' once again."

The word 'metaphysics' originally derives from the Aristotelian work of that name and was apparently employed by Aristotle's compilers merely to designate the work placed after (*meta*) the *Physics*. It soon became the favored word in philosophy to refer to that study which considers the fundamental structure of reality, or Being, *in toto*. As such, it is more or less equivalent to the phrase 'fundamental ontology' (although not in the Heideggerian sense). Insofar as religion speaks of God as the 'creator of heaven and earth,' and enjoins human beings to come to know God, religion and metaphysics would appear to have an interest in common. Both, apparently, seek to 'know' what is fundamental in Being.

And yet, in the very writing of such a sentence we immediately sense that there is something wrong with it. Indeed, we are using the word 'know' equivocally. The sort of knowledge that the religious person seeks is not the same as that sought by the metaphysician. The religious person seeks to know God in the sense in which one might speak of knowing a person. The metaphysician seeks to know the fundamentals of Being in the sense in which one might speak of knowing a scientific theory or compilation of facts. The metaphysician is seeking a rational account of the structure of Being. The religious person is seeking something on the order of a personal relationship.

---

1 Hermann Noack, "Conversation with Martin Heidegger," in James G. Hart and John C. Maraldo, *The Piety of Thinking: Essays by Martin Heidegger* (Bloomington: Indiana University Press, 1976), 64.

Must we then conclude that the religious person and metaphysician have nothing in common? Is the supposition that they have merely the result of an equivocation, a failure to discriminate between two different senses of the word 'know'? The matter is not as simple as that. Though the religious person may speak of wishing a personal relation with God, the 'knowing' of God is nevertheless *sui generis*; it is not, and cannot be, just like the knowing of a human person. God does not present himself/herself as an objective other whom one can get to know just as one would another person. Nor is God's significance reducible to that of the significance of just another person. God, for the religious person, is not a mere personal acquaintance but is, *as personal*, the very fundament of Being itself. Thus, even for the one seeking a personal relationship with God, God's metaphysical aspect as the foundation of reality remains eminently relevant.

On the other side, though the metaphysician may seek something on the order of an objective account of Being, to the extent that he/she is not a technician, the pursuit of such an account is motivated by something more than a desire for instrumental mastery. Both are seeking some relation to what fundamentally *is*, and seeking this for its own peculiar value (whatever this may be). The metaphysician pursues it cognitively, the religious person personally.

I do not wish to suggest that all metaphysicians have a secret religious intent. Perhaps there is a purely intellectual desire which finds its satisfaction in metaphysical reflection, having little or nothing to do with religion. I pass no judgment on this. Our question, however – the question for philosophy of *religion* – is how to think about the *religious* relation to God. For much of Western history an alliance has existed between Judeo-Christian spirituality and Greek metaphysical conceptuality. The religious person could borrow the terms in which he or she thought about God from the metaphysical tradition and find in this same tradition epistemic justification for his or her faith. This, perhaps, was not without its problems, as the objectivist style of metaphysical thinking, as Noack remarks, is less than ideal for the expression of spiritual concerns; nevertheless, this alliance provided some rapprochement between 'head' and 'heart' (reason and faith) for the spiritually minded person. This alliance, however, has broken down in modern times. The metaphysical concepts through which religion has hitherto understood itself have, by and large, lost their intellectual respectability. The scientific-positivistic concepts that have more or less replaced them are not compatible with the deepest concerns of religion. This situation has created, for religious thought, both a crisis and an opportunity. The crisis is that religion has lost the concepts through which it once made itself intelligible. The opportunity is that we are now in a position to seek more adequate ones.

II. Personal vs. Metaphysical Conceptuality

The critique that Heidegger and others have launched against metaphysical thinking has historical roots in Kant's rejection of what he calls 'dialectical' thinking. Ostensibly, this critique has little to do with religion, but is grounded in a critique of cognition itself. It is metaphysical thinking itself that has proven itself unsound, according to Kant. In *The Critique of Pure Reason*, Kant demonstrates that metaphysical reasoning, based, as he contends, on extrapolation from the pure (transcendental) concepts of the understanding, leads to self-contradictory results. For instance, the series of natural causes must have a first cause to initiate it, but, given that every cause must itself be caused, it cannot have such. There must be, and cannot be, a first cause. This contradiction is the result of following two divergent tendencies of human reason to their logical conclusion. The contradiction is resolved, according to Kant, by recognizing that neither tendency tells us anything about what reality is *in itself*. Metaphysical thinking, according to Kant, amounts to little more than the human intellect 'spinning its own wheels.' Our desire to know the deep metaphysical underpinnings of the universe, as it is 'in-itself,' is futile.

This conclusion bears a paradoxical relation to the religious orientation to God. On the one hand, many a religious person might agree with Kant that the 'deep things of God' are hidden from human reason. On the other hand, many would, at the same time, deny that this means we cannot know God in any direct way; that, as per Kant, God must remain a mere 'postulate of practical reason.' For the religious person, God is both knowable *and* unfathomable. There is no contradiction here because the word 'know' is being employed in the personal, not the objectivist, sense. I may not know all there is to know about my lover's circulatory system. But this does not prevent me from knowing *her*.

When Noack contends that "Heidegger's thinking moves in a dimension which alone makes room for doing genuine theological 'thinking' once again," he is suggesting, I believe, that Heidegger has provided a way of thinking about God that permits us a cognitive exploration of this *second* sense of 'knowing;' the only sense, indeed, with which religion is really concerned. Of course, though the religious person's knowing of God may be non-cognitive, this does not prevent religious philosophy from entering upon a *cognitive* exploration of just this non-cognitive knowing. Indeed, if we are to rationally explore the *religious* sense of knowing God this is just what we must do.

Heidegger, thus, has presented the philosopher of religion with a new, and perhaps more legitimate, way of reflecting upon the human relation to God than provided by traditional metaphysics. At the same time, and somewhat ironically, Heidegger – at least the Heidegger of *Being and Time* – does not himself enter into such a reflection, but provides an interpretation of human Being that emphasizes human finitude and mortality. This emphasis, of course, is based upon Heidegger's own phenomenological reflections. My thesis is that there is a phenomenology of faith that can itself be expressed in Heideggerian terms but that takes us beyond the set of existential conclusions we are left with at the end of *Being and Time*. In the following chapters, I will attempt to explore this phenomenology of faith. At present, though, we wish to examine more deeply what it is about Heideggerian conceptuality that provides us the opportunity for this exploration.

III. OBJECTIFICATION VS. RELATIONALITY

We have, to some degree, already touched upon these issues in our discussion of the construction of the factual in chapter two. Objectified thinking endeavors to consider the world as it is 'in itself' without reference to an observing subject. Given that every observation of the world must, *qua* observation, be the observation of some observing subject, however, a purely objective account of Being necessarily entails a falsification, or at least a neglect, of the way Being is indeed manifest. As we noted in chapter two, this neglect of the relationality inherent in the act of knowing has practical value. It allows the compilation of 'objective facts' that have general validity and applicability. If I say that the hammer is 'too heavy,' I provide you with no valuable information about how the hammer will be for you. If I say, however, that the hammer 'weighs a pound,' you now have information with which you can determine whether the hammer will be useable by you. In the one case, I speak of how the hammer is for me. In the other, I speak of how the hammer is 'in itself.' But these two ways of speaking are not on an epistemic par. The second case is an abstraction from the first, which is epistemically prior. I do not immediately encounter the hammer as 'weighing a pound,' but as having a certain weight *for me*. The practice whereby I speak of the hammer as 'weighing a pound,' i.e., the system of objectified thinking, is a human innovation that has practical utility but fails to accurately reflect the way in which Being is primordially disclosed.

It should be fairly obvious that such objectification must, by its very nature, lead to a distorted understanding of those matters whose very essence lies in their *relation* to an observing subject. We say, for instance, that 'beauty is in the eye of the beholder,' but what seems more truly to be the case is that beauty is in the *relation* between the beholder and the beheld. Heidegger, building on Husserl, has helped make it clear to us that such relationality is ontologically primary through his analysis of Dasein as indissolubly related to its world: There is no 'object' that can be viewed in and of itself, apart from the subject for whom it *is* an object.

This is a revolutionary discovery, especially when we consider that the word 'objective' has, in modern times, become virtually synonymous with 'real.' And yet it is the discovery of a truth that has been, quite literally, right before our eyes all along. We have not so much been prevented from *seeing* it as from *thinking* it, and we have been prevented from thinking it due to a style of thinking that has not allowed its full recognition.

The recognition that Being is primordially relational, that objectified thinking is itself a construction and abstraction from a more primordial ontological relationality, is, in and of itself, already confirmatory of an essential aspect of the religious point of view. The religious person claims to be able to know God, the fundament of Being, *relationally*. The religious person speaks of having a personal relation to that which is ontologically primary. But the term 'relationality' does not yet express all that is intended in *personal* relation. To speak of a personal relation is to speak of a relationship that involves the *concerns* native to human personhood. Heidegger has defined the human being as *essentially* concerned; i.e., as 'Care.' Dasein's relation to its world, thus, is never a relation of indifference, but one in-formed by the fundamental concerns of personhood. What gets dismissed by objectivist thinking as 'emotion' is, for Heidegger, a primary mode whereby Being is disclosed to and for Dasein.

In this respect, Heidegger's phenomenological work dovetails with the religious point of view exactly. Both Heideggerian phenomenology and religion understand Being to be primordially disclosed in (and as) relations of concern. This constitutes an enormously important breakthrough in the endeavor to think about religion. The promise of this breakthrough is that, through allowing us to think about religious matters and religious claims in a way more appropriate to religion itself, we are given the opportunity to correct many distortions that creep into religion due to the application of styles of thinking inappropriate to it. For example, the notion that one must affirm certain creedal formulae as true in an 'objective' sense in order to be saved is, I would contend, a distortion of the deep meaning of faith; a distortion that is at least partly due to an objectivist style of thinking. The faith that 'saves' is relational, it has to do with the quality of relation established between person and neighbor, person and world, and, ultimately, person and God. Objectivist thinking obscures this, and thus (as Noack says) distorts the meaning of revelation.

Nevertheless, there remain two significant differences between the Heideggerian orientation to Being and the religious. First, Heidegger's language, though no longer objectified, is still abstract. The primary religious text in the Western tradition, the Bible, on the other hand, is largely imagistic. Second, Heidegger's interpretation of human Being as Being-towards-death, though expressing one dimension of the religious interpretation of human Being, takes no account of the possibility proclaimed at the heart of religious life, the possibility that the finite human being can live *beyond* its finitude, under the telic context of what I am calling 'Being-towards-*life*.' Let us consider the significance of each of these differences in turn.

IV. Abstract vs. Imagistic Conceptuality

The Lutheran theologian Rudolf Bultmann, influenced by Heidegger, coined the term 'demythologization' to speak of the translation of the imagistic language of Scripture into conceptual, existential, language. Bultmann writes: "The real purpose of myth is not to present an objective picture of the world as it is, but to express man's understanding of himself in the world in which he lives. Myth should be interpreted not cosmologically, but anthropologically, or better still, existentially ... [T]he importance of the New Testament mythology lies not in its imagery but in the understanding of existence which it enshrines. The real question is whether this understanding of existence is true. Faith claims that it is, and faith ought not to be tied down to the imagery of New Testament mythology."[2]

Bultmann's point, in calling Scripture 'myth,' is not to suggest that it is fanciful but quite the opposite. Through myth, Scripture endeavors to reveal truths to us of the utmost importance. In order for us to understand these truths, we must interpret the myth – demythologize it – so as to extract its global, yet personal, significance. But why, we may ask, does Scripture present itself imagistically at all? Why does it not simply give us the demythologized concepts from the first?

We will not be able to answer this question, I believe, without entering into a consideration of what lies at the very heart of language and meaning. A full treatment of this subject is well beyond the scope of our project, but some discussion of it is necessary if we are to make the aims of our project clear.

In his 1947 "Letter on Humanism," Heidegger famously writes, "Language is the house of Being." What Heidegger appears to mean by this is that language presents us with the terms in and through which we live. The way we see the world is necessarily conditioned by the linguistic terms through which we see it. Another set of linguistic

2 Rudolf Bultmann, "New Testament and Mythology," in *Kerygma and Myth: A Theological Debate*, ed. Hans Werner Bartsch, trans. Reginald H. Fuller (New York: Harper & Row Publishers, 1961), 10-11.

terms would yield another perspective on the meaning of the world, and, hence, a different mode of life. Being, hence, i.e., our mode of Being, has its life conditioned by the linguistic frame it inhabits. What Heidegger's work on language does not explore as fully as it might, however, is the *reason* for language's vast influence. What is it *about* language that gives it this comprehensive power over life? If we wish to understand the relationship between abstract and mythological language, necessary to an understanding of religious thought, we must make some effort to explore this question.

As the Greek word *logos* implies, language has the power to correlate and organize our discrete phenomenal experiences, permitting us to integrate them into a rational, i.e., ordered, view of the world. Let's take a simple example. Before me stands that which I am accustomed to calling 'a glass of water.' The phrase 'glass of water' does not fully describe what I encounter in observing *this* glass of water. There are things about this glass of water that are not fully expressed in the phrase; for instance, its height. There is, further, that about the phrase which makes it applicable to more than this glass of water; the same phrase might designate another glass of water. There is, then, a discontinuity between the phrase and a particular empirical instantiation of that which it indicates, a discontinuity that allows me to correlate this particular experience with another that is relevantly similar; i.e., with another 'glass of water.' This is a peculiarity of language as such. There is no one-to-one correspondence between a word or phrase and a particular empirical datum. Even proper nouns, though naming what we *call* particulars, never name a particular empirical *moment* of experience. The name 'The Empire State Building,' for instance, does not name some particular empirical encounter with the Empire State Building, but a more extensive, more 'abstract' idea.

Language is, by its very nature, 'universalizing.' That is, it represents the world through *universal terms* that always refer to more than a given moment of phenomenal experience. These terms are used to gather together, under common names, phenomena bearing similarities we deem relevant. The practical need for doing this is fairly easy to see. If I know something of what 'glass' means, then I know something of how to relate to *this* glass even if I have never encountered it before, so long, that is, as I know it to be 'a glass.' The same phenomenal item might have been introduced to me as 'a vase,' in which case I would approach it differently. The word tells me something of how I am to relate to the thing. This universalizing and ordering function of language allows me to organize my experiences and potential experiences in ways that have practical utility. Language tells me how I *should* relate to things. In this respect, language itself has axiological implications, quite apart from any explicit adoption or endorsement of a set of values. I can now also (and not incidentally) communicate my interpretation of the world to others. I can pass it down through the generations. I can teach and be taught.

Insofar as language universalizes, it also objectifies. There is an objectifying tendency in language as such. This is because language, in its universalizing capacity, necessarily transcends the immediacy of encounter, which is to say, the immediacy of *relation*, and must do so in order to fulfill its ordering function. *This* encounter with the Empire State Building is not *that* encounter with it. To speak of the Empire State Building at all is already to speak of something abstracted from the immediacy of encounter. The phrase 'The Empire State Building' does not refer to my encounter with the Empire State Building at some particular moment, but represents the Empire State Building as a thing having its own ontological standing apart from *anyone's* encounter with it. This, of course, is utterly necessary. To the extent that I am unable to develop an understanding of the world abstracted from the immediacy of encounter, the things of the world, and the world itself, would have no coherence. If I had to give each instance of encounter a unique name it would be futile to name anything at all; the world would be a chaos of immediacy.

Insofar as language orders our experience of the world, it is easy for us to confuse it with the *meanings* that it orders. It is crucial, however, for us to recognize that language, as such, is not equivalent to *meaning*. Language *organizes* and is a *bearer* of meaning, but it is not meaning itself. This, by the way, is the mistake that the advocates of 'strong AI' make when they suppose that computers can achieve consciousness through the mere sophistication of their programming. They suppose that since computers can manipulate language they can therefore apprehend meaning. But this is a mistake. Language is not meaning.

There are any number of ways in which we might demonstrate this. We might suppose, for instance, that one can get at the primal meaning of a word through definition; say, by genus and species. But meaning itself cannot be constituted through the mere ordering of terms into genus and species. This is easy to show. For instance, suppose I give the definition of *oloo* as a *tall* member of the genus *aga*. Thus, I have designated the meaning of *oloo* in terms of both genus (*aga*) and species (*tall*). This, however, has not rendered the term *oloo* meaningful. In order to do that, I would now have to give the meaning of *aga*. But if I were to give the meaning of *aga* in terms of some genus that were itself void of meaning, the same problem would recur. The mere ordering of terms into genus and species, thus, does not suffice to render them meaningful. It should be clear that any other purely linguistic endeavor to render language meaningful will have the same problem. This implies that meaning itself is extra-linguistic.

There are many direct examples of the extra-linguistic character of meaning. The expression of a human face, for instance, is meaningful but is not, strictly, language. We can attempt to express its meaning linguistically, to say that the face is exhibiting 'sadness' or 'joy' or 'surprise,' but it is not necessary to do so to experience the meaningfulness of the facial expression. Indeed, only the most accomplished writer can capture, through language, all that is meaningful in a nuanced facial expression. The rest of us are able to judge whether or not it has been adequately captured just because we are privy to the meaning, even though we may not have the linguistic skill with which to render it into words. This example – and I believe such examples could be multiplied almost endlessly – is evidence that meaning is other than, and prior to, language.

What then is it? Meaning, as we have said throughout, refers to the concernful relations we have with ourselves, others, and the world. To fully state the meaning of something is, ultimately, to state its relevance to our (or some Dasein's) concern. It is 'concern' through which the world is meaningful. If a computer is to knowingly manipulate meanings it must *first of all* be a *concernful* being. We have no reason to suppose its electronic circuitry can render it such, and hence no reason to believe computers can achieve independent intelligence. I place the word 'concern' in quotes to indicate that it is an imprecise and vague word, scarcely sufficient for the profound reality we are trying to express with it. Unfortunately, we do not have a more precise word to express this. Philosophy cannot avoid attempting to say what is true just because it cannot say it precisely. In this case, the sin of omission would be far greater than any sin of commission we commit through imprecision.

What is the relation between meaning and language? This is a difficult and complex question whose surface we can only touch upon here. Language *orders* the meaningful world for us, and, in ordering it, shapes its meaning in particular ways. As has now been well recognized, language is essential to the human experience of the world. This is due to what might be called the 'fractionability' of experience together with what Heidegger calls the 'ecstatic' nature of temporality. *This* here-and-now, *this* precise instant, does not in itself present things to me in the fullness of their meaning. The 'pen' refers to a potential project of writing which, in turn, refers to potential projects of communicating, studying, publishing, etc. Not all of that to which the pen's meaning refers, which helps constitute the pen's meaning, is presented to me in the instant of my encounter with the pen. The pen's meaning refers beyond the instant of my encounter with it, and this beyond to which it refers must somehow be available in my encounter with it in order for me to understand the pen *as* a pen. This is reflective of the ecstatic nature of concern itself.

My concern for the things revealed in this here-and-now always extends beyond the instantaneousness of this here-and-now, to past and future, through memory and anticipation. Dasein, who is always in some here-and-now, is, nonetheless, always also concernfully projected *beyond* this here-and-now. Dasein's Being has the paradoxical character of always being *in* the instant but, *within* the instant, always projected *beyond* the instant. It is language or, more generally, conceptuality, that permits Dasein to organize its world in a way that corresponds to its own projectedness beyond the instant. It is language that allows Dasein's world to be, not a chaos of instantaneous and unrelated happenings, but an ordered whole of temporally extended 'objects' with consistent meaning. This constancy of meaning cannot find expression, i.e., have its Being, within temporality as such, insofar as the temporal is ephemeral. It is the *unifying power* that finds expression in *language* that gathers the temporal phenomena together into coherent, meaningful objects, or, perhaps better, *interprets* the temporal phenomena *as* coherent, meaningful, objects; e.g. 'pen.' It is, then, only within a world whose meaning is gathered and ordered through language that human beings can live as human beings. This is the implication of Heidegger's "Language is the house of Being." Dasein is not a mere openness to a flood of discrete, unrelated, phenomena, but lives within the context of coherent, ordered, meanings. Language is the bearer of these ordered meanings.

Language, which gathers and orders the meaning of the phenomenal, is, as many have pointed out, an essential, not an incidental, feature of Dasein's Being. Through language we *interpret* the meaning of the world to ourselves; we synthesize experience into meaningful units and designate the way in which these units relate to each other and us. We thereby 'construct' the meaning of the world. I think it important to note, however, that our capacity to so order the world is dependent upon the world's *orderability*. The phenomena must, in effect, cooperate with our ordering of them. We, in turn, must order them in accordance with their orderability. We are not free to order them in any way we please. It is a great mistake to forget this. We do not invent the world, and there are physical limits to the ways in which we may, as well as ethical and spiritual limits to the ways in which we *should*, order them.

Language, then, orders meaning. Meaning, however, has a richness that language can never fully capture. There is, for instance, often more 'going on' in a facial expression than can be put into words. This itself is a function of the universalizing tendency of language, which, in order to universalize, must abstract from the particularity of experience. This is why only the most skilled authors are able to capture the nuances of those things most meaningful to us; e.g., the romantic relations between a man and a woman, the bonds that unite a mother and child, etc. This is also the reason that narrative and imagistic language is often more immediately meaningful and, at the same time, less cognitively assimilable, than more abstract, conceptual language. As the extension of our terms expand, as we gather more under them, the richness of the meanings they convey diminishes while the range of their applicability increases.

Let's take, for example, the biblical story of Abraham's near sacrifice of Isaac. We ask: what does the story *mean*? Why does it not suffice to say that it means that God asked Abraham to sacrifice Isaac? Because, though this is clearly what the story *says*, what it says does not yet convey its meaning *for us*. The story narrates an event that took place some thousands of years ago, over the course of a few days. To grasp the story's meaning for us, some thousands of years later, we must abstract from the particular occurrences that characterize that event to some meaning of *universal,* or at least very extended, applicability. The story, insofar as it is already expressed in language, is already an abstraction. Surely not everything Abraham experienced on his way to Moriah is captured in the language of the story. But now we must abstract even further if we are to say what the story might mean *for us*, and, beyond us, what it might mean for human Being in general. With each degree of abstraction, we expand the range of meaning's applicability at the cost of meaning's immediacy.

Let us suggest that the story means that one's most precious relationships (e.g., Abraham's relationship to his beloved son Isaac) achieve full sanctity only when acknowledged as gifts from God. We have now rendered the story's meaning in a form that makes it relevant to all human beings at all times, not just to Abraham 4000 years ago. The story now serves as a prototype, a paradigm example, of the significance of faith. The example serves, as all such examples serve, to link the abstract meaning to an instance of concernful living. It is this linkage to living concern (Abraham's care for Isaac) that brings forth a recognition of the full import of the meaning. The concrete richness of the story allows us to engage with it empathically in a way that a mere recitation of the abstract meaning does not. The abstract meaning only *has* import as it pertains to our lived concerns. It is, then, only in stories expressive of such concern that religious meaning finds full expression.

This, I believe, answers the question of why Scripture does not present itself in abstract language from the first; Scripture is not concerned to give us an objective account of Being, to merely satisfy our intellectual curiosity about its physical or metaphysical structure, or our purely historical interest in the past. Scripture is intent to engage us in its account of the *meaning* of Being. It is, thus, essential to the biblical message that it not present the meaning of Being (life) in strictly objectivist terms, to be contemplated with dispassion and detachment. It endeavors, rather, to express the *personal* meaning, i.e., the meaning to *each* particular person in *each* particular here-and-now, of that which is *most* universal: God. The Bible, thus, is a book of persons: of Adam, Eve, Noah, Abraham, Sarah, Moses, Jesus, etc. It is a book of particular persons in living relation to that which is most universal. It is only *in* the particular that meaning has its import.

The reason Scripture must be demythologized is not simply that it contains an obsolete cosmology or employs fantastic imagery. It must be demythologized because its particularity must be rendered universally meaningful. Even if there were no fantastic imagery, no archaic cosmology, Scripture would require demythologization in order to express its general relevance. Biblical hermeneutic is, *as such*, demythologization. Thomas Aquinas, surely one of the most influential interpreters of Christianity, is as much a demythologizer as Bultmann. But Aquinas has rendered the meaning of the Bible into the relatively impersonal, objectivist terms of Greek metaphysics. He himself, shortly before his death and after what is said to have been a personal, mystical experience of God, is reputed to have called his own work 'straw.' The religious tradition, thus, presents us with two distinct modes of religious discourse: the particular-relational language of Scripture, and the universal-objectivist language of metaphysics. Both are inadequate in their own ways; the former because its particularism does not adequately convey its universal significance, the latter because its objectivism does not adequately convey its personal relevance. Heidegger's work is exciting in that it presents us with universal terms that are, nevertheless, non-objectifying. Heidegger's language, awkward as it often is, seeks to preserve the relationality inherent to our primordial encounter with Being. We might call it, 'universal-relational.' As such, it promises a more appropriate approach to religious meaning.

V. 'Dasein' as Universal First-Person Singular

The centerpiece of Heidegger's universal-relational language is his term 'Dasein.' "Dasein," Heidegger writes, "is in *each case mine*" (my emphasis). Heidegger's term 'Dasein' is, I believe, unique to language. It is a *universal* first-person singular. The word 'I,' of course, is a particular first-person singular. Strictly speaking, when I use 'I,' I refer to me, Richard Oxenberg. But Dasein refers to *any* 'me.' Its very employment goes some distance in solving the problem of objectification. One, of course, could use the *impersonal* singular pronoun, 'one.' But it is inappropriate to employ an impersonal pronoun in speaking of personal relations; i.e., relations of personal concern. One could use the personal pronoun 'I,' but then the scope of one's statement would be, strictly, limited to oneself. If we wish to speak of the personal relationality of the world in such a way as to make our speech universally applicable, we require a universal first-person singular. Heidegger provides us one in his term 'Dasein.'

Of course, there are special problems in the use of a *universal* first-person singular. Every first-person account, after all, is private. By what right does Heidegger, or anyone, speak for *all* first-persons? But this problem may be seen as merely the unmasking of a problem that exists, but is hidden, in ordinary objectified discourse. In objectified discourse, one speaks of 'man' or 'the human being' as if one is speaking of something that can be known in general terms, some 'objective essence' we are all assumed to share. Since, of course, no one has ever examined us *all*, such a claim is presumptuous. Its presumptuousness is hidden in the implicit notion that 'man' is some objective datum that can be known as such.

We might at first think that Heidegger's use of 'Dasein' is equally presumptuous. And yet, properly considered, Heidegger's should be seen as an *exposed* and *confessed* presumption. Indeed, Heidegger cannot know what is true of us all any more than can the objectivist. But once I understand that Dasein is in each case *mine*, which is to say, *in my case me*, I should also understand that the verification for Heidegger's claims must also rest with me. Heidegger's discourse, thus, is suggestive and invitative rather than dogmatic. I am to try it on for size and see if it fits. Perhaps I will find it does *not* fit – indeed, my work contends that Heidegger's account of authenticity does not fully fit the authentic person as envisioned by the Judeo-Christian tradition, who is neither properly characterized as Being-towards-death, nor as das Man, but as Being-towards-*life*. In the following chapters we will explore this alternative account of Dasein, one that is in important ways informed by Heidegger's, but goes beyond his, one that is grounded in a reading of Jewish and Christian texts. Like Heidegger's, however, it can only be presented as a suggestion and invitation.

Through the use of the universal first-person and the body of relational concepts (and, perhaps more importantly, the relational orientation) that Heidegger provides, we are able to give a universal account that, at the same time, respects the personal relationality of Being. Heidegger's language, thus, has given us a new thing under the sun: a ***universal-personal*** conceptuality; a way of speaking in universally applicative terms about '*my*' personal relatedness with Being; therefore, also, a way of speaking of the *personal* character of Being in its universality: i.e., a way of speaking about *God*, understood as the universal foundation of (concernful) Being.

And yet, from the religious perspective, all is not well. What Heidegger gives with one hand he takes away with the other. Heidegger's philosophy, in *Being and Time* and beyond, seems increasingly to emphasize the *im*personal character of Being. John Van Buren, one prominent interpreter of Heidegger, writes: "In its most aggravated form, the later Heidegger's essentialist bent led to ... an ultimate 'impersonal there is' ... What was suspended and completely effaced here was his youthful theme of *Mir-Sein*, to-me being, and *Mir-Ereignen*, eventing/enowning to myself ... For the later Heidegger's speculative depth-hermeneutics, *Ereignis* suddenly no longer included the *Ereignis* of the 'Dasein of personal life' in any sense."[3] Theodore Kisiel, another Heideggerian scholar, speaks of "Heidegger's lifelong attempt to 'indicate' an ultimately impersonal but active giving of being (*Sinngebung*) that 'happens' in and through the personal being of situated Dasein."[4] And John Caputo, who has written extensively

3 John Van Buren, *The Young Heidegger: Rumor of the Hidden King* (Indianapolis: Indiana University Press, 1994), 381.

4 Theodore Kisiel, "The Genetic Difference in Reading *Being and Time*," in *American Catholic Philosophical Quarterly*, vol. LXIX, Spring 1995, ed. John D.

on Heidegger's relation to religion, similarly complains: "Heidegger's Being [in contrast to Meister Eckhart's 'Godhead'] is by no means 'fatherly' or 'loving' or 'benevolent.'"[5] And: "Heidegger is not talking about any sort of personal relationship [with Being], but about 'manifestness.' He does not conceive of the coming to pass of manifestness in terms of the loving care of a father but, on the contrary, in terms of 'world-play.'"[6] Caputo concludes: "Heidegger's thought seems to me to move close to the edge of despair."[7]

As Heidegger ultimately envisions it, personal Dasein is situated in that which is, finally, impersonal. What might be considered Heidegger's single most important insight from a religious perspective – that Being is primordially manifest in relations of personal *concern* – becomes, if not entirely obliterated, then strangely muddied in his later work. We might engage in biographical speculation (not entirely inappropriate given Heidegger's philosophical methodology) to understand why he finally tends in this direction when so much of his early work seemed an attempt to rescue the personal character of Being from the impersonalism of metaphysical objectivism, but I believe we can find the answer in *Being and Time* itself. Thrown-being-towards-death, considered as Dasein's *uttermost possibility* – i.e., Dasein's ultimate 'telic context' – does not as such provide Dasein with an interpretation of Being *affirmative* of Dasein's most intimate, personal, concerns.

The Judeo-Christian tradition, on the other hand, professes to provide just such an interpretation. This tradition *knows* of death, and in very much the terms in which Heidegger speaks of it, but denies its ultimacy as Dasein's 'uttermost possibility': "Though I walk through the valley of the shadow of death," says the Psalmist, "I shall fear no evil, for Thou art with me." Death is a key phenomenon in the Western religious tradition, but it is not final. Christ passes *through* death into eternal life and invites us to follow.

Might such a belief amount to nothing more than das Man's refusal to accept its finitude? Might the entire Judeo-Christian tradition, and religion in general, be nothing but another attempt on the part

---

Caputo, 176.

5 John D. Caputo, *The Mystical Element in Heidegger's Thought* (New York: Fordham University Press, 1968), 247.

6 Ibid., 250.

7 Ibid., 251.

of anxious Dasein to evade Being-towards-death – just another instance of inauthenticity? Perhaps. But now, certainly, we have a matter to consider. Heidegger's conceptuality has provided us the means to examine this matter with more penetration than ever before. Dasein's very Being, as an *issue* to itself, as self-concerned, demands that we do so. It is to this task we turn in the remainder of our work.

VII

Creation and Fall

And a lawyer stood up and put [Jesus] to the test, saying, "Teacher, what shall I do to inherit eternal life?" And He said to him, "What is written in the Law? How does it read to you?" And he answered, "You shall love the Lord your God with all your heart, and with all your soul, and with all your strength, and with all your mind; and your neighbor as yourself." And He said to him, "You have answered correctly; Do this and you will live." (Lk 10:25-28)

We have before us a somewhat daunting task. We wish to extract from the Bible its hermeneutic of Dasein. We wish to do this in a manner that will have phenomenological viability; in particular, we wish to show the way the biblical narrative addresses the existential concerns that have surfaced in the analysis of Dasein we have reviewed thus far. Finally, we wish to compare and contrast this hermeneutic with that of Heidegger's. Our claim, of course, is that the Bible does have a hermeneutic of Dasein that can be rendered in a phenomenologically viable way. Our argument for this will be the working out of this hermeneutic itself.

We begin with certain working assumptions, the foremost of which is that the Bible can be read as a whole, coherent work. Of course, there is a huge literature examining the authorship of individual biblical books, the historical conditions under which they were produced, their textual integrity as they have been passed down to us, etc. But our project is not to engage in a textual or historical criticism of the

Bible, it is to consider a religious account of Dasein that is related to, but differs from, Heidegger's account in significant ways. To facilitate this, we will take it for granted that the Bible, as we have received it, can be read as a unified work. Our intent, in other words, is not to examine the way the Bible was put together, but to compare and contrast the account it gives of Dasein with Heidegger's hermeneutic of Dasein in *Being and Time*, in an effort to more fully understand the existential implications of both.

In approaching the Bible, we are involved in a second-order interpretation; that is to say, we are interpreting the Bible's interpretation of Dasein. To interpret is to make explicit an understanding. An understanding, as Heidegger presents it, discloses something in terms of its 'for-the-sake-of-which.'[1] If we wish to understand the Bible's understanding of Dasein, then, we will do well to begin by considering Dasein's ultimate 'for-the-sake-of-which' as the Bible envisions it. This, in turn, will provide us the hermeneutical key for interpreting the biblical account as a whole.

In the passage quoted above, we are given a summation of the Bible's view of how Dasein may attain *eternal life*. We will have occasion to consider more carefully what the qualification 'eternal' may mean in relation to 'life'; but for now we simply note that the Bible presents 'eternal life' as the consummation of life, the consummation of that toward which life rightly tends; in other word, Dasein's ultimate 'for-the-sake-of-which.'

Following Heidegger's own hermeneutical principles, this biblical statement will serve as our key for unlocking the biblical interpretation of Dasein as a whole. In other words, we will read the rest of the Bible with an eye toward the explication of this passage. Besides the term 'eternal life', we find reference in this passage to 'God,' 'Law,' and 'Love.' If we are to understand the passage, we must understand these key terms. In this chapter we will consider the meaning of 'God' in relation to the biblical accounts of Creation and Fall. In the next, we will consider the meaning of 'Law' in relation to the biblical account of the giving of law at Sinai. In the ninth chapter, we will consider the meaning of 'Love' in relation to the biblical account of Christ. In a final chapter, we will consider the significance of all of

1 Martin Heidegger, *Being and Time*, p. 182, H. 143.

this in relation to Heidegger's overall hermeneutic of Dasein and, more generally, the philosophic pursuit of truth.

I. Being and Wholeness

Heidegger began his discussion of Being-towards-death in an effort to get the 'whole' of Dasein into his theoretical grasp. This theoretical project, however, quickly evolved into a discussion of Dasein's potentiality to *be as* a whole.

We must now consider this issue more carefully. What does 'wholeness' mean for a Being such as Dasein? We might endeavor to express this in temporal terms. Dasein, as temporal, always finds itself in some here-and-now. Each here-and-now is distinguishable from the next. Were there no connection between them Dasein would live a fragmentary life; indeed, it would scarcely be possible to speak of a *single* Dasein at all. There must, then, be that which connects these discrete 'here-and-nows' in order for Dasein to exist as a continuous, whole self. This, according to Heidegger, is the *for-the-sake-of-which*.

It is the for-the-sake-of-which that gives coherent meaning to Dasein's life and allows one instant of Dasein's Being to connect with the next. Thus, I enter the office in order to sit at the desk. I sit at the desk in order to write. I write *for-the-sake-of* fulfilling some potentiality of my Being. My entering the office, sitting at the desk, writing, etc. are connected to one another as elements of my project to actualize one of my potentialities. In this way I live *from* myself *to* myself. Dasein's projection upon the actualization of its potentialities links each moment of Dasein's life with the next and gives Dasein's life unity. Such unity is not something achieved only at the end of life; rather it is phenomenally manifest in each moment, in what Heidegger calls the *Augenblick* ("moment of vision"), which may be understood as an existential state in which one's orientation to the phenomenal past, present, and future (i.e., the "having-been," "making-present," and "ahead-of-itself") is integrated in some discrete here-and-now. Thus, for authentic Dasein living toward its 'for-the-sake-of-which,' temporality 'temporalizes itself,' at each discrete moment, as whole.

But inauthentic Dasein does not live as whole. Its projects do not arise from its authentic potentialities, but from 'das Man.' Dasein, as das Man, does not live toward its true potentialities and hence does not connect with itself. To become whole Dasein must become resolute; i.e., it must discover from itself, out of itself, its *own* for-the-sake-of-which and live towards this. This itself requires, according to Heidegger, that Dasein live in the anticipation of death.

What has death to do with resoluteness? Heidegger writes: "The non-relational character of death, as understood in anticipation, individualizes Dasein down to itself...It makes manifest that all Being-alongside the things with which we concern ourselves, and all Being-with-Others, will fail us when our ownmost potentiality for Being is the issue. Dasein can be *authentically itself* only if it makes this possible for itself of its own accord."[2]

Let's consider this statement carefully: "All Being-alongside the things with which we concern ourselves, and all Being-with-Others, will fail us when our ownmost potentiality for Being is the issue." What does this exactly mean? Fail us how? Presumably, this reference to failure pertains to the *issue* Dasein is to itself, the issue that has launched our inquiry. This issue, in turn, has something to do with Dasein's drive to realize its potentialities. Being-towards-death reveals that nothing in the world, nothing we achieve through our worldly dealings, can finally resolve this issue for us. This realization, as Heidegger envisions it, liberates Dasein from enslavement to the world and its dealings and allows Dasein to live as its own.

But this merely tells us how Dasein must *not* live if it is to achieve wholeness, it tells us nothing of how Dasein *is* to live. What *is* the issue Dasein is to itself? What *are* the potentialities it must live towards in order to be authentic and whole? Heidegger never tells us. Either he himself is unclear about it, or he does not feel it can be articulated, or he feels this cannot be communicated from one person to another but must be discovered by each for him- or herself.

For all intents and purposes, it is with this conclusion that *Being and Time* ends. It ends without having clearly articulated the issue Dasein is to itself, or providing a clear vision of just what authentic life would be like. We recall that *Being and Time* is a self-described incomplete work. Heidegger has told us from the beginning that the *existential* analytic of Dasein is merely preparatory for the *ontological*

2 Ibid., p. 308, H. 263.

analytic of Being as such, and that, given the entangled nature of these two, even the existential analytic of Dasein must remain tentative until the ontological analytic has been completed. Heidegger's later work is his effort to move this project forward. But *Being and Time* is especially valuable to us because, in bringing us to this point, it has brought us to the threshold of the religious understanding of human Being.

The Bible would agree with Heidegger that Dasein's ultimate *telos* cannot and should not be defined in terms of worldly accomplishment: "For what does it profit a man to gain the whole world, and forfeit his soul?" (Mk. 8:36). It would agree, as well, that Dasein is, in some significant sense, in flight from itself as Being-towards-death and that it must face up to its Being-towards-death, i.e., its finitude, in order to realize its most fundamental potentialities. But it also articulates a vision of Being *as such* that allows it to say something of what these potentialities are. Thus, it completes Heidegger's project in a particular direction, by presenting an *ontological* analytic of Being that places the *existential* analytic of Dasein in a particular context. What we now wish to do is explore this religious analytic.

II. God

What the Judeo-Christian tradition asserts (an assertion we find repeated in virtually all the world's great religions) is that finite, individualized Dasein *is not* and *cannot be* whole in itself.

Ironically, it is Heidegger's own analytic that can help us to see why this is so: "That in the face of which one has anxiety," writes Heidegger, "is Being-in-the-world as such."[3] According to Heidegger, anxiety does not come to Dasein through a threat from without but is native to Dasein's very Being. Dasein is anxious *as such*, Dasein *as such* is 'not-at-home.' As Dasein emerges from its lostness in das Man, as Dasein 'comes back to itself,' it is just then that its anxiety and not-at-homeness come to the fore. On the face of it, this seems the reverse of what one would expect. If das Man expresses Dasein's *false* self, and anticipatory resoluteness Dasein's *true* self, we would expect that Dasein would feel a *stranger* to its false self and *at home*

3 Ibid., p. 230, H. 186.

in its true self. Indeed, if we remain true to Heidegger's insight as to the disclosive character of moods, this conclusion forces itself upon us. It is, to say the very least, odd to say that just when Dasein comes into its 'wholeness' and 'truth' it should feel *not-at-home*.

Yet Heidegger's analysis is not to be dismissed. His phenomenological observations ring true. They are based upon his recognition that Care is, implicitly, for-the-sake-of-itself, and his awareness that in das Man Dasein loses touch with this. Being-towards-death wrenches Dasein out of the falsity of das Man and delivers it back to itself; i.e., delivers it back to its realization of itself as responsible to itself. But surely here we have a paradox. If this is Dasein's true Being, why does Dasein flee from it? What is the *meaning* of Dasein's anxious flight from itself?

To ask the meaning of something, we recall, is to ask what it is *for*. Is there something, then, that Dasein's anxiety might be for? Anxiety, fallen into the world, says Heidegger, is fear. We fear this or that worldly eventuality, which is to say, we regard this or that worldly eventuality as threatening to our worldly concerns. Authentic anxiety, however, is not directed to this or that worldly circumstance but is of the very Being of Dasein. Does it thereby lose its character as disclosing that which is threatening? Or is there, rather, *something about the very Being of Dasein that is a threat to itself?*

Might it be that Dasein's very *individualization* is a threat to itself? Dasein's individualization severs it from its world, the world it shares with other Daseins, and from the font of its Being, its own ontological basis. Might this be the reason Dasein feels not-at-home in itself? To be home is to abide in that *from which* one is, that which provides the basic support for one's Being. Ontologically speaking, to be 'not-at-home' is to be out of relation to the *basis* (and, hence, support) of one's Being. Heidegger's examination of Dasein reveals just such a felt lack of relation. As *thrown*, Dasein experiences its basis as *null*. What is the meaning of this felt nullity?

Heidegger himself is not very clear on this. Jean-Paul Sartre, in his Heidegger-inspired work, *Being and Nothingness*, provides a fuller phenomenological treatment of the meaning of nullity. We can learn something by looking briefly at Sartre's account. Sartre writes:

> I have an appointment with Pierre at four o'clock. I arrive at the café a quarter of an hour late. Pierre is always punctual. Will he have waited for me? I look at the room, the patrons, and I say, 'He is not here.' Is there an intuition of Pierre's absence, or does negation indeed enter in only with judgment? At first sight it seems absurd to speak here of an intuition since to be exact there could not be an intuition of *nothing* and since the absence of Pierre is this nothing. Popular consciousness, however, bears witness to this intuition. Do we not say, for example, "I suddenly saw that he was not there"?[4]

The absence of Pierre is not a mere logical judgment, but a phenomenon. One '*sees*' that Pierre is absent. The absence of Pierre does not exist for everyone in the café but only for one *looking for* Pierre, only, that is, for one whose Being is in anticipation of Pierre, longing for Pierre. How might we apply this to Heidegger's Dasein? If Dasein's thrown-Being-towards-death has the aspect of nullity, and this nullity the aspect of anxiety (i.e., threat), does this not suggest that there is that in Dasein's very Being that *looks for*, *longs for*, an *absent* basis? Dasein's nullity, then, would have the meaning of *privation*.[5]

This in turn would make clear the meaning of authentic Dasein's anxiety. Dasein's utter individualization brings anxiety because, at the most fundamental level, Dasein is *not* an *utter* individual. Dasein's anxiety reveals that Dasein, considered as *enclosed* in thrownness and Being-towards-death, is *in*complete, fragmented, de-prived, *severed* from its ontological "home." In other words, Dasein's anxious awareness of its finitude evidences its essential relation to *in*finitude, just as Sartre's intuition of Pierre's *absence* is testimony to Sartre's relation to Pierre. If Dasein is a relatedness to infinitude, then a full understanding of Dasein will demand an account of this relatedness.

---

4 Jean-Paul Sartre, *Being and Nothingness*, trans. Hazel E. Barnes (New York: Washington Square Press, 1956), 40-41.

5 There is, of course, a long theological tradition regarding evil as *privatio boni*. Aquinas writes: [T]he nature of the good consists in perfection ... [A] thing is perfect according as it is in act. A thing will therefore be imperfect according as it falls short of act. Hence, evil is either a privation or includes privation." Thomas Aquinas, *Summa Contra Gentiles, Book One: God*, trans. Anton C. Pegis, (Notre Dame: University of Notre Dame Press, 1975), chap. 39, p. 155. In their discussions of 'the nothing,' I believe, Heidegger and Sartre provide a glimpse of the phenomenological underpinnings of this metaphysical concept.

The Bible presents us with just such an account. Here it is God who is the true ontological whole. Finite Dasein is a part of this whole, but cannot hope to achieve wholeness by itself, nor through its activity in the world. What Heidegger calls Dasein's "thrownness," religion calls its creatureliness. Ontologically, Dasein's Being is not contained in itself, but exists in relation to the whole of what-is, as rooted and unified in God. Left entirely to itself Dasein is destitute – which is just why Dasein flees its self-enclosure, into the publicness of das Man.

Thus, Dasein's Being is *relational* as such. Dasein exists, and is able to exist, only *as* relation. Dasein *qua* Dasein, Dasein considered strictly in itself, is cut off from the font of its life and is, as such, towards death. But for just this reason, Dasein's ontology is not fully given when considered strictly in itself. Relationality is essential to Dasein's Being. The destruction of Dasein's relationality is the destruction of Dasein.

It appears that Heidegger's very methodology prevents him from asking *whence* Dasein is thrown; such whence not being *phenomenally* apparent. The Bible, of course, declares this whence to be God. What is the *ground* of the Bible's claim? In the Christian tradition, of course, we can find the Anselmian and Thomistic 'proofs' for the existence of God, but these proofs have their roots in Greek metaphysics, not in that which is native to the Christian tradition as such. Religion rests its claim on what it calls revelation; i.e., the disclosedness of God to human beings as recorded in the Bible. The Christ of the New Testament does not endeavor to prove his claims through Aristotelian demonstration, but asks for faith. How are we to regard such claims, and such a request?

I wish to suggest that we cannot simply dismiss them on *methodological* grounds. In the Gospel of Matthew, Jesus is recorded as saying: "Blessed are the pure in heart, for they shall see God" (Mt 5:8). One may draw the inference that the *impure* in heart will not see God, or not see God clearly. From the Christian view, all human beings are, to some degree or other, impure in heart. Then how is this claim to be assessed?

If there is a correlation between purity of heart and the seeing of God, this suggests that such 'seeing' is not an empirical experience available to anyone with physical eyes, but a mode of Dasein's Being.

It is not that one sees some being that one then identifies as God, but that one's Being-in-the-world is modified in a way that yields an experience of God. Sartre writes, "[I]f I should finally discover Pierre, my intuition would be filled by a solid element, I should be suddenly arrested by his face and the whole café would organize itself around him as a discrete presence."[6] Of course, God is not going to be visible as Pierre is visible, but what is significant in Sartre's account is not that Pierre is suddenly physically visible, but that the presence of Pierre has overcome the absence of Pierre, which has changed the character of the whole café. The whole café, which was organized around Pierre's absence, is now organized around Pierre's presence. Likewise, for the one who 'sees God,' I suggest, the whole café (i.e., the world) organizes itself around his/her sense of the presence of God. God is apparent, not as a discrete being (*Seiendes*), but as the consummate *arché* and *telos* of Being (*Sein*), through which the world achieves its ordered wholeness, and through which one finally comes to feel "at home." Dasein's individual wholeness is realized only through its relatedness to *this* wholeness, a relatedness that resolves the anxious nullity of thrownness and death.

III. The Eternal

The Bible's 'In the beginning ...,' then, may be read as a statement concerning Dasein's ultimate, ontological, basis and support – its *home*. In effect, it confirms what Heidegger's phenomenological observations have already indicated: that Dasein is neither at home in the world, nor in itself. It purports to reveal, however, something that Heidegger's phenomenology does not: that Dasein does indeed have a home, a home it shares with all other Daseins and the world at large. This home is not visible as a datum *in* the world. It is that in which the world is.

"In the beginning God created the heaven and the earth," i.e., the world of Dasein. Since Dasein is Being-in-the-world-*with-others*, the whole of Dasein's world can *be* a whole only insofar as each element within it shares with the others a common ontological ground. The revelation of God as creator is also the revelation of Dasein's poten-

6 Sartre, *Being and Nothingness*, 40-41.

tiality-for-Being-a-whole (*with others*). Dasein's potentiality-for-Being-a-whole is revealed as contingent on Dasein's establishment of some sort of healthful relationality with God.

Thus, the Bible employs the chronological notion of 'beginning' to convey the existential sense of home; i.e., that which would resolve the *not-at-homeness* native to individualized Dasein. As the infinite basis of Dasein's finitude, God is that through which the dilemma of Dasein's nullity can be resolved. Insofar as Dasein's nullity expresses itself temporally, in the null basis and null term of thrown-Being-towards-death, the *in*-finity which resolves it must also be expressible temporally. *Eternity* is the temporal expression for God's infinity. The Bible's 'In the beginning ...' expresses the eternality of God.

As we discussed in the last chapter, the Bible's language is particular-relational. It depicts one particular being (God) creating others at a particular point in time. Traditional theology translates this into the universal-objectivist language of metaphysics. The particularistic language of the Bible is translated into a language concerning God's 'eternality,' 'infinity,' 'aseity,' etc., i.e., a discussion of God's metaphysical attributes, what God objectively is 'in himself.' For the metaphysician, the significance of God's act of creation is no longer primarily historiological, i.e., an answer to the question 'how did the world come to be?', but causal, i.e., an answer to the question 'what does the world ultimately depend upon?' Both of these questions have been criticized by Heidegger as 'onto-theological', expressions of Dasein's desire to achieve mastery over Being through cognizing it objectively from 'the ground up.' It is my contention, though, that authentic religion is not onto-theological in the Heideggerian sense. Both the historiological question and the metaphysical question may be seen as expressions of Dasein's yearning for wholeness. If we are going to assess this yearning phenomenologically, we must find a way of rendering it into universal-relational language; that is, we must ask the question: 'What might eternity *mean* for Dasein?'

In considering this question, it will aid us, I think, to have before us Augustine's metaphysical treatment of the question of time and eternity in the *Confessions*:

> A fickle-minded man ... might wonder why you, who are God almighty, Creator of all, Sustainer of all, and Maker of heaven

> and earth, should have been idle and allowed countless ages to elapse before you finally undertook the vast work of creation. My advice to such people is to shake off their dreams and think carefully, because their wonder is based on a misconception. How could those countless ages have elapsed when you, the Creator, in whom all ages have their origin, had not yet created them ... You are the maker of all time ... if there was no time before heaven and earth were created, how can anyone ask what you were doing 'then? If there was no time, there was no 'then.'
>
> Furthermore, although you are before time, it is not in time that you precede it. If this were so, you would not be before all time. It is in eternity, which is supreme over time because it is a never-ending present, that you are at once before all past time and after all future time.[7]

Our concern, again, is not to assess the metaphysics of Augustine's conception of time, but to understand what meaning it might have for Dasein. The Bible's 'In the beginning...' addresses the question of Dasein's origin, a question arising out of the incompleteness Dasein experiences in its thrownness. In asking the question of its origin Dasein is asking after the possibility of its wholeness. To clarify this question, we need to become even clearer as to what 'wholeness' itself means.

Experientially, the idea of wholeness is related to that of *sufficiency*. We can see this clearly by comparing the ideas of 'whole' and 'part.' That which is partial requires connection, relation, to something beyond itself for completion. That which is whole is sufficient as itself. What Dasein ultimately seeks, in asking the question of its origin, is not an account of some first efficient cause that will help explain the mechanics of its emergence, but an account of that which can resolve the incompleteness and insufficiency it experiences in its thrown-Being-towards-death and, thereby, make of it a whole.

As we have discussed, Dasein's life is lived in time, or better, *through* time. Time itself is fragmentable; it may be segregated into discrete moments. But now we might note that Dasein's very experience of

---

7 Augustine, *Confessions*, trans. R.S. Pine-Coffin (London: Penguin Books, 1961), Book XI, 13, p. 263.

itself as *finite* is an experience of itself as but a fragment; a fragment of a whole it intuits only in the mode of *absence*; i.e., only through feeling its own insufficiency in relation to it. On the face of it, one might think that Dasein's Being, though finite, nevertheless fills its present. Dasein, after all, is not absent to itself in the present (which gives rise to the notion that if Dasein could only divorce itself from concern for past and future and focus its attention entirely in the *now*, understood as *this instant*, it would find fulfillment). But this notion proves to be the result of too superficial an analysis. Dasein's awareness of its *thrownness*, and its *Being-towards-death*, though not an awareness of what Dasein encounters in the world at present, nevertheless qualifies Dasein's experience of the present. The nullity of Dasein's past and future are somehow experienced as a *deficiency* in what Dasein *is*, i.e., Dasein's *Being*, at present.

Dasein cannot separate its concernfulness in the present from its concern for past and future, because its present concern is, as Heidegger has shown, temporally *projected* upon its future on the ground of its past. Thus, despite what may seem the plenum of Dasein's present, finite Dasein experiences itself as needing *more*, as temporally *de*ficient. In the above quotation, Augustine speaks of eternity as a "never-ending present." One might well ask: what is the value of such never-endingness, given that one can only *be* at one moment at a time? It is only insofar as *this moment* requires the next merely to be satisfied with *itself* that never-endingness has value. In Dasein's angst over its finitude we see just this. Dasein's *present* is experienced as insufficient, as *needing* its future merely to be satisfied with itself. This is just why the prospect of death brings anxiety. This, then, indicates the projective, i.e., temporally extended, nature of Dasein as Care. Dasein's self-concern is not situated in the present as divorced from past and future, but is temporally extended *over* past and future.

To the extent that Dasein experiences its finitude as anxiety-arousing (i.e., threatening), then, Dasein proves itself to be concernfully projected *beyond* its finitude. The very character of Dasein's concern, in other words, indicates a vocation to *in*-finitude, i.e., "eternal life."

And yet we encounter a paradox. Though Dasein's concern is projected beyond the present, it is still only possible for Dasein to be *in* the present. The *concern* with past and future is *in* the present. Dasein's sense of *thrownness* and *Being-towards-death* are qualifications of Dasein's *present* experience. It is Dasein's *present* that is deficient, Dasein's *present* that looks beyond itself for something more, and it is for just this reason that Dasein seeks to rush away from its present into its future.

Eternity, then (i.e., the "never-ending present"), is the expression for a mode of temporality in which this sense of deficiency is resolved. Understood phenomenologically, in other words, *eternity is the sufficiency of the now*.

This implies that eternity is essentially a qualitative, not a quantitative, modification of time. It is a temporal expression for ontological wholeness. As whole, The Eternal (God) transcends, comprehends, and completes all that is fragmented. If we endeavor to express this in temporal terms, we say that God is 'before' the beginning and 'after' the end, but the very paradoxical nature of such expressions indicates that we are using the terms 'before' and 'after' suggestively, to express God's ontological comprehension of discursive temporality.

The distinction between eternity and time, then, is not the distinction between a totality and its parts, as if one might arrive at the concept of eternity through conceptually stringing all the parts of time together and considering them at once. Rather, it is the distinction between that which is temporally *sufficient* and that which is temporally *deficient*, and, as such, needful. For eternity to be experienced at all, it must be experienced in the *now*. It must be experienced as the *sufficiency of the now*. Eternity is a kind of peace, joy, abiding contentment in the *now*. It is ultimately to be understood as an axiological, not a quantitative, qualification of time. Given this, we might now ask after the *axiological* character of eternity: How must one be from an axiological standpoint in order to experience temporality as *whole*, i.e., as eternal? Judeo-Christian religion gives us its answer in the passage quoted at the start of this chapter: human beings access eternity – *eternal life* – through the fullness of love. It is through love that Dasein overcomes its sense of ontological deficiency and participates in the eternality of God.

We can relate this notion of eternity to Heidegger's analyses of authentic and inauthentic temporality. Temporality, as Heidegger shows, is not reducible to what he calls "clock time." Clock time, to express it in the terms we developed in chapter two, may be thought of as merely the 'factuality' of temporality; i.e., it has practical value for society but does not reveal the phenomenal meaning of temporality. Temporality is the *Being-towards* of Dasein. The character of Dasein's temporality is determined by the character of its *Being-towards*. Dasein, as self-projective, is always *Being-towards* ... something. Inauthentic Dasein's *Being-towards* is dispersed in the busyness of das Man. Only when Dasein becomes resolute does its *Being-towards* take upon itself thematic integrity, which allows Dasein to consolidate itself as whole: "Everyday Dasein has been dispersed into the many kinds of things which daily 'come to pass'...So if it wants to come to itself, it must first *pull itself together* from the *dispersion* and *disconnectedness* of the very things that have 'come to pass' ... "[8] Such 'pulling itself together' is achieved, according to Heidegger, when Dasein affirms its thrownness and Being-towards-death in the 'moment' of resolute 'vision;' i.e., the *Augenblick*. Authentic temporality is unified in the *Augenblick*. The *Augenblick* is a moment whose meaning is informed by the integration of Dasein's past, present, and future *in* the present. Authentic Dasein, abiding in the *Augenblick*, lives as whole. Heidegger writes: "One's existence in the moment of vision [*Augenblick*] temporalizes itself as something that has been stretched along in a way which is fatefully *whole* in the sense of the authentic historical *constancy* of the Self" (my emphasis).[9]

Religion would question, however, whether wholeness is indeed possible under the telic context of thrown-Being-towards-death. If thrownness and Being-towards-death present themselves as in some sense *null*, and if nullity is an experience of *privation* (i.e., deficiency),

8 Heidegger, *Being and Time*, p. 441-442, H. 390. Also: "Understood existentially, birth is not and never is something past in the sense of something no longer present-at-hand; and death is just as far from having the kind of Being of something still outstanding, not yet present-at-hand but coming along. Factical Dasein exists as born; and, as born, it is already dying, in the sense of Being-towards-death. As long as Dasein factically exists, both the 'ends' and their 'between' are ... Thrownness and the Being-towards-death in which one either flees it or anticipates it, form a unity; and in this unity birth and death are 'connected' in a manner characteristic of Dasein." Ibid., pp. 426-427, H. 374.

9 Ibid., p. 463, H. 410.

then thrown-Being-towards-death is *in*complete, fragmentary, as such. This conclusion is reinforced for us by Heidegger's own emphasis on the futurity of authentic temporality: "*The primary phenomenon of primordial and authentic temporality is the future.*"[10] Temporal Dasein is concernfully projected upon its future. The prospect of no-future must be the frustration of its projectedness, not its wholeness. And this is indeed what the Bible sees – it is just for this reason that the inevitability of death is associated with a sense of despair and meaninglessness: "[H]ow the wise man and the fool alike die! So I hated life, for the work which had been done under the sun was grievous to me; because everything was futility and striving after wind" (Eccl. 2:16-17).

Augustine's metaphysical account represents eternity as a "permanent standstill."[11] But this now seems the result of too objectivistic an analysis. Eternity is not the *stopping* of time, but its fulfillment, its wholeness. We may well ask, then, in what *dimension* of Being can the temporal be said to be more or less whole? We have already answered: it is in the *axiological* dimension; eternity is realized in – *as* – love. The mystic's 'eternal now' is not a freeze-frame in which time has literally stopped. Rather, it is the present Moment experienced under the full telic context of ontological wholeness: Here-and-now, in all its finite particularity and facticity, presents itself as the *center* of eternity. Wholeness is achieved, not through being at every here-and-now 'at once,' but through being at *this* here-and-now, *centered* in the whole. The mystic is aware that *every* here-and-now is just such another center.[12]

If this analysis is correct then we cannot simply oppose eternity to time, as if the two were contraries. Rather, eternity is to be understood as a *mode* of temporality; in Heidegger's language, eternity is the way in which temporality 'temporalizes' itself as whole. Heidegger's concept of the *Augenblick* appears to be his attempt to present a secularized, finitized, version of such temporal wholeness.

10 Ibid., p. 378, H. 329.

11 Augustine, *Confessions*, Book XI, 13, p. 263.

12 The later Heidegger's story of Heraclitus warming himself at his stove where 'the gods too are present' is reflective of this. See Martin Heidegger, "Letter on Humanism," trans Frank A. Capuzzi and J. Glenn Gray in *Martin Heidegger: Basic Writings*, 256-257.

But, as we have said, the angst and not-at-homeness accompanying finitude indicate that 'finite wholeness' is an oxymoron. From the Judeo-Christian perspective finite Dasein advances on wholeness, not through the anticipation of death, but only through the anticipation (running-towards, *Vorlaufen*) of that which is whole as such: God. Significantly, such wholeness requires of Dasein not only a 'vertical' transcendence toward God but a 'horizontal' transcendence toward others, for the reality of God *comprehends* the reality of others. The vertical and horizontal transcendence, thus, must proceed apace, like the expansion of a sphere. This is what we read in the quote with which we began this chapter: Eternal life is achieved through the love of God and neighbor. Only thereby does Dasein resolve into wholeness *all* that is present to it as Being-in-the-world-*with-others*. The religious person's pursuit of wholeness cannot be divorced from the demand for ethical relation; a concern at best slighted in Heidegger's treatment of authenticity.

So, it is not temporality *as such* that is opposed to eternity, but fragmented temporality. The potential for such fragmentation is a function of the multitudinous creation itself. The Bible never tells us *why* God creates the multitudinous, finite, world; it is written from the standpoint of a creation already in place. The question of the Bible is not '*why* does God create?', but '*how* is the creation, and the multitude of things within it (especially human beings), to exist in healthful relation to one another, so as to overcome the danger of fragmentation and achieve its potential for wholeness/goodness?'. Any answer to this question requires a diagnosis of what stands in the way. The Bible gives us this diagnosis in its accounts of creation and fall.

IV. CREATION

As the Bible presents it, the creation does not emerge from God fully formed but proceeds as a process of ordering that takes place over the course of six days. At first the earth is "without form and void," i.e., chaos. Over the six days of creation God orders the world into a form which God finally declares "very good" (Gn. 1:31).

The goodness of the creation, in other words, is not inherent to each individual thing as such, but is a function of a certain order;

a way in which the individual elements of the creation are to be related to one another as whole. The creation can potentially be in dis-order, and thereby express lack of goodness, or evil. The human being shares in the goodness of the creation only insofar as he/she is in appropriate relation to the whole.

On the sixth day, the human being (male and female) is made in the 'image of God.' If we understand God as the ontological whole, then the human being, made in the image of God, may be interpreted as an image, a reflection, of such ontological wholeness. God, as whole, is for-the-sake-of-itself. The human being, as image of God, shares in God's ontological structure as 'for-the-sake-of-itself.' Heidegger has given us an analysis of this structure and dubbed it 'Care.' According to the Great Commandment quoted at the start of this chapter, however, Dasein can realize itself as for-the-sake-of-itself only in living for-the-sake-of-others as well. This does not make Dasein less the image of God, but more the image of God, as God's creativity is an expression of *God's* being 'for-the-sake-of-others.'[13] Nevertheless, Dasein's very Godlikeness, as for-the-sake-of-itself, presents Dasein with the power to enclose itself in itself and live strictly for-itself. This self-enclosure is the essential sin; it cuts Dasein off from the whole that is God. Ironically, the Bible characterizes sin in the same terms Heidegger characterizes authenticity: it is towards-death. 'Proximally and for the most part,' says the Bible, sin is the condition of humankind.

As many exegetes have noted, a careful reading of Genesis shows that there are two creation stories, the one we have been reviewing and the one beginning at Genesis 2:4 and including the story of Eden and Fall. In the first story, God completes the creation in six days and rests "from all his work" on the seventh day. In the second story, God creates Adam and Eve, and does not appear to get much rest after that. This raises the question: On what 'day' do Adam and Eve fall? There is nothing in the second story to suggest how its chronology is to be mapped to the first. If we understand the creation of Man/

13 Aquinas: "Now, goodness is in God, and the outpouring of goodness into other things. Hence, the creature approaches more perfectly to God's likeness if it is not only good, but can also act for the good of other things, than if it were good only in itself; that which both shines and casts light is more like the sun than that which only casts light." Thomas Aquinas, *Summa Contra Gentiles, Book Two: Creation,* trans. James F. Anderson (Notre Dame: University of Notre Dame Press, 1956), chap. 45, p. 137.

Woman to *culminate* in their attaining 'the image of God,' then it is possible to read the story of the Fall, and indeed the entirety of human history as we know it, as taking place on the *sixth* day of creation. On this reading, the entire story of fall and redemption, the whole of 'salvation history' from Eden to Calvary and beyond, is a *factor* in the perfecting of Man/Woman.[14] The 'seventh day' points to the *telic context* of peace and perfect relationality that is, from a temporal point of view, always *futural*; as the fulfilled 'Kingdom of God.'

Read this way, the evils of human life may be understood as due to our having not yet fully realized our ultimate ontological *telos*. The creation is still in process; still, in no small measure, 'without form and void.'[15] The sabbatical perfection to which the Bible points, further, will depend upon the further development of human beings, those made "in the image of God." The story of this development, and of what stands in its way, begins at Genesis 2:4.

V. EDEN AND FALL

Christianity represents the chaos and evil of human life as due to a 'fall from grace,' i.e., a fall from right relation with God. Heidegger also employs the term 'fallenness' to speak of Dasein's immersion in the life of das Man, which he sees as a fall from authenticity, i.e.,

14 Among philosophers of religion, John Hick is perhaps most prominent in promoting such a progressive view of the creation: "[M]an, created as a personal being in the image of God, is only the raw material for a further and more difficult stage of God's creative work. This is the leading of men as relatively free and autonomous persons, through their own dealings with life in the world in which He has placed them, towards that quality of personal existence that is the finite likeness of God." John Hick, *Evil and the God of Love* (London: Macmillan and Company Limited, 1966), 290. As Hick points out, this view is to be found in Eastern Orthodoxy, traced to Irenaeus (c. 130- c. 202), where a distinction is made between the divine *image*, in which humans are first created, and the divine *likeness*, which they achieve in becoming Christ-like. Orthodox Bishop Kallistos Ware writes: "The Incarnation, then, is not simply a way of undoing the effects of original sin, but it is an essential stage upon man's journey from the divine image to the divine likeness." *The Orthodox Way*, (Crestwood, NY: A.R. Mowbray & Co., Ltd., 1979), 71. See also Gustaf Wingren, *Man and the Incarnation: A Study in the Biblical Theology of Irenaeus*, trans. Ross Mackenzie (Philadelphia: Muhlenberg Press, 1959).

15 This interpretation, it might be noted, would support the process theodicies developed by Hawthorne and others from Whiteheadian metaphysics. In this view the material world possesses an element of spontaneity and randomness ('chaos') that escapes the complete control of God's will. God points to the sabbatical perfection but *can*not force it upon the creation.

right relation to self. These two notions of fallenness, though not identical, may be seen to bear a relationship to one another. From the biblical perspective, Dasein's right relation to self (authenticity) becomes distorted *due to* its divergence from right relation to God.

In this section, we will examine the relationship of Heidegger's notion of fallenness to the Christian notion. To do so, we will first provide a phenomenological reflection that will ground our reading of the biblical text on which the Christian understanding of the fall is based. Next, we will provide our own symbolical interpretation of this text guided by this reflection. Finally, we will compare the biblical with the Heideggerian notion of fallenness.

1. Phenomenological Reflection

Heidegger writes: "From an existentiell point of view, the authenticity of Being-one's-Self has of course been closed off and thrust aside in falling; but to be thus closed off is merely the *privation* of a disclosedness which manifests itself phenomenally in the fact that Dasein's fleeing is a fleeing *in the face of* itself."[16]

Dasein, according to Heidegger, is "closed off" from its authenticity due to its fallenness, but such 'closed-offness' is to be understood as the privation of a more *primordial* 'un-closedness,' i.e., authenticity. Similarly, the Christian doctrine of original sin bespeaks a primordial innocence lost due to the fall of Adam and Eve. In both cases, a concept of primordiality is at play that cannot be reduced to the chronological. Heidegger does not mean to say that there was once a *time*, in everyone's life, when he or she 'fell' from authenticity. Nor can the Eden story be read as history.

True, Augustine and others have insisted that the biblical account of the Fall be accepted as historical record. Considering the propriety of symbolical exegesis of the Genesis story, for instance, Augustine writes: "There is no prohibition against such exegesis, provided that we also believe in the truth of the story as a faithful record of historical fact."[17] There are, however, grave difficulties in doing so. Quite apart from the difficulty of reconciling the story with modern anthropological and biological evidence, the story, literally construed,

16 Heidegger, *Being and Time*, p. 229, H. 184.

17 Augustine, *City of God*, trans. Henry Bettenson (London: Penguin Books, 1972), 567, XIV.10

undermines itself, depicting God as startlingly unjust. To condemn the whole of humankind for a single act of disobedience, into which the first couple were seduced by a malicious fiend, and which, for all that, had the character of a victimless crime (apart from the punishment visited by God upon the hapless 'criminals'), would be in violation of virtually every principle of justice ever advanced, including those advanced by the Bible itself. The *lex talionis* rule of justice (eye for eye, tooth for tooth) would require that God, in retribution for Eve's sin, steal a bit of fruit from Eve, not condemn the entire human race to perdition. The Eden story, thus, demands a symbolical exegesis, not as a means to reconciling it with modern science, but as a means to explicating its own biblical intentions.[18] The story shows every sign of being symbolical by intent.

But this means that we must interpret its *historical* primordiality to signify a primordiality of another sort. The chronological primordiality of Eden must be taken as symbolizing an *axio-ontological* primordiality. Man/Woman are fallen, not from what they *have* been, but from what they *ought to* be. It is certainly no accident that the Bible locates this 'fall' at the very beginning of human history. It thereby indicates that every human being is always already under its sway. The implication is that human beings, in general, live in tension with their own potential for wholeness, a tension phenomenally manifest as both nullity and 'guilt' (or nullity *as* guilt, as we will discuss next chapter).

But this raises a question. In what sense may we speak of an ontological primordiality that is not also a chronological primordiality? Metaphysically, this question has traditionally been answered through an analysis of potentiality. In the Aristotelian-Thomistic metaphysic, 'act' is said to precede 'potency' universally, though potency may, of course, precede act in any individual case. Thus, the individual, in potency, is said to have an inherent predisposition for actualizing a state of Being that it may never have, chronologically, known.

18 Kierkegaard recognized this: "Innocence is lost only by guilt. Every man loses innocence essentially the same way that Adam lost it. It is not in the interest of ethics to make all men except Adam into concerned and interested spectators of guiltiness but not participants in guiltiness, nor is it in the interest of dogmatics to make all men into interested and sympathetic spectators of the Atonement [*Forsoning*] but not participants in the Atonement." Søren Kierkegaard, *The Concept of Anxiety: A Simple Psychologically Orienting Deliberation on the Dogmatic of Hereditary Sin*, ed. and trans. Reidar Thomte and Albert B. Anderson (Princeton, Princeton University Press, 1980), 36.

For instance, a child's potentiality to be an adult is inherent to the child, even though the child has never yet been an adult. If we now imagine a being who is in some resistance, for whatever reason, to its *own* fulfilled actualization, we may speak of this resistance as, in some sense, a 'fallenness' from what it *ought to* be but has never yet been. Implicit in this metaphysic is the notion of 'form.' Every being in potency is in potency to a specific form that its Being is impelled to actualize.

Heidegger's existential analytic of Dasein may be read as an endeavor to explicate the ontological *form* of Dasein phenomenologically. Dasein, as Care, says Heidegger, is 'for-the-sake-of-itself.' This is the structure (i.e., 'form') of Care. Dasein achieves authenticity only to the extent that it lives as such. The Great Commandment, with which we began this chapter, suggests that Dasein's form requires that it live for the sake of others and God as well. Are these two claims compatible? We will consider this question in chapter nine. For now, though, we may simply note that for factical Dasein the demand to love itself and the demand to love others are certainly in tension. Dasein, as 'for-the-sake-of-itself,' lives in a world of others who are also 'for-the-sake-of-themselves,' with whom Dasein comes into conflict.

Of course, were one to judge the matter universally and disinterestedly one would see that each 'for-the-sake-of-itself' has its own inherent legitimacy. In other words, each for-the-sake-of-itself, *as* for-the-sake-of-itself, has the ontological 'right' to be for-the-sake-of-itself. By use of the word 'right' I do not mean to import an ethical standard foreign to our ontological analysis, but merely to indicate the inherent appropriateness of a thing's being what it is. That is to say, it is *proper* to a 'for-the-sake-of-itself' that it *be* 'for-the-sake-of-itself.' *Were* Dasein, then, fully sensitive to the universal, ontological situation it is in, it would *implicitly* 'love its neighbor as itself,' insofar as only thus would it respond to its neighbor in a manner appropriate to the Being of its neighbor (as 'for-the-sake-of-itself'). In doing so, it would merely be responding appropriately to the *truth* of Being as a whole, i.e., universally considered.

But if, with Heidegger, we understand 'truth' to refer to a *disclosedness* of Being, we might now ask *whose* Being discloses this

universal truth? From *whose* perspective is the truth that *every* caring being deserves respect immediately apparent? It is not immediately apparent from the standpoint of individual Dasein, who, *as* 'for-the-sake-of-itself,' often finds itself in conflict with others. The notion of a ***universal*** truth of Being that includes every particular Being refers us to a being, or *mode* of Being, that transcends individual Dasein. In the Bible, this transcendent Being is represented by the figure of God. Factical Dasein, insofar as it does not 'love its neighbor as itself,' fails to abide by *God's* truth of Being. The Biblical claim is that Dasein, as 'image of God,' can only achieve its perfection and fulfillment by living in accordance with the universal truth disclosed by God. Dasein's failure to do so – Dasein's self-enclosure in its private, limited 'truth' – is, as the Bible presents it, sin and fall.

There is, of course, no evidence that there was ever a time in human history when human beings in general were not, in this sense, 'sinful and fallen.' The very structure of Dasein places its own concerns immediately before it in a manner that privileges these concerns above those of others. One must, in effect, 'wake up' to the concerns of others. I don't believe it is helpful to read the biblical story of the Fall as an effort to lay blame upon human beings for not being what they haven't had the ontological maturity to be. However, if we were willing to entertain religious claims as to the revelatory status of the biblical text, we might read the story of the Fall – and the whole of the Bible – as an effort to 'wake human beings up' through disclosing to them their ontological situation as seen from the universal perspective, i.e., from the perspective of God. From this perspective human culture is a tragedy of self-alienation and other-alienation due to a failure of love. The name the Bible gives to such alienation is 'death.' The Bible's paradigmatic account of this alienation is provided in the story of Eden and Fall.

2. Symbolical Interpretation

It is important to distinguish between the Man/Woman created 'in the image of God' at the end of the first creation story and the Adam of the Eden story. This Adam is not created 'in the image of God' but from the dust of the ground, and although God breathes the spirit of life into him, thereby making him a living soul, he is a living soul still very much 'of the dust.' We are privy to the spectacle of God trying to find a 'helpmeet' for Adam by first creating and then parading all the beasts of the earth before him to see if one is suitable; as if it is not yet entirely clear that Adam is anything more than a beast himself. Finally, no beast proving adequate, God creates Eve from Adam's side. Adam and Eve, in other words, are ambiguous creatures from the start. They are invested with the spirit of God but encased in earthen matter. This earthen matter separates them from each other, allowing them to be distinct beings.

They are placed in the garden of Eden and told they may eat of any tree in the Garden but the one growing in its midst: the tree of the knowledge of Good and Evil. On the day they eat of this tree, they are told, they will "surely die." It is sometimes wondered why God would place a tree in the midst of Eden and then forbid Adam and Eve to eat from it. The puzzle is solved if we understand Eden itself to symbolize the creation in perfect axiological balance. Adam's relation to Eve and the first couple's relation to their world are, in Eden, in perfect harmony. Each perfectly complements the other. The tree of the knowledge of Good and Evil, then, standing in the center of this garden, is expressive of the moral order that would secure this balance. In other words, the tree of the knowledge of Good and Evil represents the axiological order of God – what we have called God's 'truth of Being' – which governs the harmony of the creation. It is this harmony that is thrown off when the human being, seeking to make *herself* a 'god,' (i.e., a whole *unto* herself) eats of the fruit of this tree in order to become, in her own separate person, the supreme axiological standard.

The eating of the fruit is the biblical paradigm for all acts of sin. Every act of sin entails a usurpation of the divine axiology, which governs the harmony of the creation, through the centering of value exclusively in oneself; i.e., through an exclusionary intensification of one's 'for-the-sake-of-oneselfness.' This did not happen just *once* at the beginning of history, but it happens again and again. This exclusionary centering of self in self, of course, is the sin of pride, which produces a societal state of Hobbesian war, as each atomic individual, taking himself/herself as supreme, wars with every other in pursuit of domination. We do not wait long for such war to begin in the Bible.

The very next thing to happen after the first couple's expulsion from Eden is the murder of one of their children by the other.

But what induces Adam and Eve to commit this 'original sin?' For all of Eden's harmony, there is something already out of balance in the garden; there is a serpent slithering in the grass. This devious 'snake in the grass' – an image suggestive of the hidden danger lurking in all temptation – must, I believe, be understood to represent an element in Adam and Eve themselves. Only thus can the serpent tempt them. The serpent, we are told, is the most clever of all the animals in Eden. Might it, then, represent the burgeoning intelligence of Adam and Eve as *coupled with* their own animality? If we are able to give up the notion of Adam and Eve as *already* perfect, this interpretation recommends itself. Adam and Eve in Eden are half-formed creatures; no longer beasts but not yet fulfilled in their humanity. The strange figure of the *talking* serpent, the animal invested with *logos*, suggests just this ambiguity. It is this alliance of reason, with its universalizing capacity, and animality, with its particularized self-concern, that now rises up in self-awareness to assert its '*in-itselfness*.' Adam and Eve now seek to bring the whole of reality under the dominion of their own particular appetites and desires. Thus, the eating of the fruit is the usurpation of the divine axiology; the individual now pursues axiological supremacy *just as if* her particular, finite, and self-referential appetites were *that for the sake of which* everything else exists. In doing so, human beings sever their relation to the true Whole and plunge their world into moral chaos. The harmony of Eden dissolves to be replaced by a world of intensive rivalries – a world of violence, deceit, isolation, fury, and death: *our* world.

To take this one step further, we can recognize with Kierkegaard, Tillich, and others, that it is *freedom* itself that is the ontological condition for the possibility of such axiological self-centeredness. Freedom entails self-sovereignty, which, in turn, entails the ability to distinguish between self and other, I and not-I. Only a being who can cognitively distinguish itself from its world can be free. Such freedom is both the glory of the human being and the precondition for disharmony and discord, because it permits the individual to behave independently of its world. Ontologically, freedom is the creature's *dis*continuity with the whole. An unfree being is wholly determined by its surroundings and instincts, a mere continuation of its environs. Such a being is not a discrete self. It is through freedom that the human being attains the status (as Kant would say, the *dignity*) of a separate and distinct self.

But such separateness comes at a price. The consciousness of separateness is also the consciousness of *finitude.* To know oneself as separate is to know oneself as bordered by that which is *not* oneself. Freedom, separateness, and finitude, thus, are co-constituting. It is *freedom* that provides the human being with the potential to be an 'image of God,' i.e., an *analog* of wholeness amidst the greater whole, a finite circle within the infinite circle. But such freedom carries the danger of ethical and spiritual rupture with the whole, the danger that the free being will employ its volitional independence to seek axiological and ontological totality; i.e., to seek to center Being in itself. It is this to which the talking serpent 'tempts' Adam and Eve: to employ their newly minted rationality and freedom, which makes each of them an *analog* of God, to *become* God.[19]

Again, we must not suppose that this story refers to an actual historical event; rather it is the Bible's diagnosis, presented in mythical form, of what is wrong with human beings in general: Our freedom and rationality tempt us to seek to center the whole of Being within ourselves, which results in ethical turmoil and spiritual rupture.

We are especially concerned to understand the meaning of death in this story. That the human being, as compounded with earth, is destined to a physical death is expressed elsewhere in the Bible: "My Spirit shall not strive with man forever, because he also is flesh; therefore his days shall be one hundred and twenty years" (Gn. 6:3). But the death decreed for Adam and Eve in Eden is clearly not the physical one figured in this passage. In their expulsion from Eden, Adam and Eve lose access to the Tree of Life. Just as the Tree of the Knowledge of Good and Evil may be seen to represent the universal axiology of God, so the Tree of Life may be taken to signify the ontological wholeness (i.e., sufficiency) of God. It is the Tree of *eternal life* that Adam and Eve lose access to when they seek to make their own finite lives absolute. Dasein loses eternity, its sense of abiding in eternity, due to its axiological self-centeredness. In seeking to center

19 This discussion of freedom owes much to Paul Tillich. See *Systematic Theology, vol. I* (Chicago: University of Chicago Press, 1951), 252-258.

all value in itself, Dasein imprisons itself in itself, uprooting itself from the whole to which it belongs, and exiling itself from its true home.

It is only now that Adam and Eve are ***thrown-being-towards-death***. Prior to the eating of the fruit Adam and Eve are "naked and not ashamed" (Gn. 3:25). Such nakedness signifies unhiddenness; the openness of self to self and self to other. Upon eating the fruit, they become, quite literally, ashamed of themselves. I think we must see that it is their ***nakedness*** they become ashamed of, not their crime. This is indicated by the fact that they seek to hide their nakedness from God. Such nakedness is now the exposure of their ontological deficiency, their vulnerability and finitude, exposed ***as*** finitude, ***as*** deficiency, only due to loss of relation to the ***in***finitude, the ***sufficiency,*** of God; an exposure made all the more dangerous for the fact that their sin has instituted a world of murderous rivalries. It is symbolically significant that Jesus, in the moment of overcoming this primal sin, is once again 'naked and unashamed' – on the Cross.

It is, we would say, the ***angst*** of thrown-being-towards-death that we see figured in the shame of nakedness that now overwhelms the humans. It is no longer safe for each to be exposed to the other, nor even to themselves. Their only relief from the anxiety and not-at-homeness of death is the illusion that they can indeed make themselves little gods, i.e., that they can achieve wholeness in their own finitude; if not altogether by themselves, then at least ***corporately***.[20] But for this they must ***hide*** their thrown-Being-towards-death, the proof of their ontological ***in***sufficiency, not merely from each other, but principally from themselves. Adam and Eve now cover themselves up, hiding themselves from each other and from God. The reign of loneliness and alienation is instituted. The dictatorship of das Man has begun.

The curses now pronounced upon them by God merely articulate the ontological exile they have thrown themselves into. They are banished from the Tree of Life, and the harmony of Eden is now overcome by discord: discord between mother and child (Gn. 3:16), man and nature (Gn. 3:17), husband and wife (Gn. 3:16) and, as we

---

20 The biblical story of the Tower of Babel expresses such a corporate 'drive to totality.' Levinas' concept of totality, conjuring up, as it does, the spectre of totalitarianism, must be sharply distinguished from our concept of wholeness. Wholeness is for the sake of *all* participants. Totality is only for the sake of the 'total.' The drive to totality is essentially a drive to *capture* and *subsume* the whole by the finite. Totalitariansm is the drive to corporate totality.

shall soon find, brother and brother. God, who once walked in the Garden in the 'cool of the day' (Gn. 3:8), now becomes increasingly remote. His visage, from here to the incarnation, will primarily be a visage of wrath.

But this is myth and, as we have said, we must *insist* upon its mythical character if we are to extract its meaning. The Eden story refers us to something universal in the human condition: the moral and spiritual desolation consequent upon human Being's tendency to self-enclosure. This is a problem inherent to the human condition as such, a problem, as the Bible will propose, whose ultimate solution is Christ: the fully integrated God-man. Christ is not a *second* Adam, but a *perfected* Adam; an Adam who has realized his full ontological potential to become a willing, conscious partner of God.

In the Eden story, we also have the revelation of a potentiality for *homefulness* that the human being – factical Dasein – only knows as *longing*. To such longing there is attached a sense of ruptured *be*-longing; hence a vague nostalgia for a *lost* home. But *just because* Dasein has been banished from the Tree of Life, it can only know of this banishment from the *perspective* of death. It can only know of its own lack of wholeness-sufficiency, its own angst and not-at-homeness. In Heidegger's treatment of Being-towards-death, may we not recognize a phenomenological account proffered from just this perspective?

3. Heidegger And Eden

The Heidegger of *Being and Time* does not speak of *life*. Life does not appear as a category in Heidegger's thought. The fall of which Heidegger writes is a fall from *death*, from the authenticity of Being-towards-death into the inauthenticity of das Man. Significantly, Heidegger conflates the symbols of fall and flight, which in the Bible are carefully distinguished, often using the terms interchangeably. We see this in the quoted passage at the beginning of this section. Dasein's *flight* into das Man is its *fall* from authenticity. Dasein's *fall* into the 'world' is its *flight* in the face of itself. In the Eden story, on the other hand, the moments of fall and flight are sharply discriminated. First Adam and Eve *fall* from God's grace (from *life*), and only then *flee* from their nakedness; i.e., from the exposure of their finite vulnerability. The *fall* is from life into death. The *flight* is from death into hiddenness. The flight is not the fall, but a flight *from* the fall. In fleeing from their nakedness, their finite vulnerability, Adam and Eve are fleeing from the 'death' brought on by the fall.

In the Eden story, in other words, we can note three distinct moments, as three *stages* of Dasein's fallenness. There is, first of all, the primordial moment of *life*, of harmony with God, which is to say, with all Being. Then there is the moment of *fall*, of rupture with God and the remainder of Being. Finally, there is the moment of *flight*, of hiding from self, God, and the rest of Being. The angst of guilt and shame is a function of the rupture with *life*. The rupture has opened a *gap* of nothingness between Dasein and its own ontological groundedness in God. In response to the anxiety associated with this rupture, Dasein flees from the truth of itself.

In Heidegger's account, these three moments are collapsed into two; what the Bible sees as a moment of rupture is, for Heidegger, the *primordial* moment, there is nothing prior to it, nothing conditioning it, and hence it is *not* a moment of rupture, nor of guilt in the ordinary sense, but merely of angst-ridden nullity. Such nullity, according to Heidegger, is itself the paradoxical 'ground' of Dasein. The angst associated with it has no meaning beyond itself. It reveals Dasein to be an *issue* to itself but tells us nothing of what this issue portends. Having arrived at this angst we have arrived at the *bottom* of meaning. The angst just *is*.

The Bible places this angst in a larger context. The angst and the nullity are symptoms of rupture, of axiological disorder. It is only sinful Dasein who experiences its *basis* as null, and, hence, itself as 'not-at-home.' At a deeper level than Heidegger's phenomenology yet knows, says the Bible, is *another* possibility; a possibility of harmony and peace, of *homefulness*. Such is the *true* bottom of Dasein. The Eden story professes to reveal this true bottom, but it is a revelation 'as in a dream.' It is for factical Dasein only a hope, an invitation to hope. Factical Dasein lives outside the gates of Eden, amidst the reality of alienation and rupture.

Heidegger's phenomenology and the Eden myth, then, may be seen as presenting the same phenomena from two different perspectives. Heidegger traces Dasein from its alienation in das Man *back to* its prior *flight* from death. The Edenic myth follows Dasein from its primordial homefulness in God *forward to* its subsequent *fall* into death. At the juncture of the two is the moment of death itself, which the Bible suggests has to do with a *mis*relation to the categories of good and evil; i.e., a misrelation to the universal axiology of God. The Heidegger of *Being and Time* does not yet see the possibility of homefulness and thus takes Dasein's truth to consist in an affirmation of its *not*-at-homeness. But the Bible professes to see farther. Dasein has a home but must re-form itself axiologically to know it.

Thus, the biblical perspective places Heidegger's account of the flight into das Man into a new context. There is a peculiar, even touching, moment at the end of the Eden story. After God has pronounced his awful curses upon Adam and Eve, he makes "garments of skin" for them to wear as they are about to embark into the world outside of Eden (Gn. 3:21). Adam and Eve are no longer able to be naked and unashamed, as they were in their 'innocent' animality. Rather than abandon them to their angst-ridden nullity, however, God now makes clothes for them himself. It will be a long time before they will be able to return to healthful nakedness. In the meantime, it is better for them to be covered up than exposed in their forlornness. Ironically, the Bible seems here to suggest that the life of das Man, for all its inauthenticity, is preferable to the life of radical self-involvement. Even an inauthentic social norm is better than none at all.

It is possible to read the Eden story and Heidegger's phenomenology as mutually reinforcing. The Bible would agree that factical Dasein *is* subsumed in Being-towards-death, and that Being-towards-death *does* refer to the 'utter individualization' of Dasein. Further, the Bible would agree that Being-towards-death *does* bring with it a sense of angst, not-at-homeness, and guilt, which, indeed, *does* drive Dasein to flee from itself and cover itself up in the inauthenticity of das Man. We find all this confirmed in the biblical account. But the Bible claims to be privy to something about Dasein that Heidegger is not. It professes to know the *whence* of Dasein's experience of Being-towards-death. It knows this – so anyway it says – because it knows something of the whence of Dasein itself.

And it is from this biblical perspective that we can also make sense of the imperative force of Heidegger's 'call of conscience.' *Why* this difficult call back from the tranquility of das Man if it is only a call *into* the angst and literal 'point-lessness' of Being-towards-death? The game seems hardly worth the candle. But if the call to face death is itself only a *prelude* to a further call into *life*, then the insistence of the call makes sense; it is an implication of Dasein's very Being *as* Being-towards-life. It is the imperative implicit in *life* that calls Dasein back from its lostness to face itself. This call *out of* das Man, *through* death, *into* life, is biblically figured in the story of the Hebrews' exodus from slavery in Egypt to freedom in the promised land. To get from the one to the other, however, the Hebrews must pass *through* the desert, the land of death and austerity, where the Law is issued.

VIII

The Revelation of Law

I. Outside Eden

Cain murders Abel in a moment of envious fury over Abel's success. In a different world, Cain might have celebrated his brother's happiness; Abel might have invited Cain to share in it. But the axiological presuppositions of the world outside of Eden, as the Bible presents them, are those of rivalry and war, as each competes with the other for supremacy. It is significant, I think, that envy is at the root of the first biblical murder as opposed to competition for material goods. The Bible sees the rivalry between human beings as centered in a spiritual, not a material, battle for preeminence. Each wants to dominate *for the sake of* domination itself.

Heidegger calls Dasein's concern with its status vis-à-vis the other 'distantiality': "In one's concern with what one has taken hold of, whether with, for, or against, the Others, there is constant care as to the way one differs from them, whether that difference is merely one that is to be evened out, whether one's own Dasein has lagged behind the Others and wants to catch up in relationship to them, or whether one's Dasein already has some priority over them and sets out to keep them suppressed."[1] Distantiality is one way in which Dasein is in thrall to others: "[T]his distantiality which belongs to Being-with, is such that Dasein, as everyday Being-with-one-another, stands in *subjection* [*Botmässigkeit*] to Others. It itself *is* not; its Being has been taken away by the Others."[2]

---

1 Martin Heidegger, *Being and Time*, pp. 163-164, H. 126.

2 Ibid., p. 164, H. 126.

Applying this to the biblical text, we might read Cain's murder of Abel as an expression of Cain's ontological subjection to Abel. Cain experiences his own ontological status as strictly relative to Abel's. In murdering Abel, Cain seeks to free himself from the oppressive weight of Abel's supremacy. Abel must die for Cain to live. What are the dynamics that account for this?

On Heidegger's interpretation, Dasein's subjection to others is due to its failure to fully differentiate itself from them; a function of its flight into das Man. Heidegger doesn't spend a great deal of time examining what he calls 'distantiality.' He notes it and moves on to a treatment of the life of das Man in general. But what Heidegger, rather abstractly, calls 'distantiality,' is at the heart of the Bible's understanding of human sinfulness. We must, then, consider it more fully.

From the biblical perspective, at Dasein's *root* is a desire for communion with infinite Being (eternal life) stemming from Dasein's primordial ontological provenance in God. Factical Dasein, cut off from communion with God, is a desire for infinite Being frustrated within the bounds of finitude. Frustrated Dasein seeks to overcome these bounds through domination of its world. Fallen Dasein (now in the biblical sense of fallen) seeks to become infinite in its own finite person, to take full command over its 'Being-in-the-world,' which involves the subjugation of 'its' world (and, *therefore*, all other persons) to itself. This desire for infinite dominion, however, is perpetually frustrated and troubled, as Dasein continues to be haunted and plagued by the limitations of its finitude. It is this troubled desire for infinite dominion that drives the dynamics of what Heidegger calls 'distantiality': Dasein's status in relation to others becomes the measure by which it assesses its own status in Being.

We recall that eternity is available only as a qualification of the *now*. Through its expansion of dominion over the world, Dasein is able to persuade itself, in the now, of its progress in securing its ontological standing; of course, always only in a troubled, haunted, self-deceptive way. When Dasein suffers defeat at the hands of the other its self-deceit is unmasked, it is hurled back into the angst of its finitude, which then releases itself as rage at the defeating other. The other is now testimony to Dasein's ontological impotence. In murdering, subjugating, or simply denigrating the other, Dasein eliminates and/or refutes the testimony of its impotence and reinstates itself in its own eyes. Here we have the birth of every form of malice.

Thus, the Bible does not see a Darwinian struggle for survival at the root of human rivalry, but a spiritual struggle for supremacy. Ironically, this struggle for dominion *over* the other is itself an expression of Dasein's subjection *to* the other. Dasein is, in effect, dominated by its *need* to dominate the other. Envy is the quintessential spirit of this struggle. One's progress toward dominion is not only measured by, but indeed has its very *Being* in, one's status vis-à-vis the other.

It is in this context that we may understand the meaning of the Hebrews' enslavement in Egypt. Such slavery is a symbol, and more than a symbol, for the self-enslavement of sin. The symbolic richness of the biblical narrative is extraordinary at this point. On the one hand, the Hebrews are, in effect, a people born as slaves. Prior to their enslavement in Egypt, they are not a people but merely a family; a family rife with envious rivalries. Jacob deceives his father Isaac in order to steal his brother Esau's birthright. Jacob's envious sons sell their brother Joseph into slavery, which results, through a convoluted turn of events, in their *own* descendants becoming slaves. The enslavers have become the enslaved. The Hebrews have now become a people *as* slaves. As such, they express humanity's self-victimage. The sins of the fathers have been visited upon the children; not as an expression of justice, but of the *injustice* bred of sin. There is nothing at all in the Bible to suggest that the Hebrew slaves are a morally exemplary people. But they are a people with moral potential, expressed in the righteousness of their father Abraham. They are, additionally, a people whose craving for freedom, a craving intensified by the hardships and injustices of slavery, will allow God to imprint his divine law of righteousness upon them – in order, eventually, to have them convey it to the world.

In the biblical Egypt, the possibilities of human life are reduced to two: the overweening arrogance of Pharaoh and the miserable destitution of the slave; i.e., the life of one who has succeeded in possessing 'his' world, and the lives of those who, by that very fact, have been dispossessed of theirs. The Hebrews are enslaved to Pharaoh and Pharaoh is enslaved to his need to enslave them, i.e., his own hardened heart, which brings disaster.

God now interrupts this all-too-human dynamic by issuing a law from a vaster sphere of Being. It is God who now demands 'possession' of the world. But God's demand for possession is not on the order of Pharaoh's, for there is an ontological difference between God and Pharaoh with the most profound axiological implications. God is the One from whom, in whom, and toward whom *all* have their Being. God's axiology is universal, inclusive of all. God is the only one whose possession of the world does not entail dispossession of others; thus, God's law has a universal legitimacy that Pharaoh's cannot. If we are to understand the nature of divine authority, we must explore the basis of this legitimacy.

II. THE LEGITIMACY OF DIVINE LAW

> For this commandment which I command you today is not too difficult to you, nor is it out of reach. It is not in heaven that you should say, "Who will go up to heaven for us to get it for us and make us hear it, that we may observe it?" Nor is it beyond the sea that you should say, "Who will cross the sea for us to get it and make us hear it, that we may observe it?" But the word is very near you, in your mouth and in your heart, that you may observe it. (Deut. 30:11-14)

"The word is very near you, in your mouth and in your heart": These words express the fundamental paradox of law, which we must consider if we are to understand the claim to legitimacy of divine law. From a phenomenological standpoint, divine law bears some parallels to what Heidegger names the 'call of conscience.' In this section, we will look at the ways these two notions relate.

Whence does law derive its *right* to command? Heidegger writes that the call of conscience "comes *from* me and yet *from beyond me and over me*."[3] This expresses the paradoxical nature of law as such. On the one hand, law speaks from beyond the individual's will. One's will is addressed *by* the law and, if law is legitimate, should be subordinated *to* the law. But were law to speak merely in the name of some *other* will, it would be indistinguishable from despotism and

3 Heidegger, *Being and Time*, p. 320, H. 275.

bullying. Law, to be legitimate, must speak in the name of that toward which the will is *properly* ordered; that is to say, law must be in some sense proper to the one commanded by it, it must be "in your mouth and in your heart," otherwise it would not be law but tyranny.

Law implies a schism in the one to whom it is issued, between what one factically is at any given moment and what one ought to be. For Heidegger, the call of conscience calls from Dasein's *authentic* self to Dasein's *inauthentic* self, calling the latter to return to the former. Biblical law implies a similar schism. It calls to *fallen* Dasein for the sake of *redeemed* Dasein, subjecting Dasein to law in order to liberate Dasein from sin. When Dasein is fully liberated from sin it will no longer be in need of an extrinsic law; then the law will have been 'written on its heart' (Jer. 31:33), its 'is' and 'ought' resolved. This reconciling of self with self is the process of sanctification, through which Dasein is made 'holy,' i.e., whole. As the above quote indicates, then, the legitimacy of divine law is a function of its rootedness in the ontology of Dasein.

The Jewish prayer over the Sabbath candles expresses the sanctifying intent of law: "Blessed art thou O Lord our God, King of the Universe, who *sanctifies* us with His commandments and has commanded us to light the lights of Shabbat." We now wish to consider in what way biblical law 'sanctifies.'

As Heidegger envisions it, the call of conscience has its value and purpose in bringing Dasein back in touch with its authentic self. It demands that Dasein wrest itself away from the tranquilizing, but self-alienating, comfort of das Man and face itself squarely and honestly. From the Heideggerian standpoint, then, the source and purport of "law" (conscience) is the individuality of Dasein. In the call of conscience, Dasein's individuality calls it back to itself, so that Dasein can live authentically *as* itself. We see something similar in the biblical call to abide by divine law. Dasein is called to a new responsibility that forces it to take stock of itself as a whole – a responsibility that calls it out of the 'dictatorship of das Man,' and calls it beyond the pushes and pulls of immediate inclination.

But from the biblical perspective, Dasein's individuality is itself rooted in the *universality* of God. Thus, divine law does not have its ground in the individuality of Dasein *per se*, but in the universality of God, to which Dasein, *as a whole self,* is called. It is not merely in returning Dasein to itself, but in lifting Dasein up beyond itself to partake in the universal, that biblical law sanctifies.

To grasp this, it is critical that we come to some understanding of the nature of divine universality. Kierkegaard, in *Fear and Trembling*, opposes universality to particularity, and thus speaks of the need for a 'teleological suspension of the ethical' (understood as universal law) for the sake of affirming the particular.[4] But in this, it seems to me, Kierkegaard (or his pseudonym, De Selentio) fails to take account of the infinite *inclusivity* of divine universality. Aquinas, on the other hand, argues that, though *human* apprehension of the universal always entails some abstraction from the particular, the same limitation does not apply to God: "God knows whatever proceeds from Him immediately. When this is known God once more knows whatever proceeds from it immediately; and so on for all intermediate causes down to the last effect. Therefore, God knows whatever is found in reality."[5] According to Aquinas, it is not God, but we who have trouble knowing particulars.[6] Yet Kierkegaard's point is not entirely to be

4 "The ethical as such is the universal, and as the universal it applies to everyone, which may be expressed from another point of view by saying that it applies at every instant... Conceived immediately as physical and psychical, the particular individual is the individual who has his telos in the universal, and his ethical task is to express himself constantly in it, to abolish his particularity in order to become the universal." Kierkegaard now contrasts this with *faith* : "[F]aith is this paradox, that the particular is higher than the universal..." That the particular is higher than the universal, presumably, justifies Abraham in 'suspending' the ethical and sacrificing Isaac: "if this be not faith, then Abraham is lost..." Søren Kierkegaard (alias Johannes De Selentio), *Fear and Trembling: A Dialectical Lyric*, trans. Walter Lowrie (Garden City: Doubleday & Company: 1941), 64-65. It might be noted that Kierkegaard, or perhaps we should say Kierkegaard's pseudonyms, are not always consistent in understanding the universality of the ethical to entail an abolition of particularity. In *Either/Or* Judge Williams expresses an understanding of the ethical more inclusive of particularity itself, and very much more along the lines that we are developing here: "The person who views life ethically sees the universal, and the person who lives ethically expresses the universal in his life. He makes himself the universal human being, not by taking off [*afføre*] his concretion, for then he becomes a complete nonentity, but by putting it on [*iføre*] and interpenetrating it with the universal." *Either/Or, part II*, ed. and trans. Howard V. Hong and Edna H. Hong (Princeton: Princeton University Press, 1987), 256.

5 Thomas Aquinas, *Summa Contra Gentiles, Book One: God*, trans. Anton C. Pegis, (Notre Dame, University of Notre Dame Press,1975), 182.

6 "All knowledge takes place through the assimilation of the knower and the known. There is this difference, however, that the assimilation in human knowledge takes place through the action of sensible things on man's knowing powers, whereas in the case of God's knowledge the assimilation takes place contrariwise through the action of the forms of the divine intellect on the things known. Hence, since the form of the sensible thing is individuated through its materiality, it cannot extend

dismissed. Aquinas often speaks as if God's universal knowledge is impersonal and static, a vast organizational chart so to speak, with human beatitude consisting of little more than a glimpse of this chart: "Since the vision of the divine substance is the ultimate end of every intellectual substance [e.g., man], as is evident from what we have said, and since the natural appetite of everything comes to rest when the thing reaches its ultimate end, the natural appetite of an intellectual substance must come to rest completely when it sees the divine substance ... Now the natural appetite of the intellect is to know the genera and species and powers of all things, and the whole of the universe."[7]

What this *seems*, anyway, to neglect is what Heidegger calls the disclosive character of moods, and what we have emphasized as the concernfulness at the root of Being and meaning. To properly ***know*** Dasein is not simply to know the genus and species to which Dasein belongs, but to know the character of Dasein's concerns, its fears and longings, its hopes and dismays. It is only insofar as God knows *this* that God can be said to know Dasein in Dasein's particularity. Aquinas' metaphysical reasoning (informed, as it is, by Aristotle) commits him to a belief in a wholly dispassionate God, but such is inconsistent with the biblical portrait. To get a correct understanding of the biblical view of God's knowledge, then, we must couple the Thomistic notion of the inclusivity of divine universality with the Heideggerian notion of the disclosive character of moods. Only thereby do we envision a God whose knowing is, at the same time, a *feeling for* the 'widows and orphans.'

Biblical law, then, calls the human being to 'know' the world as God does; a knowing indissolubly linked with a *feeling for* the other; i.e., ***com-passion***. Let us consider, for instance, a passage from *Leviticus*: "The stranger who resides with you shall be to you as a native among you, and you shall love him as yourself; for you were aliens in the land of Egypt" (Lv 19:34). What is noteworthy here is

the likeness of its singularity so that it be absolutely immaterial ... Thus, the likeness of the singularity of a sensible form cannot reach up to the human intellect. But the likeness of a form in the divine intellect, by reaching to the least of things to which its causality extends, extends to the singularity and material form. The divine intellect, therefore, can know singulars, but not the human intellect." Ibid., 216.

7 Thomas Aquinas, *Summa Contra Gentiles, Book Three: Providence, part I*, trans. Vernon J. Bourke, (Notre Dame, University of Notre Dame Press,1975), 194.

the rationale given for the injunction to love the stranger: "for you were aliens in the land of Egypt." The *wrongness* of mistreating the alien is disclosed in the suffering caused by such mistreatment; a suffering only another alien can fully understand. It is just because the Hebrew slaves have themselves suffered the injustice of slavery that they are able to *understand* the wrongness of injustice – the moral 'law' is but an implication of this. In Heideggerian terms, the *truth* of ethical violation is disclosed only through existential participation in the moods (*Stimmungen)* associated with it. But how, we might ask, can *God* know what it is like to suffer as an 'alien in the land of Egypt?' We can only conclude that God's knowledge is, or entails, an empathic participation in suffering itself.[8]

This is to say that God's knowledge is not primarily 'objectivistic,' but personal. It is universal-personal, or, in the terms we developed in chapter six, universal-relational. This suggests, again, why Heidegger's conceptuality, as Noack remarks, "moves in a dimension which alone makes room for doing genuine theological 'thinking' once again." Heidegger has found a conceptuality that allows us to convey the *universality* of God without obscuring the *personal relationality* – the intimacy – of God, which is critical to the *meaning* of God from a spiritual-religious point of view.

The law calls upon the human being to adopt the universal perspective of God; to care for those God cares for; to live as a partner of God. It is *this* that is sanctifying, dignifying, and ennobling. Far from requiring a 'suspension of the ethical' to affirm the particular (as per Kierkegaard), the ethical law commands Dasein to enter into empathic participation with each particular and ennobles Dasein by lifting up *its* particularity, not into abstract generality, but into the wholeness of divine Being, manifest as compassion for every caring being. Far from inducing in Dasein an 'utter individualization' (as per Heidegger) the law directs Dasein to an 'utter universalization' through which *every* individual in Dasein's world (every 'neighbor') is to be

8 It may well be asked: If God's knowledge entails an empathic participation in suffering itself, in what sense can God also be regarded as sufficient unto himself? Would not such suffering, as something needing to be resolved, detract from God's eternal self-sufficiency? An answer would be that God's knowledge entails *both* this empathic suffering *and* the awareness that such suffering finds its redemption and resolution in the reality of God's Being. It is just this awareness that the suffering creature, alienated from God, lacks.

respected and cherished as kin. Biblical law calls Dasein to full, ethical involvement in the particular *as* particular, and does so in the name of that which comprehends every particular: the universality of God.

Biblically, then, law calls Dasein out of its alienation in das Man back to its self-responsibility, but *then* calls Dasein beyond a *mere* responsibility to self into the life of God. It is only through participation in the life of God, so the Bible asserts, that Dasein is able to overcome the dilemma of its finitude and thereby *fulfill* its self-responsibility. From the biblical perspective, it is this failure to live by the law of God that abandons Dasein to its finite "nullity," resulting in the angst of death and guilt. In the next few sections, we will explore the concepts of nullity, guilt, and sin in dialogue with Heidegger's phenomenological interpretations, but as these may now be understood from the perspective of the biblical texts.

III. Law and Nullity

> [The] calling back in which conscience calls forth, gives Dasein to understand that Dasein itself – the null basis for its null projection, standing in the possibility of its Being – is to bring itself back to itself from its lostness in the 'they.'[9]

As Heidegger presents it, the call of conscience calls Dasein back from its lostness in das Man to an awareness of the true structure of Care as 'for-the-sake-of-itself,' an awareness that includes an acknowledgement of Being-guilty and Being-towards-death, which are accompanied by a sense of not-at-homeness and anxiety. The call of conscience, in making Dasein aware of its utter individualization, at the same time makes Dasein aware of its nullity. We now wish to enter into a deeper reflection on the meaning of *nullity* in light of the biblical understanding of Dasein. In doing so, we hope to be able to shed some light on the meaning of the phenomenon of guilt as well.

We recall that Dasein's nullity has three aspects, corresponding to the three temporal modes of past, present, and future. First, Dasein's past is null insofar as Dasein is *thrown*; i.e., released into a world that is already there from a somewhere it does not know. Second,

9 Heidegger, *Being and Time*, p. 333, H. 287.

Dasein's present is null insofar as Dasein is *free*; i.e., confronted with options it must choose between, thus, not determined to any one thing in particular. Finally, Dasein's future is null insofar as Dasein is *towards death*; i.e., projected upon the possibility of no further possibility. Dasein, says Heidegger, "*is permeated with nullity through and through.*"[10] Such nullity, says Heidegger, is the basis of Dasein's primordial guiltiness: "Thus 'care' – Dasein's Being – means, as thrown projection, Being-the-basis of a nullity (and this Being-the-basis is itself null). This means that *Dasein as such is guilty*, if our formally existential definition of 'guilt' as 'Being-the-basis of a nullity' is indeed correct."[11]

But Dasein's nullity, for both Heidegger and the Bible, though problematic, is not altogether bad. Indeed, Dasein's nullity, in respect to past (thrownness), present (freedom), and future (death), may be recognized as constituting the *borders* of Dasein's Being, allowing Dasein to be a *separate* being, not a mere continuation of that from which Dasein issues, nor a mere extension of that to which Dasein relates. Dasein's nullity has a positive aspect; it is the very possibility of Dasein's status as a 'being unto itself,' having an ontological standing of its own. A rock, for instance, though distinguishable spatio-temporally from its environs, has, we presume, no sense of self. In order for it to acquire one it would have to know itself as *dis*continuous in some way with its environment. If it did not experience itself as discontinuous, it could not be '*this* rock,' but merely an extension of the whole of which it is a part. Finite consciousness, as Sartre has perhaps most elaborately pointed out, involves a rupture, a disruption, in the continuity of 'being-in-itself.' It is such discontinuity that is then manifest as the 'nullity' of 'thrown-free-projection.'

Indeed, from a religious perspective we might say that the possibility of such nullity, the possibility of a being defined by such nullity, is the very possibility of *creation* itself. Were there no possibility of circumscribing a being with 'nothingness,' i.e., separateness from the whole, there would be no possibility of any self distinguishable as a finite self. Religiously speaking, without 'nullity' there could be no one but God. The Jewish Kabbalist Adin Steinsaltz makes this point

10 Ibid., p. 331, H. 285.

11 Ibid., p. 331, H 285.

when he writes: "The very essence of creatureliness is the feeling of being separate, of being itself. And this capacity of a thing to be itself, even though its very life and existence, physically and spiritually, are incessantly dependent on Divine mercy, on His Chesed, is the miracle of His concealment."[12]

In the last chapter we suggested that Dasein's nullity might be thought of as a kind of privation. Our present considerations now seem to suggest something else. Indeed, there is a passage in which Heidegger appears to flatly deny any privative character to Dasein's nullity. He writes: "Existential nullity has by no means the character of a privation, where something is lacking in comparison with an ideal which has been set up but does not get attained in Dasein; rather, the Being of this entity is already null *as projection*; and it is null in advance of [*vor*] any of the things which it can project and which it mostly attains."[13] Heidegger's point is that Dasein's nullity is essential to Dasein's Being as such. It is a feature of what Dasein essentially *is* rather than a symptom of some distortion or privation of what it is. Nullity is an ontological condition for the very possibility of a being such as Dasein; i.e., a finite, self-aware, being situated in a world not of its making. Dasein's nullity is not a consequence of its having been deprived of something it should have in order to realize itself as Dasein. On the contrary, such nullity is an essential condition for the possibility of Dasein.

In light of this, must we now retract our suggestion that Dasein's nullity be regarded as privative? On the contrary, from a Judeo-Christian standpoint, Dasein's nullity, which is also its finitude, may be regarded as its privation of that very *in*-finity of Being which is God. This privation is what Steinsalz calls "the miracle of His concealment."

From the religious perspective, in other words, one might imagine three 'strata' of Dasein's Being. There is, first, the stratum of Dasein's discrete Being-in-the-world, Dasein's finite individuality, concerned for itself. There is, second, the stratum of 'nullity,' which borders Dasein's Being, *allowing* Dasein to be a discrete being, separate from the whole. But, thirdly, there is the stratum of God, of infinite Being, *from* which Dasein is (properly) separated, but *in* which it is

12 Adin Steinsaltz, *The Sustaining Utterance: Discourses on Chasidic Thought*, ed. and tr. Yehuda Hanegbi (Northvale, New Jersey: Jason Aronson, Inc., 1989), 54.

13 Heidegger, *Being and Time*, p. 331, H. 285.

to find its proper home, the resolution to its nullity. Heidegger, good phenomenologist that he is, never ventures in thought beyond the second stratum. He does not see past the impersonal Nothing to that to which religion attests, the personal ground of Being. Others, however, report that they have seen farther. The Catholic theologian Karl Rahner, for instance, writes: "[W]e can say without hesitation: a person who opens himself to his transcendental experience of the holy mystery at all has the experience that this mystery is not only an infinitely distant horizon... He experiences rather that this holy mystery is also a hidden closeness, a forgiving intimacy, his real home, that it is a love which shares itself, something familiar which he can approach and turn to from the estrangement of his own perilous and empty life."[14]

The nothingness is indeed a *not*-at-homeness, insofar as Dasein, *as* concernful Being, is only at home *within* concernful Being. But such nothingness, though privative, is not essentially evil or bad. It becomes such only to the extent that Dasein becomes closed in upon itself. Only then is Dasein *abandoned* to the nothingness that delimits it as a separate being. It is the Judeo-Christian contention that Dasein is not essentially, or properly, closed in upon itself but open to the remainder of what-is: to the world of others, and, ultimately, to the infinity of God. Such openness is not, and cannot be, an unbreachable connectedness, for were it so Dasein would lose its dignity as a separate self, would be subsumed in the whole. Such openness, then, must be realized through a volitional act, i.e., a *choice* for openness.[15] Biblically, Dasein is directed to such choice by the divine command, the law:

---

14 Rahner continues: "It is the person who in the forlornness of his guilt still turns in trust to the mystery of his existence which is quietly present, and surrenders himself as one who even in his guilt no longer wants to understand himself in a self-centered and self-sufficient way, it is this person who experiences himself as one who does not forgive himself, but who is forgiven, and he experiences this forgiveness which he receives as the hidden, forgiving and liberating love of God himself, who forgives *in that* he gives himself, because only in this way can there really be forgiveness once and for all." Karl Rahner, *Foundations of Christian Faith: an introduction to the idea of Christianity*, trans. William V. Dych (New York: Crossroads, 1990), 131.

15 This finds expression in the idea of 'covenant.' Ontologically, Dasein *must* choose the covenant with God, if it is to live at all healthily. Why, then, speak of it as a 'covenant,' suggesting an agreement into which one enters freely and voluntarily, and which, presumably, one may freely reject? Because axiologically, Dasein must *choose* the covenant willingly, if it is to live with dignity. Life, finally, is something Dasein must

> Hear, O Israel! The Lord is our God, the Lord is one! You shall love the Lord your God with all your heart and with all your soul and with all your might.
>
> These words, which I am commanding you today, shall be on your heart. You shall teach them diligently to your sons and shall talk of them when you sit in your house and when you walk by the way and when you lie down and when you rise up ... You shall write them on the doorposts of your house and on your gates. (Dt 6:4-9)

Dasein is commanded to *transcend* the nullity bordering its finitude through relation to – *love of* – the infinitude of the One God. The Oneness of God bespeaks God's ontological wholeness and inclusivity. *Every* separate being derives its Being from the Being of God. The proclamation of God's Oneness is the proclamation that separateness and the nullity that makes it possible are not ontologically fundamental. Underlying separateness is a more primordial unity. The wholeness of God stands on the other side of Dasein's nullity as that *to which* Dasein is to be open. From the biblical perspective, Dasein is only, finally, "towards-death" to the extent that it becomes somehow shut off from its openness to the infinite life of God. It is only then that Dasein is subject to the not-at-homeness (*Unheimlichkeit*) of its self-enclosure. That Dasein should *feel* not-at-home when shut up in itself, when shut off from God, is fully confirmatory of this point of view.

Jesus supplements the central command of Deuteronomy with the command in Leviticus to "Love your neighbor as yourself" (Lv 19:18) thereby giving us the Great Commandment quoted at the start of the last chapter. In both the Jewish and Christian traditions, love of God is to be actualized *through* love of neighbor. The vertical relation to God cannot be divorced from the horizontal relation to neighbor, and this because God is not merely one being among others, but the fundament of *all* beings. Through such love, then, Dasein relates

---

choose of its own volition, and it has the option to opt out (with the proviso that in so doing it opts out of its own self). Of course, this is highly paradoxical. The paradox in the idea of covenant reflects Dasein's paradoxical standing in relation to God, as both free and utterly dependent; a standing that is itself but an implication of finite creatureliness.

itself, opens itself, to the whole of Being. In this way, Dasein's nullity is transfigured into what we might call a *transparency*. The metaphor 'transparency' suggests a medium through which communication takes place. Dasein's nullilty, which allows for Dasein's separateness, is not thereby cancelled, but, to use a religious term, it is *redeemed*; i.e., restored to its true purpose and value. Dasein retains its separateness, its individuality, but this separateness is now in communion with the whole of Being and the font of Being. Dasein does not thereby forfeit its individuality, but first of all secures it. All of this is to provide Dasein with a life that may be characterized as *Being-towards-life*; through which Dasein overcomes the 'sting' of death.

From the biblical perspective, Dasein's true 'call of conscience,' figured in the giving of law at Sinai, is ultimately a call *out of* an orientation defined by death *into* one defined by life. In responding to it, Dasein *overcomes* the not-at-homeness of its nullity. Thus, the biblical account does not so much deny Heidegger's phenomenological findings as place them in a broader context from which they appear in a new light. Dasein's nullity is affirmed but seen to have a dual aspect: it is indeed the condition for Dasein's individualization and separateness, but it is also the possibility of Dasein's openness to infinity. The angst accompanying such nullity is now seen as symptomatic of Dasein's closure upon itself; a closure that is not ontologically inevitable. When Dasein opens itself in love, its nullity is unveiled as transparency, its angst transformed into awe.

From this perspective, as well, we are able to answer one of the questions we asked at the end of chapter three: Why should the flight into das Man be tranquilizing? The answer now becomes apparent. It is because Dasein, *not* at home in itself, has its ultimate home in God and its *proximate* home in the society of others. Dasein, shut off from God and others, shut in on itself, is furthest from home and, hence, most anxious. The society of others, even lostness in the society of others, provides some tranquilization for Dasein because it opens Dasein, in however limited and distorted a fashion, to *some* of the life of which it is, in itself, bereft. Still, such relation to others remains lostness just to the extent that Dasein seeks to ground itself in these relations. This endeavor turns out to be the meaning of what Heidegger calls 'distantiality': Dasein seeks, through its comportment to others, to provide for itself the ontological standing that can only be found through God. This perverts its relation with others, enslaving itself to its need to enslave them, in its desperate effort to fill the void of its nullity.

IV. NULLITY AND GUILT

> [W]e define the formally existential idea of the 'Guilty!' as 'Being-the-basis for a Being which has been defined with a 'not' – that is to say, as *'Being-the-basis of a nullity'*.[16]

As we have seen, Heidegger takes pains to dissociate his concept of guilt, *Schuld*, from the conventional one of moral transgress, wishing to signify rather the ontological condition for the possibility of any kind of *indebtedness*, including moral indebtedness. He does make some effort, in Section 59 of *Being and Time*, to suggest a relation between his ontological notion of *Schuldigsein* and the moral notion of guilt, but his treatment of this, in my view, is strained and unconvincing. The question we now wish to consider, however, is the relationship between nullity, indebtedness, and guilt from the perspective of the religious analytic of Dasein that we have been developing.

Thomas Aquinas writes: "[T]hat which is necessary to the perfection of each thing is *due* to it"[17] (my emphasis). If we posit, with Christianity, that eternal life is necessary to the perfection of Dasein, then Dasein's Being, considered strictly in itself, is *deficient* with respect to itself. It is this deficiency that constitutes Dasein's primordial *indebtedness*. Dasein owes it to itself to overcome its deficiency. Its nullity *discloses* this primordial deficiency, insofar as it discloses Dasein's finitude, but it does not itself constitute it. Dasein's deficiency is a function of its finitude *in relation to* its drive for wholeness and infinitude. What Dasein's nullity discloses is that, *as* finite, Dasein hasn't the power to fully actualize itself through itself. Thus, the existential indebtedness of Dasein might be expressed thus: Dasein's Being requires infinity of itself, but finds that it hasn't the means to 'pay' for it.

---

16 Heidegger, *Being and Time*, p. 329, H. 283.

17 Aquinas, *Summa Contra Gentiles, Book One: God*, 286.

This sense of ontological deficiency manifests itself as anxiety; Dasein is anxious over its need, and inability, to provide a solid basis for itself. It is this that is represented as the *shame of nakedness* in the Eden myth. Such anxiety becomes *guilt* when Dasein comes to see itself as somehow responsible for its deficiency. In this respect the revelation of law is ambiguous: it reveals the way to eternal life and, *by* revealing this way, reveals Dasein's default in respect to it. From the Christian perspective, the revelation of law is, at once, the *disclosure* of Dasein's true *telos* and the *exposure* of its, often willful, divergence from it. Dasein comes to see that the very tendency of its Being is in resistance to the axiology (the law) of God. As Paul laments: "The good that I want, I do not do, but I practice the very evil that I do not want" (Rom. 7:19). Thus, the revelation of law is *also* the revelation of sin.

V. GUILT AND ORIGINAL SIN

Finite Dasein, *as* for-the-sake-of-itself, is for-the-sake-of-eternal-life. Eternal life is not an abstraction but, reading from the Great Commandment, is realized in the life of love for God and neighbor. Eternal life is the perfection (i.e., completeness, wholeness) of life. Every Dasein, insofar as it lives at all and knows something of life, implicitly knows something of eternal life, even if only in a privative mode. This privation is manifest as loneliness, isolation, angst, despair. But finite Dasein cannot at first fully grasp the character of eternal life. The call to eternal life first comes to Dasein from without. Biblically, this takes place through the revelation of law.

The law makes explicit Dasein's implicit vocation to infinitude. It calls Dasein to rise above the confines of its finitude and live in accordance with the dictates of infinitude. The law reveals to Dasein that the very finitude of its Care is in default in respect to the demands of Infinite Care. It is in relation to law that the 'simple' angst of Being-towards-death is *revealed* as the angst of guilt. Thus, Paul writes: "The Law brings about wrath, but where there is no law, there also is no violation" (Rom 4:15). Had Dasein no vocation to infinitude, to self-transcendence, there could be no guilt, as there is none for animals. This suggests a two-tiered origin for what the tradition calls sin. First, there is the origin of the existential proclivity for exclusionary self-involvement. Next, there is the first awareness of it as *wrong*. It is only in the light of this awareness that sin becomes, in Paul's words, "utterly sinful" (Rom 7:13). This distinction, I think, will allow us to give a phenomenological interpretation of the Christian doctrine of original sin.

The human being, as we know her, begins her career outside the gates of Eden. We have no recollection of an historical fall, nor any reason to suppose that such a thing actually occurred in human history. Nevertheless, the divine law gives us to understand that our exclusionary self-involvement is itself guilty; now in the moral sense, i.e., in the sense of that which *should not be*. The actual developmental, historical, and/or biological origin of such self-involvement is of no account, so long as we understand that the purpose of law is to change us, not to blame us. Our selfish inclinations are guilty in respect to the true values of life, in respect to our true vocation, in respect to those we hurt, even if, until the encounter with law, we cannot clearly understand this.

It is this sense of *ontological* guiltiness, guiltiness with respect to the *way we are* in our basic inclinations – for which we are not really to blame but nevertheless, now, for the first time, responsible – that, I suggest, underlies 'original sin' as a *phenomenon*. The Christian doctrine of '*original* sin' (*primordial* sin) arises from the conviction that the human being is to turn, not from this or that questionable doing, but from her fundamental axiological orientation, an orientation she did not consciously choose, but that nevertheless de-fines (and con-fines) her. It is not predicated upon a past transgression, but upon a vision of human perfection. The law calls for a *metanoia* (change of heart and mind); in Paul's terms, a turn from the life of the 'flesh' to the life of the 'Spirit,' from egoity to love. Paul complains that the law demands change but cannot produce it, a complaint that constitutes one of the fundamental arguments between Judaism and Christianity. Nevertheless, even Paul recognizes that the law, though convicting us of guilt, is not essentially a curse but a blessing, for the very fact that we are called to it reveals the possibility of an escape from our self-enclosure.

Thus, from a Judeo-Christian perspective, Heidegger – at least the Heidegger of *Being and Time* – fails to identify the ultimate thrust of the call of conscience in supposing it to be a call that terminates in the awareness of Being-towards-death. As a result, Heidegger's concept of Being-towards-death acquires a disturbing ambiguity that it never sheds in the pages of *Being and Time*. Through anticipatory resoluteness, writes Heidegger, Dasein is to "take over in its thrownness that entity which it itself is, and take it over wholly."[18] By 'take over' here, Heidegger appears to mean 'take over' from its prior subjection to das Man. With this, the Bible would agree. But, from the religious perspective, such liberation from das Man is to be but the first stage in a process through which Dasein comes to recognize its thrownness *as* creatureliness, and thereby recognize its rootedness in, and responsibility to, the life of God. To the extent that Dasein endeavors to 'take itself over wholly' without such recognition, it closes itself up in itself and shuts itself off from the very Life it seeks.

Thus, anticipatory resoluteness might signify two distinct, even diametrically opposed, modes of Being, depending upon the broader context in which we understand it. On the one hand, to the extent that it involves an honest acceptance of one's finite limitations, it is suggestive of the attitude of Christian humility, which Christianity sees as essential to the life of faith. On the other hand, to the extent that it involves a willful insistence upon the axiological ultimacy of one's finite, individualized being, it is suggestive of the attitude of hubristic pride, which Christianity sees as at the root of sin. Which attitude does Heidegger have in mind in *Being and Time*? It is not altogether clear.

In Heidegger's later work, with the development of his concept of *Gellassenheit*, Heidegger moves decisively in the direction of humility. At the time of his writing of *Being and Time*, however, there is much to suggest that this ambiguity was unresolved, and perhaps even unrecognized, by Heidegger himself – which might go some distance in explaining his disastrous attraction to Nazism. It appears that Heidegger saw in 'authentic' National Socialism the potential to wrest Dasein from its lostness in das Man, and either

18 Heidegger, *Being and Time*, p.434, H. 382.

failed to understand, or, for a time, was positively enamored of, the catastrophic hubris at Nazism's core.

VI. Sin and Despair

The ambiguity in Heidegger's account of Being-towards-death bespeaks a duality in the phenomenon itself that we will do well to consider. Indeed, given this duality, we can identify *three* distinct existential modes Dasein might occupy in its relation to death. Let us call the first '*self-enclosed* Being-towards-death.' The anxiety arising from such self-enclosure conditions the flight into das Man. Das Man, then, is the second mode, which we might label '*self-concealed* Being-towards-death.' Many never progress beyond such self-concealment. In *Being and Time* Heidegger suggests (although, again, with some ambiguity) that authenticity involves a return from this second mode to the first.

And yet religion sees *both* the life of self-enclosure *and* the life of das Man as existentially inadequate, and posits a third mode. Let us call this '*self-transcendent* Being-towards-death.' Through this third mode, Dasein, finally in acceptance of its finite limitations, turns, in humility, to that *from which*, and *upon which*, it *is*. This is faith. From the Christian point of view, this third mode is the passageway from death to eternal life, a passageway figured (as we will discuss in the next chapter) in the Cross of Christ.

In his work *The Sickness Unto Death*, Kierkegaard presents an account of these three existential modes. A brief look at Kierkegaard's work, I believe, can help deepen our understanding of their relationship to one another and to the life of faith we wish to explore. Kierkegaard writes:

> The human self is ... a derived, established relation, a relation that relates itself to itself and in relating itself to itself relates itself to another. This is why there can be two forms of despair in the strict sense. If the human self had itself established itself, then there could be only one form: not to will to be oneself, to will to do away with oneself, but there could not be the form: in despair to will to be oneself. This second formulation is ...

> the expression for the inability of the self to arrive at or be in equilibrium and rest by itself, but only, in relating itself to itself, by relating itself to that which has established the entire relation.[19]

Let us make some effort to unravel this rather convoluted passage.

Kierkegaard notes, first of all, that the human being's self-relation is "a derived, established relation." In other words, we do not first bring ourselves into existence, but find ourselves already here – 'thrown' into existence, as Heidegger says.

Thus, our own self-relation is, essentially, related to something beyond itself. As Kierkegaard puts it, we are "a relation that relates itself to itself and in relating itself to itself relates itself to another." This is a rather elaborated way of pointing to the ontological structure that Heidegger calls "Being-in-the-world." Dasein relates itself to itself *through* its relation to its world. But Kierkegaard would add that for Dasein to be *properly* related to itself it must *also* relate itself to that which establishes the entire self-world relation: God.

Our failure to do so yields two forms of despair. The first mentioned – the despair of not willing to be oneself – corresponds closely to Heidegger's conception of the inauthentic life of das Man, into which Dasein flees in order to escape itself.

And yet, what Heidegger sees as *authentic* life corresponds to Kierkegaard's *second* form of despair, the despair of 'willing to be oneself.' Indeed, as Kierkegaard presents it, the first form of despair (to will *not* to be oneself) arises in *response* to the second form: He writes: "This second form of despair (in despair to will to be oneself) is so far from designating merely a distinctive kind of despair that, on the contrary, all despair ultimately can be traced back to and be resolved in it."[20] What Kierkegaard means by "the will to be oneself" is the desire to establish oneself in and through oneself; to become the basis of one's own existence; i.e., to become God. It is this futile desire, says Kierkegaard, that lies at the root of all despair.

To express this in simpler language: The human being has an inherent and fundamental desire for life but cannot finally secure its life through itself nor through its world. Its futile endeavor to do so

19 Søren Kierkegaard, *The Sickness Unto Death: A Christian Psychological Exposition for Upbuilding and Awakening*, ed. and trans. Howard V. Hong and Edna H. Hong (Princeton, New Jersey: Princeton University Press, 1980), 14.

20 Ibid.

is what Kierkegaard calls the "will to be oneself." When this breaks down, as it must, we flee from the truth of ourselves. This flight is "the will *not* to be oneself."

For both Heidegger and Kierkegaard, then, the flight into das Man, the will *not* to be oneself, is a response to the distress native to a prior (more primordial) encounter with self. Heidegger writes: "Only to the extent that Dasein has been brought before itself in an ontologically essential manner through whatever disclosedness belongs to it, *can* it flee *in the face of* that in the face of which it flees."[21] Heidegger sees this more primordial self-encounter as Dasein's authenticity – and if by 'authenticity' we mean 'honest self-encounter,' perhaps it is. But from Kierkegaard's perspective *it is just this authenticity* – this honest self-encounter – that is at the root of despair.

Why is authentic Dasein in despair? Because Dasein is ontologically deficient in itself; it cannot resolve what Heidegger calls the 'issue' it is to itself, an issue religion would identify as the need for infinitude; eternal life. An honest encounter with self reveals this deficiency, which is just why Dasein flees from itself, into self-forgetfulness.

Is there a solution to this dilemma? One may well read Heidegger's later work as his struggle to find one. It is not clear that he succeeds. For Kierkegaard, however, and for the Judeo-Christian tradition in general, there is indeed a solution: the solution of *faith*.

Kierkegaard defines faith thus: "in relating itself to itself and in willing to be itself the self rests transparently in the power that established it."[22] The despair of Dasein's self-enclosure is finally resolved only through a self-opening, a "transparency," to the divine ground upon which Dasein's life rests.

It is this opening to the divine – and to the mode of life that such an opening entails – that is commanded by divine law. The law reveals that neither the life of das Man *nor* the life of self-enclosure constitutes the *true* life of Dasein. Opposed to both is the life of the Spirit, the life of faith and love. For Christianity, this life of the Spirit is most fully revealed in the life of Christ.

---

21 Heidegger, *Being and Time*, p. 229, H. 184.

22 Kierkegaard, *The Sickness Unto Death*, 49.

IX

Christ

The word "Christ" is the Greek translation of the Hebrew for "Messiah." In the Jewish tradition, the Messiah is envisioned as a divinely-ordained King who will be sent by God to initiate a reign of peace and righteousness on earth. In the days of the Messiah, so we read in Isaiah: "The wolf shall lie down with the lamb, and the leopard shall lie down with the kid ... They shall not hurt or destroy in all my holy mountain; for the earth shall be full of the knowledge of the Lord as the waters cover the sea" (Is. 11:1-4). Similarly, the prophet Jeremiah writes:

> "Behold, the days are coming," says the Lord, "when I will make a new covenant with the house of Israel, not like the covenant which I made with their fathers when I took them by the hand to bring them out of the land of Egypt... But this is the covenant which I will make... I will put my law *within* them, and I will write it upon their hearts; and I shall be their God and they shall be my people. And no longer shall each man teach his neighbor and each his brother, saying, 'Know the Lord,' for they shall all know me, from the least of them to the greatest." (Jer. 31:31-34, my emphasis)

In the Christian tradition, the figure of the Messiah – the Christ – is identified with the person of Jesus as presented in the New Testament. Judaism, of course, traditionally rejects this identification. I have no desire to adjudicate this controversy here. Rather, we will use the New Testament's portrayal of Christ to explore a broadly 'Judeo-Christian' understanding of fully actualized Dasein, i.e., a

Dasein fully realized as "image of God," in whom the divine law – to which Dasein is called – is no longer experienced as an imposition from without but as "written on the heart," that is, as fully integrated with the human will and understanding.

This vision of Christ as *perfected* Dasein marks a basic difference between the biblical conception of Dasein and Heidegger's. Heidegger supposes that Dasein can achieve a finite wholeness, a wholeness of itself in its own individualization. The Bible, in contrast, sees Dasein's Being as standing always in relation to the whole of Being and the font of Being. Dasein can either live in concord with this whole or as alienated from it, but in no way can Dasein escape it. As we have seen, Heidegger's own phenomenological observations suggest as much: Confined to itself, Dasein is *not*-at-home.

Nevertheless, the Bible fully recognizes that everyday Dasein, cut off from its experience of God, will try to overcome its not-at-homeness through pursuit of a finite, "worldly," wholeness. It will try to subsume the world in itself, either in its own individuality (e.g., Pharaoh) or in various forms of tribalism, nationalism, etc. (as symbolized in the Tower of Babel story). This pursuit of finite wholeness closes Dasein in on itself and creates what Hobbes calls "the war of all against all." It is the principal spiritual malady of human beings.[1]

Heidegger's phenomenological findings, then, are largely affirmed by the Judeo-Christian tradition. Heidegger has faithfully, and with great penetration, detailed the very mode of Being this tradition considers typically human. But, from the religious perspective, Heidegger's interpretation of it is skewed. Heidegger attempts to interpret the meaning of human existence in its own terms, a procedure only hermeneutically sound to the extent that human meaning is consummated in itself. If, however, human Being bears an essential relation to infinitude, then its meaning must be given in terms of this relation. For Christianity, Christ reveals the relation to infinitude through which human life finds its true meaning. Indeed, Christ, as the *God-man*, is the perfect instance of the relation itself. Through active comportment toward the truth revealed in Christ, the human

1 "This then is the original evil; man regards himself as his own light, and turns away from the light which would make man himself a light if he would set his heart on it." Augustine, *City of God*, XIV.13.

being overcomes existential death and enters upon its genuine telic context of *life*. In this chapter we will explore the meaning of this.

I. Love and Transcendence

The central axio-ontological claim of Christianity is that "God is love" (1 Jn 4:8). The central spiritual claim is that, as called to participate in this universal love, one is to "love God with all one's heart, mind, and soul" (Mt 22:37). The central ethical claim is that such love of God entails "loving one's neighbor as oneself" (Mt 22:39), where neighbor is defined as *anyone* in need of love (Lk 10:30-37). To the extent that one achieves this, one lives the life of Christ (1 Jn 2:3-6), becomes participant in God's love (1 Jn 4:16), and enters into eternal life (Jn 17:3). In this and the following sections, we will try to make sense of these ideas.

The apostle Paul makes a distinction between what he calls the life of the "Spirit" and the life of the "flesh": "For those who are according to the flesh set their minds on the things of the flesh, but those who are according to the Spirit, the things of the Spirit. For the mind set on the flesh is death, but the mind set on the Spirit is life and peace" (Rom 8:5-6). By 'flesh' Paul does not mean the physical body *per se*, but – in the terms we have received from Heidegger – that of us that is circumscribed by "nullity"; i.e., our separate Being. The term 'flesh' metaphorically suggests that by which our separateness is contained. 'Flesh,' thus, may be read as an expression for finite self-enclosure. If Paul were writing today he might speak rather of 'ego.' As Paul presents it, the flesh is concerned for itself, and ready to subsume the world in itself and for the sake of itself: "the mind set on the flesh is hostile toward God; for it does not subject itself to the law of God, for it is not even able to do so" (Rom 8:7). But the human being is not doomed to the life of flesh, because it has the capacity for the life of Spirit: "However, you are not in the flesh but in the Spirit, if indeed the Spirit of God dwells in you" (Rom 8:9). Spirit is the capacity for transcendent relation with God and others, the capacity for love: "[T]he fruit of the Spirit is love..." (Gal. 5:22).

Sin, then, is the domination of flesh over Spirit in the human being,[2] a domination that leads to transgression against others and alienation from God.

As we suggested in the last chapter, from the Christian perspective *both* the life of das Man and the life of anticipatory resoluteness must be seen as variations on the life of the flesh. What Paul calls the life of the Spirit does not appear as a possibility in Heidegger's thought.[3] It is not that Heidegger overtly denies its possibility, it is that he takes no notice of it – true, in his later work, with the development of his concept of *Gelassenheit* (itself bearing some relation to the thought of the Christian mystic Meister Eckhart[4]), we begin to detect a groping toward it – still, in my estimation anyway, his thought remains far from it to the very end. Nevertheless, Heidegger's phenomenological insights, categories, and distinctions can serve us in explicating the meaning of the life of the Spirit.

II. Transcendent Interest

The life of 'the flesh' is the life of exclusionary self-interest. Dasein, as Care, is inherently, even necessarily, self-interested, i.e., for-the-sake-of-itself. Self-interest, in and of itself, is not sin. It becomes sin only when restricted to itself; when it becomes, for the person whose self-interest it is, the sole criterion of value. Sin is primarily a spiritual, not an ethical, category (though, of course, with ethical ramifications); it is alienation from God. Dasein's axiological self-centeredness creates a rupture in its relation to God.

As we interpreted it in chapter seven, such exclusionary centering of value in oneself is the symbolic meaning of 'eating from the Tree of the Knowledge of Good and Evil,' which closes off access to the

2 This distinction finds its parallel in Judaism, as the distinction between the *yetzer ha ra* and the *yetzer ha tov*.

3 One might suggest that Heidegger's notion of authentic *Mitsein*, characterized by solicitude (*Fursorge*), bears some resemblance to the spiritual community of love proclaimed by Paul, but it seems to me that Heidegger's development of this is too spare, and his concept of anticipatory resoluteness too individual, to allow for such a claim. At most one may suggest that Heidegger's conception of authentic Mitsein, *had* it ever been really developed, might have led Heidegger to modify some of his other views in the direction of Paul.

4 See John D. Caputo, *The Mystical Element in Heidegger's Thought.*

'Tree of Life'; the tendency to such self-centeredness is made all but inevitable by human individualization and freedom; it is a tendency inherent to human Being as such ("the intent of man's heart is evil from youth" Gn. 8:23). The human being must be opened up to the love of God; to the love that *is* God. This is no simple process. The whole of the Bible may be read as a record of the *struggle* to enact such an opening. Indeed, the name 'Israel,' according to the Bible's own etymology, means 'one who struggles with God.'

The life of the Spirit is the life of divine love (*agape*), which is neither a life of obsequious obedience to authoritarian commands, nor a life of self-interestedness in the 'fleshly' (egoic) sense, but a life of *transcendent* interestedness; i.e., an interestedness of universal scope, of caring for the caring of *all*. This manifests itself, globally, as a concern for socio-economic-political justice, and locally, as a concern for the encountered other, i.e., the 'neighbor.'

From the standpoint of ordinary human thought, the life of agapic love appears a paradox. Interestedness seems to *imply* self-concern (as Heidegger's analyses have made clear: one is interested in the 'in-order-to' 'for-the-sake-of' some potentiality of *oneself*). How, then, can there be an *interestedness* that transcends self-concern? The New Testament is well aware of this paradox, and almost seems, at times, to revel in it: "Whoever wishes to save his life will lose it, but whoever loses his life for My sake will find it" (Mt 18:24). "Whoever exalts himself shall be humbled and whoever humbles himself shall be exalted" (Mt 23:12), "[W]hoever wishes to be first among you shall be your slave" (Mt 23:11), etc. In other words, in order to satisfy the thrust of one's self-interest one must first of all eschew self-interest.

The solution to these paradoxes is given in the formula for the fully realized human being as 'Being-in-the-world-with-others-*in*-God.' This is our Heidegger-derived expression for the ontology of Christ. Consummated human Being rises beyond its purely private self-concern to participate in the universal concern of God. Self-concern is not thereby effaced but infinitely extended, an extension that changes the very contours of the self. This transformation, extension, and elevation of self-concern is the fulfillment of the Great Commandment quoted at the start of chapter seven – it is to "love God with all one's heart, mind, and soul and one's neighbor as oneself." Such a life is *eternal life*.

Eternal life is not to be thought of as something one receives at the end of life as a reward for good behavior. Nor is it simply the endless continuation of life as we ordinarily live it. Phenomenologically (as we discussed in chapter seven), eternity is to be understood as the *sufficiency of the now*. To achieve 'eternal life' is to experience such sufficiency in an ongoing way. The Bible tells us that this is accomplished through participation in the life of divine love; a participation that has its own mode of temporalization, its own projects, its own moods, its own desires and goals. Commitment to such a life, then, may be thought of as commitment to a particular *telic context* – i.e., an ultimate hermeneutic of life under which one may live – a telic context distinct from the telic contexts of das Man *and* Being-towards-death.

Still, given that most human beings do not yet have the psycho-spiritual maturity to fully live the life of divine love, the *struggle* for it may be thought of as the pursuit of a specific *telos*; i.e., a specific goal to be realized. To realize this telos, to transcend the telic contexts of das Man and Being-towards-death and enter upon the telic context of eternal life, I suggest, is the deep meaning of 'salvation.'

III. Love and Salvation

Whoever wishes to save his life will lose it... (Mt 18:24)

The Jewish philosopher-theologian Emmanuel Levinas complains that Christianity, as a religion of 'salvation,' dangerously misprioritizes the ethical relation. He writes: "[T]he fact that the monstrosity of Hitlerism could be produced in an evangelized Europe shook within the Jewish mind the plausibility which Christian metaphysics could have for a Jew used to a long acquaintance with Christianity. This plausibility involved *the primacy of supernatural salvation with regard to justice on earth*. Has not this primacy made at least possible a great deal of confusion on earth, and this extreme limit of human dereliction? The famous incomprehension towards supernatural salvation shown by supposedly worldly Jews ... appeared abruptly not as an example of pigheadedness but as a moment of supreme lucidity, and the Jews began to believe that their stiff necks were the most metaphysical part of their anatomy."[5]

Although I believe Levinas' critique to be justified with respect to much traditional and popular Christian doctrine, a careful reading of the New Testament suggests that any prioritization of concern for salvation *over* concern for the ethical relation misconstrues Christ's message; whose entire thrust is the *perfection* of the ethical relation. It is just for this reason that, as quoted above, "whoever wishes to save his life will lose it..." One is not to pursue the ethical as a *means* to salvation (such is legalism), but as salvation itself. Salvation (eternal life) is the overcoming of self-enclosed Being-towards-death. The life of divine love, which *entails* the perfection of the ethical relation, *is* this overcoming: "Love is the fulfillment of the law" (Rom. 13:10).

Then whence the emphasis on salvation? I believe, again, we can use Heideggerian concepts and categories to clarify the relation between salvation and the ethical, and, in the process, perhaps, identify some of institutional Christianity's historical failings.

First, we must attempt to clarify what salvation saves *from*. Although a few isolated passages in Scripture may be read as supportive of the common conception that Christ's sacrifice saves from the supernatural punishment to be visited upon the unjust, the overwhelming testimony of Scripture, both Hebrew Bible and New Testament, makes it clear that the Messianic salvation made available through Christ is not a salvation from punishment *per se*, but from *sin* itself. Isaiah, as we have seen, depicts the Messianic age as an age of universal peace and harmony: "The wolf will dwell with the lamb, and the leopard will lie down with the young goat. They shall not hurt or destroy in all my holy mountain; for the earth shall be full of the knowledge of the Lord as the waters cover the sea" (Is. 11:1-4). This passage depicts a world in which *sin* has been overcome, not punishment. The angel who reveals Mary's pregnancy to Joseph tells him: "She will bear a Son and you will call his name Jesus, for He will save His people from their *sins*" (Mt 1:21, my emphasis). Jesus, explaining the meaning of the freedom he brings, declares "Everyone who commits *sin* is the slave of *sin*" (Jn 8:34, my emphasis). We could multiply such passages almost endlessly. Christ's salvation is from *sin*, not punishment.

5 Emmanuel Levinas, "Jewish Thought Today," *in Difficult Freedom: Essays on Judaism*, trans. Sean Hand (Baltimore: John Hopkins University Press, 1990), 161.

Sin is alienation from the love of God. This alienation has a dual consequence. It leads to ethical transgressions among the unloving: the problem of justice. And it leads to alienation from the eternal (hence, 'death') for the one bereft of love: the problem of salvation. That concern over personal salvation should take precedence over concern for the other is *itself* a function of sin; i.e., an instance of failing to love one's neighbor as oneself. This, I take it, is the gist of Levinas' complaint against the traditional Christian emphasis on salvation. There is every reason to believe it would be Christ's complaint as well.

Still, given that Christ's message is first of all broadcast to 'sinners,' this distortion is not only to be expected but even, in some sense, to be recognized as a necessary stage in spiritual development. Dasein, as Care, is implicitly concerned for itself. As said, this is not itself 'sin,' but simply the ontological structure of finite Care. Care becomes 'sin' only when *con-fined* to itself. Viewed from the biblical perspective, such confinement may be seen as opposed to the fundamental thrust of Care itself. As Heidegger has shown, Dasein's self-concern is ec-static; i.e., it stands out from itself. Even Dasein's self-concern is not restricted to the Being of Dasein *at the present instant*, but is a concern for self *temporally extended* into the past and future.

There is a sense, then, in which the Dasein of *this instant* may be said to have an implicit 'empathic regard' for its extended self (although sinful Dasein, living for 'today,' can often be deficient even in this). Were we to assume that Dasein's ec-static concern were ontologically restricted to itself then we could not envision the possibility of agapic love. But Dasein's very thrownness, or, in religious terms, 'creatureliness,' suggests the possibility of something else. Dasein's Being is not grounded in itself, but, from the religious perspective, in God. It is God who is the basis of Dasein's ecstatic temporality. This suggests the possibility that Dasein's ecstatic *reach* can extend beyond its own finite personhood; can potentially reach as far as *God's*. Dasein, as 'child of God,' whose ecstatic temporality is *of* God, may be thought to have the potentiality for *universal* empathic regard. And, indeed, this is just what is commanded in the Great Commandment. This is life in the Spirit of God, through which Dasein's concern ecstatically transcends its finitude while, nevertheless, remaining centered in Dasein as a discrete, finite self.

It is interesting to note that this provides a vision of infinite transcendence more nuanced and complex than found in strictly monistic accounts of divine unity. Christ does not meld into the Father like a drop of water into the ocean. Rather, Christ retains his own separateness and individuality, i.e., finitude, while participating in *in*finitude through love. Separateness is not undone, but redeemed.

Suggested here is that the very temporal-projective structure that makes possible Dasein's *self*-concern also makes possible Dasein's *other*-concern. The former is merely a limitation of the latter, the latter an extension of the former. It is the ecstatic nature of Care that allows for *both* 'selfishness' *and* love. Sin is smallness. Christ calls upon Dasein to *grow* in Care. One is to love one's neighbor *as* oneself. The ec-stasy of Care, which constitutes Dasein's own self-relation, is now to constitute Dasein's relation to the other as well, thereby extending Dasein's concernful domain. In this way, Dasein fulfills *itself* as 'image of God,' satisfies the demand for *justice*, and *also* resolves the issue of its own finitude, i.e., the demand for *salvation.*

Thus, there is a continuity between concern for *self* and concern for the *transcendence* of self. The first is an instance of *self*-love, the latter an instance of *other*-love, but *both* are expressions of divine love. The problem is that self-enclosed self-love, by the very fact of its self-enclosure, fails to fulfill self-love. Given its finitude and its vocation to infinitude, the self must transcend itself in order to fulfill itself. This is the root of all the Christian paradoxes that suggest that one must deny oneself to save oneself, e.g. "Whoever wishes to save his life will lose it, but whoever loses his life for My sake will find it" (Mt 18:24). One must give up exclusionary involvement in one's private self-interest in order to fulfill the true thrust of one's self-interest.

This paradox leads to another: What should properly motivate Dasein's love of the other? Should it be motivated by the desire for 'salvation' (the desire to escape the angst of death), the desire to fulfill itself as 'image of God' (the desire for the joys of eternal life), or by recognition of the inherent worth of the other (love itself)? The first two may be thought of as corresponding, loosely, to the categories of 'servile' and 'filial' fear as developed in classical Christian theology.

Thomas Aquinas writes: "Through faith there arises in us an apprehension of certain penal evils, which are inflicted in accordance with Divine Judgment. In this way, then, faith is the cause of the fear whereby one dreads to be punished by God; and this is servile fear. It is also the cause of filial fear, whereby one dreads to be separated from God.... Of the first fear ... formless faith is the cause, while formed faith is the cause of the second."[6]

Fear of punishment is prompted by one's sense of guiltiness, which motivates one to change one's behavior so as to escape the punishment it threatens. This produces faith in the form of 'servile fear,' an inferior form of faith, according to Aquinas. Superior is the faith characterized by 'filial fear'; the faith of one who has attained a certain nearness to God and is anxious to preserve it. Servile fear dreads the presence of guiltiness. Filial fear dreads the loss of blessedness. I suggest, however, that even filial fear is deficient in respect to the true beatitude forecast by Christ. To be anxious to be 'like unto God' is, by that fact, *not* to be 'like unto God.' God is not anxious to be like unto God but anxious (so to speak) for the good of the creation. Ultimately, the proper motivation for love is just love itself. We do not require an ulterior motive for our own self-concern, nor, *ideally*, do we require an ulterior motive for our concern for the other. But in saying that 'love' is to motivate love, we must be careful to note that it is not the empty ideal of love that is to be valued, but the *other*. To value the other *is* love (As any mother understands in respect to her child. She does not value 'love,' she values the child. That *is* love.).

But this presents religion with a dilemma. Love can only motivate to the extent that love is present. What is to motivate us to love when love is not present? Only the negativity of the *absence of love* can do so; i.e., the threat that one may be enclosed in death. When only 'death' is present, only death can motivate. Love motivates to love, it is inherently self-affirming. Death motivates an *escape* from death, it is inherently repulsive. Again, we note the striking concord of Heidegger's phenomenological findings with Christianity, while, at the same time, noting the (perhaps equally striking) discord in the way those findings are interpreted. Heidegger characterizes Being-

6 Thomas Aquinas, *The Summa Theologica, vol. I1*, trans. Fathers of the English Dominican Province (Westminster, Maryland: Christian Classics, 1948), P IIb, Q 8, A 1.

towards-death as repellent; Dasein *flees* it into the life of das Man. Christianity agrees. But whereas Heidegger concludes that one must reconcile oneself to this inherently negative state to remain true to oneself, the Bible tells us that the repellent character of death is to *motivate* us to seek Life.

What leads Heidegger to conclude that the negativity of Being-towards-death is to be embraced? It is the fact that the life of das Man is *alienating*.[7] Dasein is caught between *two* negativities. Only by accepting the repellent character of Being-towards-death, says Heidegger, can Dasein overcome its self-alienation and be *true* to itself. Christianity, again, agrees, but makes an addition that places the meaning of the entire complex in a new light. As das Man, Dasein is indeed alienated from itself. Dasein must wrest itself away from its worldly attachment and accept its finitude to be true to itself. But as self-enclosed Being-towards-death, Dasein is *still* alienated, although now from God. Since Dasein's Being is rooted in God, alienation from God is still alienation from self. To fully resolve its alienation, then, Dasein must move *beyond* Being-towards-death to a recognition of its vocation to Life. This movement, from world to death to Life, is figured in the crucifixion and resurrection of Christ.

This suggests that salvation is a process that takes place in stages. The first stage may well produce in Dasein 'servile fear,' as Dasein comes to see the deathly implications of its own self-enclosure. The second stage may well produce 'filial fear,' as Dasein comes to see the possibility of transcending such self-enclosure in the life of God. But fully consummated Being-towards-life is perfect love. John writes: "There is no fear in love; but perfect love casts out fear" (1 Jn 4:18). If perfect love casts out fear, it follows that the life of one consummated in love is free of fear, and must, therefore, have another motivation. This motivation, as we have said, can only be love itself.

7 "The cultivation of such a 'superior' indifference [to death, as one finds in das Man] alienates Dasein from its ownmost non-relational potentiality-for-Being." Heidegger, *Being and Time*, p. 298, H. 254.

IV. Love and the Oneness of God

Sanctification is the *process* of salvation; it refers to Dasein's gradual transformation into one who lives the Life of God. In Paul's writings, we can see this process proceeding through three ethico-spiritual phases. There is, first, the separated human being prior to the reception of the law; pursuing her own private, finite, interests, free of guilt *per se* but nevertheless full of anxiety and towards-death. Then there is the human being who has received the law and come to realize her deficiency (guilt) in respect to it, a guilt which makes manifest the desolation of unredeemed finitude. In effect, under the law the 'simple' anxiety of Being-towards-death *becomes* the anxiety of guilt, as one comes to see one's deathliness as a function of one's failure to abide by the law (the imperatives) of God. This is what Paul calls the 'curse' of the law. These two phases may be thought to correspond more or less with Dasein as das Man, on the one hand, and Dasein as called by conscience on the other.

But Paul now sees a third phase. With the help of the Holy Spirit the human being is to be transformed from the life of exclusionary self-involvement (flesh) to the life of love (Spirit). Love is at once the tacit fulfillment of the law and freedom from the 'curse' of the law. The transformed human being loves spontaneously and joyously, as the expression of her own perfected will – no longer from fear of reprisal. This resolves both the existential *and* the ethical dilemma consequent upon nullity/separateness, which is the dilemma of human finitude itself. Given individualization, each Dasein's Care is centered upon itself, separating it from God and others. Were separateness ontologically fundamental there would be no escape from the state of Hobbesian war. But the *Oneness* of God bespeaks the axiological unity of the creation. Love is the form of this unity. Through love, Dasein fulfills its *own* Being-towards-life in its very caring for, and communion with, the other. Through love Dasein participates in the Oneness of God.

Thomas Aquinas expresses the unitive character of love: "[S]ince each thing in its own way wills and seeks its proper good, if it is the nature of love that the lover will and seek the good of the one he loves, it follows that the lover is to the loved as to that which in some way is one with him. From this the proper nature of love is seen to consist in this, that the affection of the one tends to the other as to someone who is somehow one with him. On this account it is said by Dionysius that love is a 'unitive power'."[8] Love is the reflection in the creation of the unity of God; as such it is the overcoming of radical separateness (i.e., 'alienation') and, hence, 'not-at-homeness.' Such is eternal life.

Eternal life, then, is neither a reward for the 'good work' of ethical behavior, ***nor*** is it essentially divorced from the demands of the ethical. Rather, it is Dasein's full participation in the truth of Being – not the truth of this or that particular being, nor a truth that hovers above every particular being in empty abstraction, but the truth of ***each and every*** being as seen from the universal perspective, the perspective of divine Oneness. To live in accordance with such divine truth is the ***fulfillment*** of the ethical. Dasein's self-enclosure severs it from this divine truth. The redemption of Dasein's separateness through love is its reunion with it.

For Christianity, the ***way*** to this salvific reunion is through the life revealed by – and ***as*** – the Christ.

V. The Christ

Expressed in Heideggerian terms, the figure of Christ reveals ***perfected*** Dasein, Dasein instated in the universal truth of Being. As such, Christ is the 'Son of Man'; i.e., the perfect realization of human potentiality. But, from the Christian perspective, this perfect realization of human potentiality is such only ***as*** 'Son of God'; i.e., only as the realization of the potentiality of God's creative logos. The human does not stand on its own. Its perfection is accomplished ***in, through, and with*** the Spirit of God. Dasein's spirit of ecstatic ***self***-concern must be joined with God's Spirit of ecstatic ***universal***-concern. Only thereby is Dasein's spirit brought into its ***own*** perfection. Only thereby does it enter the telic context of Life. This ***joining*** of the human spirit with the divine Spirit is the meaning of Christ, the ***God-man***.

---

8 Thomas Aquinas, *Summa Contra Gentiles, Book One:God*, trans. Anton C. Pegis (Notre Dame: University of Notre Dame Press, 1975), 277-276.

In the Gospels, Christ is not presented as an object of worship but of emulation-participation; we are to become *like* Christ. In the Gospel of *Mark*, for instance, Jesus is depicted as specifically discouraging a worshipful attitude toward himself: "As He was setting out on a journey, a man ran up to Him and knelt before Him and asked Him, 'Good Teacher, what shall I do to inherit eternal life?' And Jesus said to him, 'Why do you call me good? No one is good except God alone" (Mk. 10:17-18). Jesus goes on to say that the way to eternal life is through observance of the principle commandments, and, beyond this, 'following me' (Mk 10:19-21). In *Matthew* Jesus says: "Not everyone who says to Me, 'Lord, Lord,' will enter the kingdom of heaven, but he who does the will of My Father who is in heaven will enter" (Mt 7:21). Even in the Gospel of *John*, where Christ's identification with God is most pronounced, Jesus makes it clear that devotion to him is to take the form of participation in the life he discloses: "He who has My commandments and keeps them is the one who loves Me; and he who loves Me will be loved by My Father, and I will love him, and will disclose Myself to him" (Jn 14:21). The commandment referred to here is that of love: "A new commandment I give to you, that you love one another as I have loved you, even as I have loved you, that you also love one another" (Jn 13:34).

It is only in this light that we can read what is perhaps the central biblical statement on the significance of Christ: "I am the way, and the truth, and the life; no one comes to the Father but through Me" (Jn 14:6). The 'through' here is clearly a 'through' of existential participation: i.e., one achieves nearness to God only through participation in the mode of Being disclosed by Christ; or, in Heideggerian terms, only through a mode of Being-in-the-world characterized by the *Befindlichkeit* of Christ-like love. Although this text is often cited as a proof-text of Christian exclusivism, what is touted here is not the need for exclusive worship of Christ as a divine personage, but the need for adoption of the *existential disposition* revealed by Christ. In the very same Gospel, Jesus repudiates the chauvinistic particularism so common to institutional religion in general, and so prevalent in historical Christianity. He says to a Samaritan woman who asks him whether the proper place of worship is on the holy mountain of Samaria or in the Temple of Jerusalem (representing two contending religious institutions): "Woman, believe Me, an hour is coming when neither in this mountain nor in Jerusalem will you worship the Father ... an hour is coming, and now is, when the true worshippers will worship in spirit and truth; for such people the Father seeks to be His worshippers. God is spirit, and those who worship Him must worship in spirit and truth" (Jn 4:21-24).

'Spirit and truth,' of course, are neither places nor institutions. To worship in 'spirit and truth' is to enter into a new mode of Being-in-the-world; to become, in Paul's words, "a new creation" (Gal 6:15). This new mode of Being is one that overcomes human self-enclosure. Dasein is no longer to be 'of itself' but 'of God': "[A]s many as received Him, to them He gave the right to become children *of* God...who were born, not *of* blood nor *of* the will of the flesh nor *of* the will of man, but *of* God" (Jn 1:12-13, my emphasis). Birth, of course, is the beginning of finite Dasein's earth-career, as physical death is its end. One born *of* 'the will of the flesh,' then, is one whose existence is con-*fined* within the borders of birth and death. But she who 'receives Christ,' i.e., participates in the 'truth,' or, as we might now say, the 'disclosedness,' of Christ, has her beginning and end transparently opened to the infinity of God, thereby overcoming finitude. Heidegger writes: "Understood existentially, birth is not and never is something past in the sense of something no longer present-at-hand; and death is just as far from having the kind of Being of something still outstanding, not yet present-at-hand but coming along. Factical Dasein exists as born; and, as born, it is already dying, in the sense of Being-towards-death. As long as Dasein factically exists, both 'ends' and their 'between' *are*, and they *are* in the only way which is possible on the basis of Dasein's Being as *care*. Thrownness and that Being towards death in which one either flees it or anticipates it, form a unity; and in this unity birth and death are 'connected' in a manner characteristic of Dasein. As care, Dasein *is* the 'between.'"[9]

But the 'between' of Christ and the 'between' of Heidegger's finite Dasein are different. The former entails the breaking open of the borders encasing the latter. Christ lives 'between,' i.e., as centered in, eternity, whereas finite Dasein lives only as centered in the nullity of its own null-basis and null-term. Insofar as Dasein *is* its between,

9 Heidegger, *Being and Time*, pp. 426-427, H. 374.

Christ and Heidegger's Dasein constitute two distinct modes of Being for Dasein, each with its own distinct kind of unity. The unity of Heidegger's Dasein is enclosed in its own finitude. The unity of Christ is projected infinitely toward God and neighbor. Given the Bible's claim that the very *Being* of Christ is revelatory ('I *am* the truth'), Christ's mode of Being cannot be regarded as available only to Jesus. Traditional Christian emphasis on the metaphysical uniqueness of Jesus, it seems to me, tends to obscure this. *All* who participate in the Being of Christ, says Paul, are "sons of God through faith in Christ Jesus" (Gal 3:26). Jesus is the perfect embodiment and exemplar of a mode of Being to which *all* are called.[10] To 'believe in' Christ, then, is to devote oneself to ('project oneself upon') the potentiality for Being revealed in Christ. This, not intellectual assent to a creed, is the basic meaning of Christian faith.

Christ provides a picture of human wholeness in decided contrast to Heidegger's. Christ is whole *as* a continual and limitless transcendence toward the infinite. Conceptually, Christ's wholeness is not predicated upon the termination (or anticipated termination) of self-projectivity, i.e., death, but upon the infinity of self-projectivity native to the divine life. The Christian idea of Trinity captures the eternal *livingness* of God. The Son is eternally ec-static toward the Father and the Father eternally ec-static toward the Son. The Son, incarnate as the Christ, calls for *all* to participate in this eternal ec-stasy of Father and Son: "The glory which You have given Me I have given to them, that they may be one, just as We are one; I in them and You in Me, that they may be perfected in unity..." (Jn 17:22). This, finally, is a conception of wholeness consistent with the infinite self-projective thrust of ek-sistence. Yet wholeness is not compromised by such endless projectivity. For wholeness is realized, finally, not temporally but *axiologically*. Eternity is the *axiological* wholeness of time; the *sufficiency* of *every* now. That which is still outstanding – the future – is *comprehended and contained* within the spirit of love. Time doesn't cease; there is still the surprising, the new, the

10 Rahner writes: "This union [of God and Man in Jesus] is distinguished from our grace not by what has been offered in it, which in both instances, including that of Jesus, is grace. It is distinguished rather by the fact that Jesus is the offer for us, and we ourselves are not once again the offer, but the recipients of God's offer to us." *Foundations of Christian Faith*, 202.

unexpected, the astonishing ... but no longer the *utterly* alien. Even the horrible and terrible are comprehended by love: "Even though I walk through the valley of the shadow of death I fear no evil, for You are with me" (Ps 23:4).

Being-towards-life, then, is the telic context under which Dasein lives its ec-static wholeness. Given the self-projectivity of existence it entails, I believe, a hope and expectation of continued existence beyond physical death; but this is not its essence. It is the axiological *quality* of existence that is expressed in the idea of eternal life, not the temporal *quantity*. Christ reveals life lived under the telic context of eternal life. The Christian is one who accepts Christ's call to such a life as his or her supreme *telos*, a telos which is itself but an *opening into* the *telic context* of eternal life.

The telos of Christ is opposed in the Christian tradition to the telos of Anti-Christ, expressing the one who lives wholly under the telic context of self-enclosure. Though these are figuratively represented as warring parties, the weapons of this war are *axiological*, and the battleground is the 'soul' of man/woman. There is a sense in which Jesus only fully becomes the Christ through overcoming the temptations of Anti-Christ. The encounter of Christ with Anti-Christ is graphically depicted in the Gospels as the 'temptation in the desert.' An examination of this will allow us a fuller appreciation of the meaning of Christ.

VI. CHRIST AND ANTI-CHRIST.

There is a parallel between the temptation of Christ in the desert and the temptation of Adam and Eve in the garden. Adam and Eve succumb to the Satanic temptation and thereby turn their garden into a spiritual desert. Christ overcomes the temptation of Satan and thereby turns the spiritual desert back into a garden: "He who believes in Me..." says Christ, "From his innermost being will flow rivers of living water" (Jn 7:38). If we understand Christ to be expressive of perfected *ek*-sistence; i.e., transcendent regard, then Satan may be thought of as expressing the principle of perfect *in*-sistence; i.e., self-enclosed regard.

And yet Satan's in-sistence is a paradox in a way that Christ's ek-sistence is not. As perfect ek-sistence, Christ has regard for all that is. But Satan's in-sistence cannot be regard for *only* himself; for the self, as such, is Being-in-the-world-with-others. In other words, exclusionary self-regard is never *merely* a concern with self; it entails an attitude toward the world and others as well. The one of exclusionary self-regard will seek to subsume the world *within* the self. Both Satan and Christ, thus, are projected toward the world, but, of course, with a difference. Whereas Christ wishes to honor the Being of all that is, Satan wishes to subsume it in the self. Christ wishes to be open to infinity, Satan wishes to enclose infinity within himself. Both, in effect, have their eye on infinity. Christ loves it. Satan lusts after it.

It is significant that the temptation of Christ takes place in the desert, for the desert surroundings make the temptations all the more tempting. One of the problems biblical exegetes have always had in treating of the temptation of Adam and Eve in Eden is explaining why, amidst such lush surroundings, they would have succumbed to sin. Even if we explain it as a moment in which 'curiosity got the better of them' such would hardly seem to warrant the horrific penalties and curses brought down upon them. Nor do we entirely escape the problem by insisting that the story be taken as symbolic. We still need to say *what* the story symbolizes: The story, as we interpret it, intends to disclose the axio-spiritual destitution of humankind. The symbol of Eden, then, serves as an image of that *of which* human life is destitute. The symbol of ejection from Eden indicates, not only *that* humankind is 'fallen,' but that *from which* it is fallen; i.e., the 'garden.'

But for factical Dasein, sin does not tempt from the garden but from the desert. Satan offers a way out of the desert of death. This is by no means an inconsiderable part of Satan's allure. But, says the Bible, it is a false way: all that glitters is not gold.

Each of the temptations of Jesus may be seen as expressing one or another way in which the human being seeks ultimate satisfaction through worldly acquisition. One might pursue material goods ('wealth'); turn the rock into bread (Mt 4:4). One might pursue self-glorification ('fame'); entice the angels to honor one (Mt 4:6). One might pursue imperial dominion ('power'); conquer the kingdoms of the earth (Mt 4:8-10). Each of these are ways in which the human being might seek to subsume the goods of the world within the self. They are tempting just insofar as the self is impoverished, for they promise, in their various ways, to alleviate the self's poverty. But the Christian message is that the poverty of the self cannot be, and is not to be, alleviated through *subsumption* of the world. *First*, the pursuit of such is ethically problematic, insofar as it necessarily involves transgression against the other. *Second*, the pursuit of such is spiritually problematic, insofar as infinity cannot be contained within the finite. Even the most wealthy and powerful remain 'thrown-Being-towards-death': "Truly I say to you," says Jesus, "it is hard for a rich man to enter the kingdom of heaven" (Mt 19:23). The rich man becomes attached to his riches and bloated in self-importance. Such attachment and bloatedness close the self upon itself. The way to Life is otherwise.

Christ's life is, at once, the repudiation of these ways and the pointing to another way. Rather than extract bread from rock, Christ offers himself as 'living bread' for the nourishment of the spirit (Jn 6:51). Rather than be elevated to the heights by angels, Christ falls to his knees to wash the feet of his own disciples (Jn 13:3-5). Rather than conquer the kingdoms of the world, Christ stands silent as the might of imperial Rome crucifies him. Life, Being-towards-life, is won through the *giving* of oneself to the other and to God. Only thereby does one *open* oneself to communion with infinity. Only thereby does the desert become the garden. It is through such givingness that human Being is transformed from deathliness to life. The New Testament's principle expression of this is in the death and resurrection of Christ.

VII. THE CROSS OF CHRIST

The crucifixion and resurrection of Christ bespeaks a great hope: that death is *not* Dasein's 'uttermost possibility.' It is an image extraordinarily rich in meaning, in Paul Ricoeur's phrase, 'multivocal,' straining our very capacity to express it. The Cross denotes, almost all at once: sin, violence, horror, despair, death, repentance, redemption, sanctification, forgiveness, love, and, finally, reunion with the divine. On the cross Christ – representing humanity – surrenders to the death consequent upon sin in order to be reborn into the life of the Spirit of God. And on the cross, Christ – now representing God – lovingly undergoes this death *with* human beings in order to conduct us into this new life. In this section we will, again, employ Heideggerian categories in an effort to penetrate into the meaning of the Cross.

"The wages of sin is death," writes Paul in his epistle to the Romans (Rom. 6:23). What are we to understand by this? Heidegger has made it clear that, existentially, death can only be understood as Being-*towards*-death. We can have no experience of death *per se*. Strictly speaking, death is the end of experience. The meaning of death, then, is exhausted in our experience of being subject to it. What is the nature of this experience? Heidegger writes: "Dasein does not, proximally and for the most part, have any explicit or even theoretical knowledge of the fact that it has been delivered over to its death, and that death thus belongs to Being-in-the-world. Thrownness into death reveals itself to Dasein in a more primordial and impressive manner in that state-of-mind which we have called 'anxiety'."[11] "Being-towards-death is essentially anxiety."[12]

Our experience of subjection to death is, in essence, an experience of anxiety. Heidegger never gives us an interpretation of the meaning of anxiety itself, but our own analyses have shown that anxiety has its meaning as an experience of *threat* to the fundamental thrust of life. The human being is not essentially Being-towards-death but Being-towards-life. Our subjection to death brings anxiety because it contravenes our fundamental nature as towards-life.

In this respect human Being is a paradox. Our basic nature, as towards-life, is in conflict with our basic existential condition, as finite. The claim of Christianity is that this paradox can be resolved through communion with the font of life itself: God. The experience of such communion is, at heart, an experience of peace, love, and joy, not anxiety. Paul speaks of it as a peace that "passes all understanding" (Ph. 4:7). Through such communion, the thrust of life, as towards life, finds its satisfaction.

It is the rupture of such communion that yields the *experience* of death. Such rupture is the essential meaning of sin. It is in just this respect that "the wages of sin is death."

---

11 Ibid., p. 295, H. 251.

12 Ibid., p. 310, H. 266.

What conditions this rupture? The Bible presents its answer, in somewhat enigmatic form, in the Garden of Eden story. The moment of rupture is traced to the moment when Adam and Eve reach out to eat from the Tree of the Knowledge of Good and Evil. As we have said throughout, this story must be interpreted symbolically and paradigmatically. It is not a story about a choice made by two individuals, but about an inclination inherent to human ontology as such: the inclination to center all value in oneself, to prioritize one's finite interests and desires above all. This inclination is the "original sin." It ruptures our communion with others, with the remainder of Being, and with the font of Being. It prevents us from "loving God with all our heart, mind, and soul and our neighbor as ourselves." It thereby exiles us from the experience of "eternal life." In the Eden story, this exile is represented as banishment from the Tree of Life. Hence, this inclination yields 'death,' i.e., the intensive anxiety of subjection to death.

But this inclination is not the result of a simple, conscious choice we make. Again, it is native to our ontology. As the Bible puts it: "The intent of man's heart is evil from youth" (Gn. 8:21). The Bible illustrates this 'evil intent' through the very next story it narrates following the Eden story – the story of brother murdering brother.

What is required, then, is what the New Testament calls a "*metanoia*." The Greek word 'metanoia' is generally translated 'repentance', but its Greek meaning is richer than this. It means, more literally, a transformation of heart and mind. The 'Christ' is a revelation of what the transformed human being is like. This path of transformation (*metanoia*) is represented by the Cross. Jesus tells his disciples: "If anyone would come after me, let him deny himself and take up his cross" (Mt 16:24). We are now in a position to try to unravel the multi-layered meanings of the Cross.

Perhaps the very first thing to note about the crucifixion of Christ is the obvious: it is a spectacle of ghastly violence. The Romans used crucifixion as a way of publically torturing their opponents to death. Death by crucifixion was an especially horrific one. The victim of crucifixion would die of asphyxiation, his physical position on the cross making it all but impossible to breathe. In order not to suffocate he would have to pull himself up by his nailed arms, inhale a tortured breath, and then let himself drop, only to do it again a moment later. This would go on until he died. Throughout he would suffer heat, thirst, exhaustion, wrenching pain, and the anguish of knowing there was no escape. All in full public view. The typical crucifixion could last for days.

Surely, at this level, the Cross is one of the more startling of the world's religious symbols; a symbol of human Being torturing and tormenting itself. It is significant, of course, that it is *Christ* who is on the cross; Christ, who represents the 'image of God' in us. The crucifixion of Christ is both an expression for, and an instance of, the tragic self-victimage of human existence; the cruelty and brutality to which we are prone and of which we are, at the same time, victim; the excruciating violence we inflict upon one another, and contain within ourselves. It is a graphic depiction of the "fallenness" of human Being, the darkness that envelops us, our alienation from God and one another. On the cross, Jesus gives vent to this experience of darkness and despair in his mournful cry, "My God, my God, why have you forsaken me?" (Mt. 27:46).

But, of course, the message of the Cross is that God has *not* forsaken us. Even in the extremity of our suffering and sin God remains *with us*.[13] And this brings us to a second meaning of the Cross. The crucifixion of Christ expresses *both* the self-victimage of humanity *and* God's compassionate, and ultimately redeeming, *participation* in this self-victimage. On the Cross, Christ, as God, takes upon himself the sinfulness of humankind, absorbs it into himself, and thereby redeems it. As Paul says: Christ becomes "sin on our behalf" (2 Cor 5:21). Christ journeys into the heart of darkness and vanquishes it with the light of love: "In Him was life, and the life was the Light of men. The Light shines in the darkness, and the darkness did not overcome it" (Jn 1:4)[14].

13 In the Gospel of Matthew the name *Jesus*, which literally means 'God saves,' is associated with the name of the Messiah as given in Isaiah, *Emmanuel*, which literally means, "God with us."

14 In many translations, including the New American Standard from which we have been quoting, the word I have replaced with 'overcome' is rendered 'comprehend.' The original Greek *can* mean comprehend in the cognitive sense, but also 'encompass' in the sense of 'subsume' or even 'overwhelm.' I believe that the latter meaning is more apt to the sense John is trying to convey, hence I have modified the translation to reflect this here.

How are we to understand this ontologically? Perhaps we can do so by recalling the three 'strata' of Dasein's Being we discussed briefly in chapter eight. First, there is the stratum of Dasein's finite individuality, concerned for itself. Next, there is the stratum of 'nullity,' which borders Dasein's finite individuality, separating Dasein from the remainder of Being and *allowing* it to be a distinct self, separate from the whole. But, finally (from the religious perspective), there is the stratum of God, infinite Being, *from* which Dasein is separated, but *in* which it is to find its proper home and the resolution to its nullity. For 'sinful' Dasein, this nullity has become opaque, clogged with self-involvement. Dasein cannot see through it or past it. Hence Dasein feels closed in upon itself, abandoned to itself. This is what gives rise to the intensive anxiety that impels Dasein to flee itself into the inauthentic life of das Man, where Dasein strives, in futility, to escape the confines of its self-enclosure.

But Christ is presented as one for whom the nullity has become a *transparency*; this is the meaning of Christ as the "God-Man." Christ's humanity is a continual openness to – communion with – the Being of God in which we rest. Christ is not closed in on himself but open, in love, to the Being of all. It is this that allows Christ to forgive his tormentors, even from the Cross: "Father, forgive them, they know not what they do" (Lk. 23:24). Christ sees the horror of sinful existence, undergoes this horror in its most extreme form, but at the same time sees beyond it, to the infinite grace of God. Such grace is the redemption of sin; i.e., alienation from God.

We are *all* to become what Christ is, to experience the grace through which sin is redeemed. This is the clear message of the New Testament, a message betokened in the Hebrew Bible as well. Christ is the ultimate *telos* of human Being, revealed in the person of Jesus but not restricted to him; Christ is that into which we are *all* to be transformed. This – not 'death' – is our "uttermost possibility." This is the "good news" of the gospel.

And this yields a third meaning of the Cross: the Cross symbolically depicts the transformational process we must all undergo in order to transition from life under the "reign of death" (as Paul puts it) to life under the grace of God; or, in the terms we have developed, from a life lived under the telic context of Being-towards-death to a life lived under the telic context of Being-towards-life.

Paul writes: "[I]f we have become united with Him in the likeness of His death, certainly we shall also be in the likeness of His resurrection, knowing this, that our old self was crucified with Him, in order that our body of sin might be done away with, so that we would no longer be slaves to sin; for he who has died is freed from sin. Now if we have died with Christ, we believe that we shall also live with Him" (Rom 6:6-8).

For Paul, the Cross represents the passage from everyday life (das Man), *through* death (being-towards-death), *to* eternal life. Let us take a moment to consider the stages of this passage.

Paul writes: "I was once alive apart from the Law; but when the commandment came, sin became alive and I died. I found that the very commandment that was intended to bring life actually brought death. For sin, taking an opportunity through the commandment, deceived me and through it killed me" (Rom 7:9-11).

Paul seems here to be doing his best to provide his own phenomenological account of what Heidegger names 'the call of conscience.' It parallels Heidegger's account in significant ways but, of course, diverges from it in critical ways.

As with Heidegger, Paul experiences the call of conscience (given form through the Law) as convicting him of living wrongly (for Heidegger, 'inauthentically'). As with Heidegger, conscience makes Paul aware of himself as towards-death. But Paul has no doubt as to the negativity of such a state: "Wretched man that I am! Who will set me free from the body of this death?" (Rom 7:24).

Of course, there is a significant difference between Heidegger's experience of the "call of conscience" and Paul's, a difference traceable to the different 'telic contexts' under which they interpret it. For Heidegger, the "call of conscience" is a call from Dasein to Dasein; from authentic Dasein to inauthentic Dasein, calling the latter to return to the former. For Paul, the Law is a call from God, calling Paul to responsibility before God.

And this difference conditions a difference in their understanding of 'death' as well. Heidegger sees death as "repellent" but, nevertheless, as something one must embrace in order to live authentically. Paul agrees that death is repellent, but sees it as something to be overcome by entry into the new life betokened by Christ.

Still, there is a fascinating moment of coincidence between the biblical and Heideggerian understanding of death. For both, our *flight* from death must be renounced if we are to confront our existential situation honestly. It is the *flight* from death that yields the "war of all against all" that Paul calls the "reign of death." As Paul expresses it, we must "die with Christ" so that we may "live with him" (Rm. 6:8). It is through the humble acceptance of our finitude that the Spirit is able to open the windows of our 'nullity' and allow us to look out upon the Being of God.

And this is the final meaning of the Cross. Jesus' surrender to God on the Cross represents the reversal of the Edenic impulse to make ourselves gods *unto* ourselves; it is an acceptance of finitude, of being *part* of the greater whole rather than a whole unto ourselves: "Unless a grain of wheat falls to the earth and dies," says Jesus, "it remains by itself alone; but if it dies, it bears much fruit" (Jn. 12:24). What must 'die' is our disposition to axiological self-enclosure, biblically represented by the eating of the fruit from the Tree of the Knowledge of Good and Evil. Ironically and paradoxically, it is this yielding to death that is the condition for liberation from death; for it is through such humble yielding that the Spirit of God is able to break through from the bottom up.

Finally, as Paul envisions it, it is this death of the sinful inclination that finally yields rebirth – resurrection – into a new life of participation in the love of the divine. Such is *eternal* life. That is the surprising good news – that a reverent yielding to death results, not in death, but in a transformed life in the Spirit of God.

VIII. The Spirit of Truth

> I will ask the Father, and he will give you another Counselor to be with you forever – the *Spirit of truth*. The world cannot accept him, because it neither sees him nor knows him. But you know him, for he lives with you and will be in you. (Jn. 14:16-17, my emphasis)

The one who dies is not the same as the one who is reborn. Prior to the resurrection, Jesus' life is largely pedagogic; he is, primarily, a moral and spiritual teacher. After the resurrection Jesus is a bestower of the Spirit of God: "He breathed on them and said to them 'Receive the Holy Spirit' (Jn 20:22). In a sense, Jesus is only completed *as* Christ through the crucifixion-resurrection. Christ discloses the path each human being is to follow, from death to life, from self-enclosure to openness to the divine Spirit. Christ, as the 'Way,' reveals it.

In the above passage, the Holy Spirit is referred to as 'the Spirit of *truth*.' What are we to understand by this phrase?

In its Latinate roots, the English word 'spirit' is related to the word for 'breath,' as in the word re-*spirat*-ion. This connection can be found as well in the Hebrew and Greek words for spirit: *ruach* and *pneuma*. It is easy to see the relationship between the idea of breath and life, as the most immediate sign of death is the cessation of breathing. The Greek word for spirit, *pneuma*, can also mean *wind*, as can the Hebrew *ruach*. It is easy, again, to see an analogical relation between the idea of 'breath' and the idea of 'wind.'

But we might note that these bear more than an analogical relationship. The wind *is* just that which we breathe when we breathe in. That which we breathe out *is* just the wind. Wind and breath are, in other words, physically *continuous*. The wind is the 'objective' of which the breath is the 'subjective.' The wind is the 'public' of which the breath is the 'private.' The word wind, further, expresses the stirring of the environing atmosphere. In some sense, all things are *within* that which is stirred when the wind is stirred. In this much broader sense, then, spirit may be understood as referring to that *within which* things *are*. The spirit is that 'livingness' *within which* things have their relation to us and for us. I suggest that its meaning is more or less equivalent to what Heidegger means by *Being* (*Sein*), when he takes pains to distinguish Being from beings (*Seiendes*).

Spirit always manifests itself with a certain *quality*. We can speak of a spirit of *anger*, a spirit of *peace*, a spirit of *hatred*, a spirit of *love*. As Heidegger has pointed out, these words express something more than mere subjective emotion. They are ways in which Being is *disclosed*. But what do we mean when we say that things are *disclosed* in these ways? What is modified in these modifications of spirit are not the spatio-temporal (empirical or sensible) attributes of things, but the way in which they *matter* to us. *Meaning*, we have said, expresses the way in which things *matter* to us. Such mattering cannot be rendered in spatio-temporal terms, and it is for just this reason that *meaning* cannot be reduced to empirical categories: this is just where the logical positivists went wrong. To *hate* someone, to *love* someone, expresses a quality of relation that is independent of spatio-temporal relations and, therefore, cannot be explicated in purely spatio-temporal terms. Nevertheless, love and hatred are not mere private emotion. They are qualities of concernful *relation*. They express ways in which things and people are related to one another in the sphere of *spirit*.

Spirit is also the domain of meaning. When Christ says "I am the truth" he is professing to reveal ('disclose') the true *meaning* of human existence. Such meaning cannot be rendered in spatio-temporal terms; it is axio-relational.

The Judeo-Christian claim is: *God is Spirit*. That which ultimately *Is* is spirit. The spatio-temporal has its Being *within* spirit, but spirit cannot be reduced to it. It is because Heidegger's concept of Being is, in effect, a concept of *spirit* that Heidegger's philosophy has such resonance for religious thought. The whole of Scripture concerns the relationship between the human spirit and the divine Spirit. The human spirit, says the Bible, is derived from, 'created by,' the divine Spirit, but has its own separateness and volitional independence. God's endeavor to conform the human spirit to the divine Spirit would have to be construed as abject despotism were it not for the fact that the former is already and always ontologically embedded in the latter. The human being, ontologically grounded in God, finds its own truth only in right relation to the Spirit of God, which, in turn, entails right relation with every other spirit grounded in God. Such right relation is love. This, then, is the meaning of the Great Commandment quoted at the start of chapter seven: We achieve eternal life, the consummation of life, through love of God and neighbor. Our love, inclined to self-enclosure due to individualization and freedom, must open itself up toward God and others. Such opening conducts us *through* death (as self-enclosure) to eternal life. Christ's crucifixion and resurrection reveal the *way* from death to life.

In the end, Christianity envisions a *partnering* of the human and the divine, a partnering that resolves the dilemma of human finitude; the dilemma of 'death.' This partnering is the meaning of Christ, as the God-man. Christ says to his disciples: "I no longer call you servants, because a servant does not know his master's business. Instead, I have called you friends, for everything that I learned from my Father I have made known to you" (Jn. 15:15). The human spirit is to commune with – 'befriend' – the divine Spirit, such that human love and divine love fuse. In this way God becomes, in Paul's evocative phrase, "all in all" (1Cor. 15:28).

It is the Judeo-Christian claim that it is only through such love that Being is disclosed in *truth*. In our final chapter, we will reflect on the significance of this claim for both the religious and the philosophical pursuit of truth.

X

Philosophy, Religion, and the Pursuit of Truth

> *When anyone hears the message about the kingdom and does not understand it, the evil one comes and snatches away what was sown in his heart. (Mt. 13:19)*

In the Gospel of Matthew, Jesus relates the parable of the sower. A sower goes out to sow some seed. Some of the seed falls on the open path where it is immediately eaten by birds who descend upon it and devour it; this seed has no chance to grow at all. Some of the seed falls on rocky ground from which plants immediately spring to life, but because the rocky soil has no depth these plants die just as quickly. Some of the seed falls among thorns, and these thorns, growing together with the plants, eventually choke the life out of them. Some of the seed, however, falls on good soil, and this seed yields much grain. "He who has ears to hear," Jesus concludes, "let him hear."

In the parable of the sower, Jesus foresees the misunderstanding of his message. The words of the message (the seeds) are insufficient in themselves to preclude such misunderstanding; everything depends upon the manner in which the words are received. Heidegger's work is important for religious hermeneutic because he presents us with a new, and more appropriate, way of hearing these words. In Part Two of our work we have tried to use Heidegger's phenomenological method, along with the analytic of Dasein he develops through it, to hear anew "the message about the kingdom."

This has not been a simple task. Heidegger's work is complicated by the fact that his analytic of Dasein is, at once, an explication of the ontology of Dasein and, at the same time, an exploration of just how such an explication must proceed. Logically speaking, we would prefer to know how to proceed before we begin the process, but such is not possible in the examination of Dasein, where the one inquired about is also the one who inquires. Understanding the subject requires the employment of the very features of the subject we are seeking to understand.

Our work has exhibited a similar complexity. On the one hand, I have wanted to say something about religion and, in particular, the Judeo-Christian religious message, the "message about the kingdom." On the other, I have entered into questions concerning *how* such an examination of religious claims must proceed, given their peculiar nature. These cannot be separated from one another. *What* we can know is inextricably bound up with *how* we can know it. This is especially true in the religious sphere. God does not appear as an 'objective datum,' visible to anyone with physical eyes. God is *Spirit*, disclosed only in the context of human concern, and, therefore, only through an openness to oneself *in* one's concerns. As we have now said a number of times, this makes Heidegger's examination of the ontology of human concern of particular relevance to philosophy of religion.

But, as we have also now said a number of times, Heidegger's explication of Dasein does not finally penetrate into that about Dasein that would legitimize faith. Heidegger – at least the Heidegger of *Being and Time* – does not see the possibility of an authentic relation with the infinite. Thus, from the religious point of view, Heidegger's analytic of Dasein is incomplete. It has been my contention that just as Heidegger's work can help us uncover religious meanings, so these very religious meanings can help us penetrate more deeply into the existential structure of Dasein as Heidegger himself presents it. In this final chapter, I would like to try to pull the entire argument of this work together so as to bring out, in sharper relief, the manner in which both these claims prove to be true. In doing so, I hope also to indicate the intimate relationship between the philosophic and religious pursuit of truth.

I. PHILOSOPHICAL INQUIRY

"Philosophy," writes Heidegger, "is universal phenomenological ontology, and takes its departure from the hermeneutic of Dasein, which, as an analytic of *existence*, has made fast the guiding-line for all philosophical inquiry at the point where it *arises* and to which it *returns*."[1] Philosophical inquiry, as Heidegger here notes, has its point of departure and point of return in the existence of Dasein. It is Dasein who asks the questions of philosophy, and Dasein who is to be the peculiar beneficiary of the answers. Philosophical inquiry is distinguished from technological inquiry in just this respect: whereas technical knowledge is pursued for an end other than the knowledge sought, philosophical knowledge is pursued 'for its own sake'; i.e., pursued for the peculiar value of knowing itself.

What is this peculiar value? Heidegger writes: "In existing, Dasein understands itself, and in such a way, indeed, that this understanding does not merely get something in its grasp, but makes up the existentiell Being of its factical potentiality-for-Being."[2] Dasein's self understanding (which entails Dasein's 'world' understanding, given that Dasein is 'Being-in-the-world'), is not merely the understanding *of* something that Dasein can then manipulate for other ends (i.e., is not *technical* knowledge), but is a determining factor in *who* Dasein is. Dasein *is*, in some significant sense, its understanding of itself. Given, further, that what Dasein is, at any point in time, conditions the possibilities of what Dasein may become, Dasein's self-understanding determines, as well, what Dasein *may be*.

Dasein, Heidegger tells us, is a being whose Being is an issue to itself; i.e., a being intrinsically concerned with what it *may be*. Philosophy, then, far from an idle pursuit, is an expression of Dasein's concern to realize itself, to actualize its onto-noetic potentiality to fully *be* itself through fulfilling the Socratic dictum to fully *know* itself. The quality of Dasein's self-knowing determines, in no small degree, the quality of Dasein's Being.

The question Dasein asks about Being, then, is also the question Dasein asks about itself. "This question," Heidegger tells us at the start

---

1 Martin Heidegger, *Being and Time*, p. 62, H. 38.

2 Ibid., p. 372, H. 325.

of *Being and Time*, "has today been forgotten."[3] Heidegger's point is not that we are no longer asking this question at all, but that we have lost touch with what is *essential* to it; we are no longer asking it from out of the authentic concern that motivates it, but as if it were an *objective* question, a *technical* question. There is, indeed, a place for asking such technical questions about human Being; sociology, psychology, anthropology, etc., all seek knowledge about the objective structure of the characteristically human. But philosophy is, or should be, something else. Philosophy is the pursuit of *self*-knowing, where 'self' is understood as every first-person singular, every discrete *me*, concerned for itself.

This is an understanding of philosophy we see already expressed in the works of Plato. In the *Gorgias*, for instance, Socrates says to his dialogue partner Polis, "I believe that nothing worth speaking of will have been accomplished in our discussion unless I can obtain your adhesion, and yours alone, to the truth of what I say..."[4] Philosophical truth has no value, perhaps no meaning, apart from the concerned subject who pursues that truth. Its value is precisely in its power to address the fundamental concerns of that subject.

It is convenient to point to Descartes as the one whose philosophy, in establishing a strict dichotomy between subject and object, conditions the 'forgetting of the question' for modern thought. We discussed this at length in chapter one. It is, however, a bit unfair to lay the full burden on Descartes. At worst Descartes' philosophy is symptomatic of a human tendency the Platonic Socrates is already protesting at the inception of Western philosophy:

> Men of Athens, I honor and love you, but I shall obey God rather than you, and while I have life and strength I shall never cease from the practice and teaching of philosophy, exhorting anyone whom I meet after my manner, and convincing him, saying: O my friend, why do you who are a citizen of the great and mighty and wise city of Athens, care so much about laying up the greatest amount of money and honor and reputation, and so little about wisdom and truth and the greatest improvement of the soul, which you never regard or heed at all? Are you not

3 Ibid., p. 21, H. 2.

4 Plato, *Gorgias*, trans. Walter Hamilton (London: Penguin Books, 1960), 58

> ashamed of this? And if the person with whom I am arguing says: Yes, but I do care; I do not depart or let him go at once; I interrogate and examine and cross-examine him, and if I think that he has no virtue, but only says that he has, I reproach him with undervaluing the greater, and overvaluing the less. And this I should say to everyone whom I meet, young and old, citizen and alien, but especially to the citizens, inasmuch as they are my brethren. For this is the command of God, as I would have you know; and I believe that to this day no greater good has ever happened in the state than my service to the God.[5]

Knowledge that allows for "laying up the greatest amount of money and honor and reputation" is, of course, technical knowledge. It is controlling knowledge, 'know-how': *Ge-stell*.[6] But philosophy, as the Platonic Socrates here envisions it, has another end: the establishment of virtue, i.e., *arête*, perhaps best translated as 'perfection of the soul.' Such virtue is achieved, according to Socrates, primarily through self-knowing, which, then, is the particular task of philosophy.[7]

---

5 Plato, "Apology," trans. Benjamin Jowett in *The Works of Plato, vol. 3* (New York: Tudor Publishing Co.: 1937), 118.

6 Heidegger's most complete statement on the meaning of technology is to be found in his "The Question Concerning Technology." There he employs the German word '*Gestell*' to express the self/world understanding of technological Dasein. *Gestell* means 'set within a frame'; its meaning, as Heidegger uses it, is perhaps best captured by what we have been calling 'objectification.' Technological Dasein seeks to set the world 'over against' him/her, to objectify it, to set it within an explanatory 'frame' so as to better control it. Enframing, says Heidegger, has had its impact on theology as well: "[W]here everything that presences exhibits itself in the light of a cause-effect coherence, even God can, for representational thinking, lose all that is exalted and holy, the mysteriousness of his distance. In the light of causality, God can sink to the level of a cause, of *causa efficiens*. He then becomes, even in theology, the god of the philosophers, namely, of those who define the unconcealed and the concealed in terms of the causality of making, without ever considering the essential origin of this causality." Martin Heidegger, "The Question Concerning Technology," trans. William Lovett, in *The Question Concerning Technology and Other Essays* (New York: Harper & Row, 1977).

7 Robert Cushman emphasizes this aspect of Plato's philosophy in his book *Therapeia*: "In Plato the prime data of metaphysical knowledge are taken from the realm of man's distinctive experience, namely, the axiological. These data are given; but, as Socrates perceived, they are not given by way of the *exteriorized standpoint* occupied by the earlier 'nature philosophy.' Philosophic knowledge has its inception by way of *man's honest encounter with himself*. This Socratic alteration of standpoint is, above all else, responsible for the Socratic-Platonic conception of philosophy" (my emphasis). Robert E. Cushman, *Therapeia: Plato's Conception of Philosophy*, (Chapel Hill: The University of North Carolina Press, 1958), xx.

What conditions the 'forgetting of the question'? This is a question we must ask, not only in order to get philosophy back on track, but as an authentic philosophical question in itself. Dasein 'forgets' the question through some tendency in him/herself. Dasein, Heidegger tells us, is a being who is, to a considerable degree, *in flight* from its Being. Dasein, as das Man, is in flight from itself as Being-towards-death. Dasein's forgetting the question of itself is part and parcel of Dasein's desire to *escape* itself.

Heidegger's prescription for Dasein, which he takes to be Dasein's prescription for itself (rendered in the call of conscience), is to face up courageously to its Being-towards-death. Only thereby can Dasein live authentically, and only thereby can the authentic philosophical project be resumed; a project which, in his later work, and to distinguish it from inauthentic philosophy, Heidegger simply calls 'thinking.'

I have suggested, however, that there is a deep ambiguity in Heidegger's concept of Being-towards-death, one that Heidegger himself is never able to resolve. Why, we have asked, should Dasein feel *not-at-home* in its very Being? That Dasein should feel *not*-at-home with itself implies, at very least, that Dasein intimates a sense of 'home' that it experiences as somehow missing. What is the significance of this?

On reflection, it is Heidegger's own phenomenology that allows us to answer this question: Dasein, Heidegger tells us, experiences its ultimate basis and ultimate term as null; it feels no connection

---

Oddly, Heidegger, in contrast, accuses Plato of being responsible for the shift in the conception of truth from disclosedness (*aletheia*) to 'correctness.' See "Plato's Doctrine of Truth," trans. Thomas Sheehan, in *Pathmarks*, where Heidegger gives a reading of Plato's allegory of the cave. Heidegger's argument is almost entirely etymological, however, based upon the concrete sense of *idea* and *eidos* as 'visible form,' which he takes, apparently, to imply objective otherness. He discusses, but then all but dismisses, the metaphorical significance of the 'cave' as signifying a 'hiddenness' from which the philosopher is gradually liberated through entry into the light that 'discloses.' Yet even a moderately generous reading of Plato's cave allegory would recognize that Plato well understood that 'truth' entails an 'unconcealment' and that the *ideas* are, precisely, that through which 'unconcealment' occurs. As such, they are not alien to Dasein, such that Dasein encounters them 'objectively,' but modes of Dasein's knowing (*Verständnis*) when Dasein's knowing is liberated from illusion ('inauthenticity'). Only this reading is consistent with the passage from the *Apology* quoted above. That the '*ideas*' are ontologically *native* to what Dasein is in truth is also expressed in Plato's concept of *anamnesis*. Thus, they cannot possibly signify 'objective' (and, hence, alien) norms of 'correctness.' They are, rather, noetic modes of Dasein's own Being as 'disclosed.' Given this, as Michael Inwood writes, "Heidegger is far closer to Plato, properly interpreted, than he acknowledges." Michael Inwood, *A Heidegger Dictionary* (Malden, MA: Blackwell Publishers, 1999), 15.

with where it has come from nor with where it is finally going. This sense of nullity gives rise to a feeling of anxiety (threat) and not-at-homeness (alienation), which leads it to flee into the life of das Man, in an effort to find there the home it cannot find in itself. In other words, Dasein experiences its very Being, as enclosed in finitude, as a *threat* to the basic *thrust* of its Being. A simple inference (which Heidegger does not make) yields the insight that human existence is inherently inimical to finitude. The thrust of life is *towards-life* (not death), *hence* Dasein seeks to escape its thrownness upon death.

This means that *finite* Dasein is, inherently, a dilemma to itself. Were this the last word on the matter there would be no hope for a restoration of the philosophical project (as Socrates and Plato envision it), for there would be nothing for this project to pursue. The soul cannot be perfected if the very tendency of its Being is in opposition to itself. It can fly into das Man, or stoically resolve upon its finitude, but neither will allow it to escape the dilemma that it is to itself; i.e., the 'sickness unto death' that Kierkegaard identifies as despair.

It is just here that religion has something to say of relevance to the philosophical project itself. Being-towards-death is not, says religion, Dasein's 'uttermost possibility.' On the contrary, Dasein's 'uttermost possibility,' a possibility derived from its provenance in God, is *eternal life*. Heidegger is right in recognizing 'everyday' Dasein as in flight from Being-towards-death, but he has failed to see this in its broadest context. Being-towards-death is not primordial for Dasein, but the expression of a rupture in Dasein's rootedness in God; a rupture Dasein must overcome if it is to fully actualize itself.

But has traditional religion expressed itself, or even understood itself, in a manner that has made all this clear? In chapter six, we noted that traditional theology has itself been characterized by the same inappropriate objectivism that Heidegger complains has distorted philosophy. Indeed, in later works Heidegger notes this explicitly and dubs this distortion, evident in *both* the philosophical and theological traditions, 'onto-theology.'[8] Onto-theology approaches the question of Being, and the question of God, as if asking a technical question.

---

8 A general discussion of Heidegger's notion of Onto-theology can be found in Jeff Owen Prudhomme's *God and Being: Heidegger's Relation to Theology*, chapter four, "How the Deity Gets into Philosophy: The Onto-Theo-Logical Character of Metaphysics" (New Jersey: Humanities Press, 1997).

It seeks to know Being and/or God as an objective datum that might then be dealt with to serve this or that end. Salvation becomes a matter of doing this or that thing, professing this or that belief, so as to affect a change in the condemnatory disposition of God. It is perhaps insufficiently noted that Jesus' strongest protest was reserved for the religious authorities of his time, whose 'legalistic' (in our terms, 'objectivistic') distortions kept their adherents from a genuine experience of divine grace: "Woe to you, scribes and Pharisees, hypocrites, because you shut off the kingdom of heaven from men; for you do not enter in yourselves, nor do you allow those who are entering to go in" (Mt 23:13).

A full critique of the theological tradition is outside the scope of our work. We have had to content ourselves, in chapter six, with indicating the problematic nature of metaphysical objectivism for religious understanding.

Heidegger's hermeneutical phenomenology, we've argued, provides a more appropriate approach to religious ideas than metaphysical objectivism. Our task in the second half of this work, then, was to employ this very method in a reading of the Bible, with the aim of unveiling the Bible's alternate understanding of human Being; an understanding with the potential to resolve the dilemma that *finite* Dasein is to itself. In the next section we will briefly summarize the conclusions we have come to in this regard.

II. Contending 'Telic Contexts'

Neither 'death' nor 'eternal life' can be understood as temporal eventualities that Dasein may some day arrive at. One who has literally died is no longer there to notice it. On the other hand, however long one may live, one will never have lived forever. 'Death' and 'eternal life,' then, do not have their meaning as future eventualities, but, as we have said, as ultimate 'telic contexts' through which Dasein may understand itself and its relation to its world. Their meaning is hermeneutical-existential. Although, literally construed, both are set in the future, the notion of future here is used as a symbol for what might be called 'axiological ultimacy.' Heidegger does not use the term 'telic context,' but it is Heidegger who has made its meaning clear in his analysis of Being-towards-death. Being-towards-death is a qualification of the self-understanding of Dasein and has meaning only as such. According to Heidegger, authentic Dasein recognizes itself as (or in the 'telic context' of) Being-towards-death. Inauthentic Dasein flees from this self-understanding into the life of das Man.

Heidegger takes no note of the possibility of an authentic overcoming of Being-towards-death; a possibility we find proclaimed at the very heart of the Bible: "I have set before you life and death, the blessing and the curse. So choose life that you may live" (Deut. 30:19). The Bible cannot here be speaking of physical life and physical death, since it must have been as clear to the biblical authors as it is to us that all human beings, regardless of their choices, are subject to the latter. 'Life' and 'death' here, and throughout the Bible, refer to alternate telic contexts under which Dasein may live.

Briefly stated, Being-towards-death is characterized by Heidegger as accompanied by a state-of-mind of ***not-at-homeness*** and a mood of ***angst.*** As we have noted, Heidegger never questions the fact that Dasein's authenticity should be accompanied by such repellent moods; he accepts it as a phenomenological given. Nevertheless, it clearly makes Dasein into a questionable being; a being who is a dilemma to itself; indeed, it is just this dilemma that induces Dasein to flee into the inauthenticity of das Man.

Though Heidegger evidences little awareness of the possibility of eternal life as proclaimed in religion, religion seems to know a great deal about Being-towards-death as developed by Heidegger: "He who does not love abides in death," declares the apostle John (1 Jn 3:10). "Wretched man that I am! Who will set me free from the body of this death?", cries Paul (Rom 7:24). "[T]he people living in darkness have seen a great light; on those living in the land of the shadow of death a light has dawned," pronounces Jesus (Mt 4:16). And, of course: "The Lord God commanded the man, saying, 'From any tree of the garden you may eat freely; but from the tree of the knowledge of good and evil you shall not eat, for in the day that you eat from it you will surely die'" (Gn 2:16-17).

The 'death' of which the Bible speaks in these passages is not physical death; it is rather a mode of life; a life of being *cut off* from one's rootedness in the eternal life of God, hence a life of rupture, a life in which one feels oneself to be (now in Heidegger's terms) 'not-at-home.' We have called this the life of 'self-enclosed finitude,' in which Dasein's self-concern is wholly encased in itself. In contrast, the Bible proclaims the possibility of Being-towards-*life*, which might be characterized as a life of rootedness in the *eternal life* of God, which is itself a life of self-transcending love. It is through love, says religion, that Dasein achieves the infinite wholeness finite ek-sistence longs for. Through love Dasein overcomes the self-enclosure of death and comes *home*. The Bible's understanding of *eternal life* is expressed in the Great Commandment, quoted at the start of chapter seven: "You shall love the Lord your God with all your heart, and with all your soul, and with all your strength, and with all your mind; and your neighbor as yourself... Do this and you will *live*" (Lk 10:25-28, my emphasis).

The ontological possibility for such self-transcending love lies in the Oneness of God. In this respect, the biblical story of the Creation may be read, not as a metaphysical claim about temporal origins, but as a statement concerning the possibility of love and the overcoming of death. That from which Dasein derives its Being is not *nothing*, says the Bible, but the life of God; an *infinite life* from which *every* finite life proceeds; in which all "live and move and have their being" (Acts 17:28). Hence, the Oneness of God implies the fundamental relationality of all things, which Dasein, as "image of God," is to recognize and open itself to.

From the religious perspective, it is only through such recognition, and adoption of the telic context of Being-towards-life (i.e., through 'faith'), that Dasein can resolve the dilemma of its finitude and become whole. Further, the imperatives (i.e., the 'law') that derive from this telic context demand more than a commitment to *self*-responsibility (anticipatory resoluteness), but a commitment to *other*-responsibility (love of neighbor). The Bible's hermeneutic of Dasein, then, is distinguished from Heidegger's in this most important respect: it has moral implications entirely absent from the latter. One who loves his neighbor as himself cannot become a Nazi.

Heidegger's hermeneutic is grounded in his own phenomenological reflections. The Bible's hermeneutic is based, we are told, on 'revelation.' As we discussed briefly in chapter seven, the Bible tells us that it is only the one who is "pure in heart" who "sees God": "No one can see the Kingdom of God," says Jesus, "unless he is born from above" (Jn 3:3). On the face of it, this is no different in principle from Heidegger's suggestion that it is only the one who has answered the 'call of conscience' who 'sees' authentic Dasein. Epistemologically, then, the Bible's hermeneutic (although, of course, written in an entirely different genre) need not be considered intrinsically less sound than Heidegger's. One can imagine a depth of disclosedness that would reveal, to those privy to it, ontological insights that transcend those available to Heidegger (and, indeed, the average human being), from which perspective the biblical texts (some or all) are written.[9]

The Bible, then, puts forward an interpretation of human Being that affirms, but then qualifies in important ways, the interpretation advanced by Heidegger; through which many of the ambiguities, paradoxes, and limitations of Heidegger's account can be resolved. Eternal life, as Christianity envisions it, is characterized by peace and joy (Gal 5:22), whereas Heidegger's authentic Dasein is characterized by angst and not-at-homeness. Again, given the disclosive character of moods, it would seem that only the former could, even in principle, indicate a fully integrated self.

This, then, might be thought of as a religious response to Heidegger's existential analytic of Dasein, a response that confirms it in many of its essentials, but then takes us beyond it. In our next section we will consider the implications of this response for the ***philosophical*** project.

III. PHILOSOPHICAL INQUIRY REVISITED

If philosophy has gotten off track, if authentic philosophical questioning has been 'forgotten' due to the inauthenticity of Dasein, then the Bible's alternate understanding of Dasein is of the utmost *philosophical* significance. It would suggest that, though Heidegger may have correctly identified the disease, he has failed to identify the cure. This cure is not to be had through a commitment to oneself as 'Being-towards-death,' but through an acknowledgment of oneself as

9 Rahner: "Looked at theologically and correctly, the prophet is none other than the believer who can express his transcendental experience of God correctly." *Foundations of Christian Faith*, 159.

'Being-towards-life.' It is only through Being-towards-life, then – i.e., through *some version* of faith – that we can hope to authentically engage in the philosophic pursuit of ***truth***.

And yet, it appears that Heidegger denied this explicitly. In his 1958 conversation with Hermann Noack, after Noack remarked that "Heidegger's thinking moves in a dimension which alone makes room for doing genuine theological 'thinking' once again...," Heidegger responded, "Within thinking nothing can be achieved which would be a preparation or a confirmation for that which occurs in faith and in grace. Were I so addressed by faith I would have to close up my shop – Within faithfulness one still thinks, of course; but thinking as such no longer has a task."[10]

Is this indeed the case? I submit that whether or not thinking has a 'task' in faithfulness entirely depends upon what we suppose the task of thinking to be. Indeed, one might wonder what task thinking would have for one who lives entirely in 'anticipatory resoluteness.' For such a one, Dasein's ontological potentialities are strictly limited by its finite, worldly possibilities. In such a case, technological knowledge would assume primary importance, for it is through such knowledge that Dasein can achieve maximal inner-worldly power and comfort. On the other hand, it is just within 'faithfulness' that thinking ***has*** a task. It is, indeed, the very same task we read in Plato at the inception of Western philosophy: to pursue "the greatest improvement of the soul" through coming to know oneself in relation to 'the good.'[11]

---

10 Hermann Noack, "Conversation with Martin Heidegger," in *The Piety of Thinking: Essays by Martin Heidegger* (Bloomington: Indiana University Press, 1976), 64.

11 Heidegger himself writes: "It is absolutely correct and proper to say that 'You can't do anything with philosophy.' It is only wrong to suppose that this is the last word on philosophy. For the rejoinder imposes itself: granted that *we* cannot do anything with philosophy, might not philosophy, if we concern ourselves with it, do something ***with us***?" Martin Heidegger, *An Introduction to Metaphysics*, trans. Ralph Manheim (New Haven: Yale University Press, 1959), 12. But Heidegger never clearly articulates what he supposes philosophy is to do with us, whose 'uttermost possibility' is '*im*-possibility.' In the same work Heidegger refers to 'Christian philosophy' as a 'round square' (p. 7) because Christianity has already answered the fundamental philosophical question 'why is there something rather than nothing,' hence, philosophically speaking, Christians have nothing left to consider. But this is true (to the extent that it is) only insofar as we consider the 'why' of this question in a causal, rather than in a teleological, sense; which is contrary to Heidegger's own approach to such questions. If we consider the 'why' in a teleological sense then Christianity still provides an answer of sorts (viz. 'for the glory of God') but the *meaning* of this answer very much calls for thought.

Jesus says: "When anyone hears the message about the kingdom and does not ***understand*** it, the evil one comes and snatches away what was sown in his heart" (Mt 13:19, my emphasis). Hence, a principal task of thinking within Christian faithfulness is to come to 'understand the message about the kingdom.' But since the message about the kingdom is a message about the ultimate good of Dasein (who is 'Being-in-the-world-with-others'), such an understanding cannot be had without an understanding of self, world, and other. The task of thinking within faithfulness, then, is to understand self, world, and other within the telic context of Being-towards-life.

Does faith, however, prejudice its results by adopting this telic context? On the contrary, as Heidegger writes: "All interpretation ... operates in the fore-structure [of self/world-understanding] ... Any interpretation which is to contribute understanding, must already have understood what is to be interpreted ... This circle of understanding is not an orbit in which any random kind of knowledge may move; it is the expression of the existential fore-structure of Dasein itself ... In the circle is hidden the positive possibility of the most primordial kind of knowing."[12]

Every thinking moves within the orbit (or spiral) of self-understanding. One who has come to see her life as *towards-life* does not see herself as traversing a lesser, but a greater, orbit of self; a self whose farthest reaches touch upon infinity itself; a self whose responsibilities extend equally as far. Every conceivable inquiry is comprehended by the inquiry into the infinite good. Fully consummated self-understanding, in this context, is *infinite* understanding. There is no end to the task of thinking within faithfulness. Faithfulness does not entail an end to philosophical questioning, such that we can then 'close up shop,' it gives such questioning axiological *direction*. It makes it clear that all inquiries, as the inquiries of a being who is a self-relation of *infinite* concern, are ultimately inquiries into 'the good.' To inquire into this *is* the task of thinking.

And this task of thinking – as, again, Plato understood – is also a task of *becoming*. To know the good is an essential part of actualizing the good, for, as Heidegger's work has itself made clear, knowing is itself a mode of Being.

12 Heidegger, *Being and Time*, pp. 194-195, H 154-155.

As we move beyond the objectivist ("onto-theological") distortions to be found in both the religious *and* the philosophical traditions, we come to see religion and philosophy as natural partners, mutually supporting one another. Religion points to that which philosophy must struggle to understand. Philosophy's struggle to understand, further, is not incidental to the religious pursuit, but essential to it. Authentic faith requires, and involves, the careful and thoughtful *examination* of faith. Thus, religion and philosophy, rightly construed, must work together to advance us toward 'the good.'

IV. Conclusion

From the religious perspective, Heidegger's philosophy appears limited because it fails to fully and properly grasp the axiological character of Being, and the ultimate thrust of that axiology. Truth (as dis-closedness of Being) is desirable only because Being, in its axiological character, is *good*. It is the good of Being that makes death (as the prospect of *not* being) threatening, and, hence, angst-provoking. Da-*Sein*, as a participant in *Being*, is at home in Being. The 'possibility of im-possibility' (i.e., *no* Being), as Kierkegaard teaches us, does not render Dasein whole, but brings Dasein to despair. Desperate Dasein, then, flees from itself in order to flee from its despair. The solution to this is not an embrace of death *per se* – death is precisely what Dasein, as *concerned* for its Being, cannot embrace (without doing violence to itself) – its solution is *some version* of faith. Only through faith, says religion, can Dasein fully open itself to Being. Only through faith can Dasein stand 'resolutely' in the truth.

I say 'some version' of faith because there are, of course, many versions of what gets *called* faith. Many are, themselves, just further instances of flight into das Man. We have tried to indicate what *authentic* faith might look like in the latter half of this work. Of course, much more needs to be said; a fuller work would have explored more thoroughly inauthentic modes of faith. To think about what authentic faith would be like is yet another of the all-important 'tasks of thinking' within faithfulness.

Heidegger has had much to say about the etymology of the Greek word for 'truth,' *aletheia*. I believe it will be worth our while, in closing, to consider the etymology of the *English* word 'truth.' The English word 'truth' is related to the Middle English 'troth,' whose principal meaning is 'trust' (to be-*troth* someone, for instance, is to enter into a relation of trust with him or her). A truthful account, then, is one that is maximally *trustworthy*.

This gives us the axiological meaning of the word 'truth.' The true is that which can be trusted. The pursuit of truth is the pursuit of that which is trustworthy. It is in this sense, finally, that we can understand Christ's pronouncement 'I am the truth.' Christ professes to disclose that which can be trusted and invites us to enter into it in faith. That Plato had a similar understanding of truth is evident from his association of the true and the good.[13] It is just to the extent that philosophy has forgotten this association, in my view, that it has forgotten 'the question of the meaning of Being.'

From the religious perspective anyway, Heidegger also seems to have forgotten, or, at least, to have not fully remembered, this question. Yet any criticism of Heidegger's work from this perspective must be tempered by the recognition that it is Heidegger himself who has helped us unveil the existential meaning of the Judeo-Christian message, in terms of which such criticism might be made. Had we more time, we might have elaborated in greater detail the many existential distortions – distortions of authoritarianism, dogmatism, superstition, legalism, literalism, exclusivism, judgmentalism, elitism, bigotry, and, again and again, the most egregious uncharitableness – that have, throughout history, marred the face of Western religion. From such distortions, Heidegger, perhaps, had no choice but to turn away. It is, finally, a tribute to his work that it has provided us the wherewithal to turn back.

---

13 A relation between 'truth' and 'trustworthiness' can be found in the Greek '*aletheia*' as well. According to P. Friedländer in his book *Plato: An Introduction* one of the ways in which *aletheia* is used in Homer, Hesiod, and other early Greeks is to refer to the "genuineness, truthfulness and conscientiousness [i.e., trustworthiness] of an individual or character" (see Inwood, *A Heidegger Dictionary*, 14, where Inwood discusses Friedländer's claims). Though Friedländer proffers this as an argument *against* Heidegger's interpretation of *aletheia*, it is not difficult to see a relationship between trustworthiness and unhiddenness if we consider the sphere of *personal* relations (to which the word was, perhaps, first applied). He/she who is 'hiding something' is not to be trusted. He/she who is 'open,' and 'speaks plainly,' is worthy of trust. Hence, the trustworthy one is also the one who is 'unhidden.'

Works Consulted

Aquinas, Thomas. *Summa Contra Gentiles, Book One: God.* Translated by Anton C. Pegis, Notre Dame: University of Notre Dame Press, 1975.

_____. *Summa Contra Gentiles, Book Two: Creation*. Translated by James F. Anderson. Notre Dame: University of Notre Dame Press, 1975.

_____. *Summa Contra Gentiles, Book Three: Providence*. Part I. Translated by Vernon J. Bourke. Notre Dame: University of Notre Dame Press, 1975.

_____. *The Summa Theologica*, Vol. 1. Translated by Fathers of the English Dominican Province. Westminster, Maryland: Christian Classics, 1948.

_____. *The Summa Theologica*, Vol. 2. Translated by Fathers of the English Dominican Province. Westminster, Maryland: Christian Classics, 1948.

Aristotle. *Metaphysica.* Translated by W.D. Ross. In *The Basic Works of Aristotle.* Edited by Richard Mckeon. New York: Random House, 1941.

_____. *The Nicomachean Ethics*. Translated by W.D. Ross, in *The Basic Works of Aristotle*, p. 936, 1094b.

Augustine. *City of God.* Translated by Henry Bettenson. London: Penguin Books, 1972.

____. *Confessions*. Translated by R.S. Pine-Coffin. London: Penguin Books, 1961.

Bultmann, Rudolf. *Existence and Faith: Shorter Writings of Rudolf Bultmann*. Translated by Schubert M. Ogden. New York: Meridian Books, 1960.

____. "New Testament and Mythology." Translated by Reginald H. Fuller. In *Kerygma and Myth: A Theological Debate*. Edited by Hans Werner Bartsch. New York: Harper & Row Publishers, 1961.

____. *Jesus Christ and Mythology*. New York: Charles Scribner's Sons, 1958.

Carr, David. *The Paradox of Subjectivity: The Self in the Transcendental Tradition*. New York: Oxford University Press, 1999.

Caputo, John D. *Demythologizing Heidegger*. Bloomington: Indiana University Press, 1993.

____. *Heidegger and Aquinas: An Essay on Overcoming Metaphysics*. New York: Fordham University Press, 19992.

____. *The Mystical Element in Heidegger's Thought*. New York: Fordham University Press, 1968.

Caton, Hiram. "Tory History of Ideas." *Independent Journal of Philosophy*. 5-6 (1988): 1-9.

Cushman, Robert E. *Therapeia: Plato's Conception of Philosophy*. Chapel Hill: The University of North Carolina Press, 1958.

Descartes, René. *Discourse on Method*. In *Discourse on Method and The Meditations*. Translated by F.E. Sutcliffe. Middlesex: Penguin Books, 1968.

____. *Meditations on First Philosophy*. In *The Philosophical Works of Descartes*. Vol. 1. Translated by Elizabeth S. Haldane and G.R.T. Ross. Cambridge: Cambridge University Press, 1911.

____. *Principles of Philosophy*. In *The Philosophical Works of Descartes*. Vol. 1. Translated by Elizabeth S. Haldane and G.R.T. Ross. Cambridge: Cambridge University Press, 1911.

Emad, Parvis. *Heidegger and the Phenomenology of Values : His Critique of Intentionality*. Glen Ellyn, ILL: Torey Press, 1981.

Gall, Robert S. *Beyond Theism and Atheism: Heidegger's Significance for Religious Thinking*. Dordrecht: M. Nijhoff, 1987.

Heidegger, Martin. *Being and Time*. Translated by John MacQuarrie and Edward Robinson. New York: Harper & Row Publishers, 1962.

_____. *Introduction to Metaphysics*. Translated by Ralph Manheim. New Haven: Yale University Press, 1959.

_____. "Letter on Humanism." Translated by Frank A. Capuzzi with J. Glenn Gray. In *Martin Heidegger: Basic Writings*. Edited by David Farrell Krell. San Francisco: HarperCollins Publishers, 1992.

_____. "Phenomenology and Theology." Translated by James G. Hart and John C. Maraldo. In *Pathmarks*. Edited by William McNeill. Cambridge: Cambridge University Press, 1998.

_____. *Ontology—The Hermeneutics of Facticity*. Translated by John van Buren. Bloomington, Indiana: Indiana University Press, 1999.

_____. "The Question Concerning Technology." Translated by William Lovitt. In *The Question Concerning Technology and Other Essays*. New York: Harper & Row, 1977.

_____. *Sein und Zeit*. Tübingen: Niemeyer, 1979.

Hick, John. *Evil and the God of Love*. London: Macmillan and Company Limited, 1966.

Husserl, Edmund. *Cartesian Meditations: An Introduction to Phenomenology*. Translated by Dorion Cairns. Dordrecht, The Netherlands: Kluwer Academic Publishers, 1995.

_____. *The Idea of Phenomenology*. Translated by Alston & Nakhnikian. Martinus Nijoff, 1964.

Inwood, Michael. *A Heidegger Dictionary*. Malden, MA: Blackwell Publishers, 1999.

Kant, Immanuel. *The Critique of Practical Reason*. Edited and Translated by Lewis White Beck. New York: Macmillan Publishing Company, 1993.

____. *Critique of Pure Reason*. Translated by Norman Kemp Smith. New York: St. Martin's Press, 1929.

Kierkegaard, Søren. *The Concept of Anxiety: A Simple Psychologically Orienting Deliberation on the Dogmatic of Hereditary Sin*. Edited and Translated by Reidar Thomte and Albert B. Anderson. Princeton: Princeton University Press, 1980.

____. *Concluding Unscientific Postscript to the Philosophical Fragments*. Translated by David F. Swenson and Walter Lowrie. Princeton: Princeton University Press, 1941.

____. *Either/Or, Part II*. Edited and translated by Howard V. Hong and Edna H. Hong. Princeton: Princeton University Press, 1987.

____. *Fear and Trembling: A Dialectical Lyric*. Translated by Walter Lowrie. Garden City: Doubleday & Company, 1941.

____. *The Sickness Unto Death: A Christian Psychological Exposition for Upbuilding and Awakening*. Edited and Translated by Howard V. Hong and Edna H. Hong. Princeton: Princeton University Press, 1980.

Kisiel, Theodore. *The Genesis of Being and Time*. Berkeley: University of California Press, 1993.

____. "The Genetic Difference in Reading *Being and Time*." *American Catholic Philosophical Quarterly*. 69 (Spring 1995): 171-187.

Levinas, Emmanuel. "Jewish Thought Today." In *Difficult Freedom: Essays on Judaism*. Translated by Sean Hand. Baltimore: John Hopkins University Press, 1990.

____. *Totality and Infinity: An Essay on Exteriority*. Translated by Alphonso Lingis. Pittsburgh: Duquesne University Press, 1992.

Macquarrie, John. *An Existentialist Theology: A Comparison of Heidegger and Bultmann*. London: SCM Press, 1955.

____. *The Scope of Demythologizing: Bultmann and His Critics*. Gloucester, MA: P. Smith, 1969.

____. *Studies in Christian Existentialism: Lectures and Essays*. London: SCM Press, 1966.

Malet, André. *The Thought of Rudolf Bultmann*. Translated by Richard Strachen. Garden City, NY: Doubleday, 1971.

Nietzsche, Friedrich. *The Gay Science*. Translated by Walter Kaufman. New York: Random House, 1974.

____. *Thus Spoke Zarathustra*. Translated by Walter Kaufman. New York: Penguin Books, 1978.

Noack, Hermann. "Conversation with Martin Heidegger." Translated by James G. Hart and John C. Maraldo. In *The Piety of Thinking: Essays by Martin Heidegger.* Bloomington: Indiana University Press, 1976.

Plato. *Apology*. Translated by Benjamin Jowett. in *The Works of Plato*. Vol. 3. New York: Tudor Publishing Co.: 1937.

____. *Gorgias*. Translated by Walter Hamilton. London: Penguin Books, 1960.

Prudhomme, Jeff Owen. *God and Being: Heidegger's Relation to Theology*. New Jersey: Humanities Press, 1997.

Rahner, Karl. *Foundations of Christian Faith: An Introduction to the Idea of Christianity*. Translated by William V. Dych. New York: Crossroads, 1990.

Robinson, James McConkey. *The Later Heidegger and Theology*. Edited by James M. Robinson and John B. Cobb, Jr. New York: Harper & Row, 1963.

Sartre, Jean-Paul. *Being and Nothingness: A Phenomenological Essay on Ontology*. Translated by Hazel E. Barnes. New York: Washington Square Press, 1956.

Soffer, Walter. *From Science to Subjectivity: An Interpretation of Descartes' Meditations*. New York: Greenwood Press, 1987.

Severson, Richard James. *Time, Death and Eternity: Reflecting on Augustine's Confessions in Light of Heidegger's Being and Time*. ATLA Monograph Series No. 36. Lanham, Maryland: Scarecrow Press, 1995.

Steinsaltz, Adin. *The Sustaining Utterance: Discourses on Chasidic Thought*. Edited and Translated by Yehuda Hanegbi. Northvale, New Jersey: Jason Aronson, Inc., 1989.

Tillich, Paul. *Dynamics of Faith*. Edited by Ruth Nanda Anshen. New York: Harper, 1956.

_____. *A History of Christian Thought: From its Judaic and Hellenistic Origins to Existentialism*. Edited by Carl E. Braaten. New York: Simon & Schuster, 1967.

_____. *Systematic Theology*. Vol. 1. Chicago: University of Chicago Press, 1951.

_____. *Systematic Theology*. Vol. 2. Chicago: University of Chicago Press, 1957.

_____. *Systematic Theology*. Vol. 3. Chicago: University of Chicago Press, 1963..

Van Buren, John. *The Young Heidegger: Rumor of the Hidden King*. Indianapolis: Indiana University Press, 1994.

Ware, Bishop Kallistos. *The Orthodox Way*. Crestwood, NY: A.R. Mowbray & Co., Ltd. 1979

Wingren, Gustaf. *Man and the Incarnation: A Study in the Biblical Theology of Irenaeus*. Translated by Ross Mackenzie. Philadelphia: Muhlenberg Press, 1959.

INDEX

Note that many of the key terms listed in the Index below are used very frequently throughout the text. It would not be helpful to list every page on which they appear. I have tried, in the below, to list places where terms are introduced, significant discussion of them takes place, and/or significant points about them are made.

V

W

Y